Will Brooker is the leading academic expert on the Dark Knight, and author of the cultural history of Batman, *Batman Unmasked*. His other books include *Using the Force* and *Alice's Adventures*. He edited the *Audience Studies Reader* and *The Blade Runner Experience*, and wrote the BFI Film Classics volume on *Star Wars*. He is currently Reader and Director of Research in Film and Television at Kingston University, London, and editor of *Cinema Journal*.

'A fascinating and incredibly detailed analysis of comic fiction's most powerful and successful hero.'

– Pat Mills, author of *Batman: The Book of Shadows*

'Through the prism of poststructuralism, Will Brooker casts dazzling new light on Batman as myth, brand, and canon. Bruce Wayne encounters the likes of Foucault, Bakhtin, Barthes, and Derrida in an epic team-up across these pages. But more than just a theoretical excursion, this is a skilful, passionate argument for setting the Batman free from repressive, restrictive views of who and what the character can be. From author-function to Joker-function, Brooker illuminates the strategies and creative choices of "scriptors" such as Christopher Nolan and Grant Morrison, showing how they select, rework, and recombine elements from Batman's longer history and continuity. *Hunting the Dark Knight* is, quite simply, a brilliant study of the Batman and contemporary processes of rebooting, franchising and shaping a cultural icon.'

– Matt Hills, author of *Triumph of a Time Lord*

HUNTING THE DARK KNIGHT

TWENTY-FIRST CENTURY BATMAN

WILL BROOKER

I.B. TAURIS

LONDON · NEW YORK

Published in 2012 by I.B.Tauris & Co Ltd
6 Salem Road, London W2 4BU
175 Fifth Avenue, New York NY 10010
www.ibtauris.com

Distributed in the United States and Canada
Exclusively by Palgrave Macmillan
175 Fifth Avenue, New York NY 10010

ISBN 978 1 84885 279 2 (HB)
     978 1 84885 280 8 (PB)

A full CIP record for this book is available from the British Library
A full CIP record is available from the Library of Congress

Library of Congress Catalog Card Number: available

Typeset by Newgen Publishers, Chennai
Printed and bound by TJ International Ltd, Padstow, Cornwall

CONTENTS

ACKNOWLEDGEMENTS

'The first truth of Batman . . . the saving grace.
I was never alone. I had help.'

Grant Morrison,
The Return of Bruce Wayne (New York: DC Comics, 2011)

Thanks to:

Scholars Julian Darius, Marc diPaolo, Jonathan Gray, Matt Hills, Marc Singer.

Online, the team from www.mindlessones.com, the respondents from www.BatmanonFilm.com, the forum members of Comic Book Resources; and the Sons of the Batman.

Colleagues Simon Brown, Matthew Pateman, John Mullarkey, Simon Locke, PhD candidates Sarah Zaidan, Phillip Bevin and Billy Proctor and Sisley White for her prototype cover design.

At I.B.Tauris, Philippa Brewster.

At home, Peter, Elizabeth, Joseph and Fiona Brooker, and Maisie.

PROLOGUE: BATMAN OF MANY WORLDS

Who is the Batman? Imagine him. You have a sense of him; who he is, what he looks like. Perhaps you see Adam West in a soft grey costume and shiny cowl. Perhaps you see Frank Miller's hulking, middle-aged vigilante from the *Dark Knight Returns* graphic novel, George Clooney posing awkwardly in a sculpted plastic suit for Joel Schumacher's *Batman & Robin*, or an armour-encased, snarling Christian Bale as the brutal, militarised protagonist of Christopher Nolan's films.

Perhaps you play videogames, and see the Batman of *Arkham Asylum*, a muscle-bound tough guy with a flowing cape; or you remember the lantern-jawed hero of the animated series, built like a city block but agile as a cat. Or you're a hardcore comics fan, and you imagine the very different Batmen drawn by Frank Quitely, Dave McKean or Jim Lee.

Or you're simply a Batman fan, a lifelong lover of Batman, and when you close your eyes and conjure him, he's a combination of some or all of the above, folded in with countless other variants from other media, other moments, wrapped up with your own personal vision of what he looks like; this icon, this idea who has been guarding the cities of our imagination for over 70 years.

In Pearson and Uricchio's *The Many Lives of the Batman*, Eileen R. Meehan identifies a 'deluge of material' around the character, which

> ... has generated a complex web of cross references as the major text, [Tim Burton's 1989] *Batman*, ricochets back in cultural memory to Bob Kane's original vision of a caped vigilante, then up to the more recent dystopian *Dark Knight Returns*, with ironic reference to the camp Crusader of television and all the intervening Bat-texts. This web of cross references creates an intertext into which we fit ourselves, positioning ourselves to construct different readings of the film and positioning the film and its intertext to suit our own particular purposes.[1]

Jim Collins, in the same volume, is faced with 'seemingly endless re-articulations' of the Batman:

> multiple narrativizations of the same figure produced over a fifty-year period, appearing as simultaneous options, a simultaneity made more complicated by the fact that these narratives were not just continuations of an Ur text ... this array of texts could obviously generate any number of narrative analyses ...[2]

Pearson and Uricchio themselves claim to be witnessing 'the most divergent set of refractions of the Batman character ... now, newly created Batmen, existing simultaneously with the older Batmen of the television series and comic reprints and back issues, all struggled for recognition and a share of the market.'[3]

All of them discuss Batman in terms of multiple but simultaneous variants; Batmen of many worlds, coexisting across alternate earths. All of them were writing around the time of Tim Burton's 1989 movie. That was over 20 years ago, when Batman was a mere 50 years old. That was before Burton's sequel, *Batman Returns* of 1992; before Joel Schumacher's commercially and critically disastrous *Batman Forever* (1995) and *Batman & Robin* (1997) killed off the film franchise. That was before the various animated series (1992 onwards) and their comic book spin-offs, and long before the *Arkham Asylum* video game of 2009. That was before the comic book *Batman* – whose continuity runs on a different track to, but occasionally intersects with, that of live action movies, animated series and video games – went through numerous changes, including (in the last five years alone) meeting an English, Argentinean and Sioux version of himself (*The Black Glove*, 2007), losing his mind (*Batman RIP*, 2008) then dying (*Final Crisis*, 2009), to be replaced by his former partner and his newly discovered son (*Batman and Robin*, 2009), before returning from the dead to launch an international Batman franchise (*Batman Incorporated*, 2011). It was before the DC Comics universe relaxed its rules (in *52*, 2006–7) and reintroduced the idea of multiple worlds, many of which host alternate-universe Batmen (from the criminal Owlman of Earth-3 and the Nazi 'Leatherwing' of Earth-10 to Batman Junior of Earth-16 and the Victorian Batman of Earth-19). Perhaps most significantly, it was before Christopher Nolan's two films *Batman Begins* (2005) and *The Dark Knight* (2008), with their own range of spin-offs and merchandise that, again, maintained an ambiguous relationship with the other, previous and coexisting texts of Batman.

A lot has happened to Batman in the last 20 years: for one thing, there are a lot more Batmen. The multiplicities identified by Meehan, Collins, Pearson and Uricchio have multiplied; the sense that Batman is ungraspable, elusive, everywhere (and therefore potentially nowhere) has intensified. On one level, Batman is everything he has ever been – a combination of a thousand variations, an overlapping of alternates. But at the same time, those countless variants are policed, reduced, controlled and contained. They are branded by author, artist and director: Miller's Batman, Nolan's Batman, Lee's Batman. They are arranged in hierarchies, some personal and some public: many fans draw up their individual top tens and list their preferred versions, but more powerful voices also impose, or try to impose, a framework of quality, fidelity, 'truth' and 'reality' on the many texts of the Batman.

'Truth' and 'reality', of course, because such terms are meaningless in relation to the Batman: a 70-year old fiction, with countless authors, about a millionaire who fights crime in costume. But discourses around the real Batman, the original Batman, the Batman

faithful to 'the source', persist; they are circulated, shared and reinforced by fans, authors, artists, journalists and editors. These conversations debate – and depending on the cultural power of the person
or organisation involved, they decide – which Batman, or Batmen,
are official, in continuity and in canon. They decide how the official
versions of Batman relate to each other. They decide which type of
Batman is the current dominant, and which one is aberrant. The
approved Batman is promoted, and the Batman that doesn't fit is
pushed aside.

I use the word 'hierarchies', but in practice, the relationship
has taken the form not of a top-ten ranking but a binary opposi-
tion. For the last four decades of Batman's 70-year career, the
'good' Batman – the official Batman, pushed most vigorously by
DC and Warner Bros., and preferred by many fans – has been the
dark Batman, the gritty, violent vigilante: Denny O'Neil and Neal
Adams' 'Darknight Detective' of the 1970s, Frank Miller's *The Dark
Knight Returns* of 1986, Christopher Nolan's *The Dark Knight* of 2008.
The 'bad' Batman, ironically, has been the fun Batman, the playful
Batman, the camp Batman: the light-hearted 1950s comics that led to
Senate Subcommittee censorship for homoerotic content, the POW!
AWWK! Pop Art of Adam West's 1960s TV Batman, and the gaudy
pantomime of Joel Schumacher's two 1990s *Batman* movies.

This book examines how that policing, promotion and pushing-
aside works, using Batman as a case study to explore broader issues
of cultural meaning and cultural power. It studies the character
across a range of media, exploring *Batman Begins* and *The Dark Knight*
within the context of the twenty-first-century Batman, from comic
books to pizza promotions. As such, it asks a number of questions.

Unlike most new films, Nolan's *Batman* movies were released into
a complex network of existing, ongoing narratives, which continued
during and after their cinema exhibition. These narratives offered
similar but distinct representations of the main character, his world,
his history and his supporting cast. The films also carried their own
substantial secondary texts in other media, again to a greater degree
than most new releases. These included not just the usual posters,
trailers and merchandise, but also a comic book (*Batman Begins and*

Other Tales of the Dark Knight) that compiled a graphic adaptation of the film with a selection of existing Batman stories, a DVD of animated shorts (*Gotham Knight*) that bridged *Batman Begins* and its sequel, and an online Alternate Reality Game ('Why So Serious') that invited fans to step into the story-world of *The Dark Knight*, months before it reached cinemas. How do concepts of authorship operate in this matrix of cross-media texts? Do conventional models of the individual author still circulate, and if so, what purpose do they serve?

Nolan's movies were promoted as faithful adaptations of the comic book; this was a key aspect of their branding as distinct from previous *Batman* films. But what does adaptation mean, when the 'original' Batman is not a single literary novel but seven decades of stories? When new tales of the Batman appear every month in comic books and regularly in other media, does the normally one-way linear process shift into a multidirectional borrowing, whereby the film in turn shapes comic book, video game and animated continuity? What model of adaptation best explains this complex relationship?

Although 'fidelity' seems meaningless in this context – it is surely impossible to be faithful to such a diverse wealth of stories – the concept was fervently stressed by producers and fans alike, coupled with discourses of realism: a word that came to stand not just for Nolan's film aesthetic, but for a distinct characterisation and interpretation of Batman, which linked Nolan's films with a selective tradition of comic book texts. It signalled that Nolan had captured the 'dark' Batman, as opposed to the Schumacher Batman, the 1960s TV show and the light-hearted comics of the 1950s and 60s. What strategies were used to establish this 'dark' Batman as the dominant – not as an addition to Schumacher's interpretation, but as a clean reboot that attempted to wipe Schumacher's from public memory – and did they work? Why was it so important to enforce this single reading of Batman? What was at stake? Who did it serve? And what does it do to the concept of Batman – as a 70-year compendium of contradictory stories – when we close down his authorised, approved meaning to a selective reading from a handful of recent texts?

This book is born from, and about, a specific historical moment. It focuses primarily on the Batman of 2001–2011, against the background of the 'war on terror', and it examines the ways in which the contemporary Batman grapples with this particular sociopolitical context. But it also goes back through the character's history; through the darkness, through the play, back to the early stories.

It argues that the complexity of Christopher Nolan's allegorical engagement with the contradictions of the war on terror in *The Dark Knight Returns* is reduced to a one-dimensional political agenda – whether left or right, blue or red – if we insist on reading it only through the filter of the 'dark Batman' discourse. Through an examination of the comic book continuity that ran alongside Nolan's stories, the book draws out a new reading of Batman and his defining relationship with the Joker. Drawing on theories of carnival and deconstruction, it exposes the oppositions that sustain the 'dark Batman' against his playful opposite, and shows that they are fluid rather than fixed. More radically, it suggests that they have always been that way, and that the instability of this opposition is at the root of the character, inherent in the key traits that are consistent from the first Batman story to the last, and informing the Batman who is made up of all those collected stories. To make Batman into one thing, I argue, is a violation. To reduce him to a single dark dimension is to imprison him.

The book has five chapters. The first and second examine the ways in which Nolan's films and their paratexts were situated among the multiple surrounding and preceding texts of Batman, through discourses of authorship and adaptation. The third examines the ideas of fidelity and realism that were used to tie Nolan's films to a specific and narrow trend – the 'dark' persona – in Batman's representation and characterisation. In the fourth and fifth chapters, I suggest that Nolan's films can be prised open through a reading of the Batman/Joker relationship that is prompted and supported by the *Batman* comic book continuity that ran, semi-independently, alongside the movies. This reading opens up a new interpretation not just of Nolan's films but of the seven decades of Batman mythos to date; the body of stories that makes up 'Batman' provides evidence for such a revisionary reading, even as it changes our perspective on them and challenges our view of the central character.

So, to summarise, the book examines how Batman's meanings were locked down, why it happened, who benefited and what it did to the character. It then stages a breakout. Its aim is to set Batman free.

'Batman! It's a magic name . . .'

'The Batmen of All Nations',
Detective Comics #215 (January 1955)

'No doubt the god . . . had several faces, belonged to several eras, lived in several homes. The discordant tangle of mythological accounts in which he is caught should not be neglected. Nevertheless, certain constants can be distinguished throughout, drawn in broad letters with firm strokes.'

Jacques Derrida, *Dissemination*
(London: The Athlone Press), p.86.

'In his comprehensive history *Batman Unmasked*, published in early 2001, Will Brooker speculates on what form Batman might take in the 21st century. With reference to developments in DC's comic book line, Brooker suggests that Batman will be less "lonely avenger and more like the boss of a well-honed outfit", and that the Caped Crusader's adventures would incorporate the light touch of the 60s TV series into its mythos. Brooker could not have predicted the events of 9/11 . . .'

Vincent M. Gaine,
'Borders of the Bat: Batman's Liminal Heroism',
conference paper presented at the Society for Cinema
and Media Studies, Los Angeles, March 2010.

THE NOLAN FUNCTION:
AUTHORSHIP

When did *Batman Begins* begin? With the film's release in June 2005, or with the promotion, publicity and previews that paved its way during the previous year? Did it start, in a sense, with the comic books that inspired and shaped it – *The Long Halloween* of 1996–7, 'The Man Who Falls' of 1989, *Year One* from 1987, or the first Batman origin story in *Detective Comics* #33 (1939)? And when did it end? Did *Batman Begins* finish when *The Dark Knight* began, or were they promoted and received as part of the same story? Does the broader 'text' of Nolan's films include promotions like the Burger King 'Dark Whopper' and the Domino's 'Gotham City Pizza' campaigns, the 'Why So Serious' viral marketing and the *Gotham Knight* animated collection? Is it separate from the parallel narratives of the *Arkham Asylum* game, the regular comic books and the animated series? Did it cross over and influence these other texts, or do they all feed into a Batman metatext, a collected myth that constitutes the character as a whole?

How were these beginnings and endings, these origins and borderlines, marked within the ongoing, ever-growing, multimedia matrix of Batman stories? How were Nolan's films distinguished from and linked to all the contradictory texts of Batman, not just present, but previous – from camp crusader to dark vigilante, from Adam West's TV show to Frank Miller's graphic novels? How was their relationship, whether of sameness or difference, convergence or opposition, negotiated, established and confirmed?

The answers lie in three interrelated discourses – authorship, fidelity and realism – and the first three chapters of this book explore the ways in which those discourses were used in an attempt to lock down the meanings of Nolan's Batman films.

A few notes, before this book begins. Firstly, while I use the words 'promotion' and 'reception' as shorthand to indicate the meanings circulated by producers like Warner Bros. at one end, and audiences like online fan groups at another, I regard them as part of the same process. Every official promotion of specific meanings around Nolan's films depends on an initial interpretation of those films; every fan who posts his or her opinion on *Batman Begins* offers a reading to other fans on the internet board, and shapes their responses in turn. Journalism operates as a further intermediary, as part of a two-way process: newspaper reviewers form an interpretation of the film text, often guided by its surrounding promotional materials, and circulate this interpretation to their readers. We are all – from Dan DiDio, the executive editor of DC Comics, to a 12-year-old on an online forum, to me as author of this book – both receivers and producers of meaning around Batman.

Secondly, as I argued in the prologue, Batman is a multimedia text, with various narratives and iterations running at the same time across several platforms. This, by contrast, is a book. Issues surrounding Batman's promotion and reception are not distinct, but intertwined in a complex relay; however, the argument in a book can only really go forward, in one direction, and cross-references to other closely related ideas are inevitably clumsy. So you will often find me promising that certain themes, touched upon in passing, will be returned to in more depth later; and later discussion will refer back to previous chapters. Ideally, these would be optional links to take the reader directly to the relevant section, and back – but we are using a traditional technology here.

Thirdly, I am a Batman fan and an academic. I do not see the two as distinct, either in my own case or more broadly. The number of sites offering detailed annotations of comic book texts are testament to the close, intelligent and informed reading practiced by many fans. This book is based on the belief that Batman, as a case study, can help us to understand important ideas in contemporary popular culture, with an application well beyond these specific examples; but I also believe that 'theory' is everywhere, that we all use it, and that it can help us all to understand the way popular culture works. Ideally, I hope that this book will encourage some Batman fans to discover that theory is relevant and rewarding, and that, equally, it will encourage some theorists to discover that Batman is relevant and rewarding. That said, if you are more of an academic, and theories of authorship are already familiar to you – or if you are more of a fan, and theories of authorship are not your primary interest – feel free to skip the next section and go straight into the discussion of primary Batman data. You can always return to this part later.

Authorship Theory: A Very Short Introduction

While authorship remains a powerful device in film promotion and continues to structure its popular reception – it features prominently on posters and in reviews, and often guides our choice of film viewing – the figure of the author as an individual who governs the sole meaning of a text has been subject to significant challenges within the academic debates of the last 50 years.

Ironically, the major theories that complicated and undermined the role of the author came to prominence in the late 1960s, not long after the concept of individual authorship had finally found a place in cinema. While, David A. Gerstner notes, 'the long-standing tradition of the sole artist as creative force [had] evolved for centuries' into its twentieth-century function as a guarantor of quality, originality and capitalist exchange value, it reached cinema only in the 1950s. Cinema, 'like literature before it ... went through the hoops and hurdles of art criticism so as to overcome its vulgar associations with and reputation as mere popular entertainment.'[1]

Debates around authorship in cinema are often sourced to January 1954, with François Truffaut's essay 'A Certain Tendency of French Cinema', in the journal *Cahiers du Cinéma*, introducing the term *'la politique des auteurs'*; the term was later adapted into, and adopted as, *'auteur* theory.'[2] Truffaut argued for recognition of the *'hommes du cinéma'*, including the Continental European directors Jean Renoir, Robert Bresson, Max Ophuls and Jean Cocteau; articles published later that year in the same journal celebrated English and American directors such as Alfred Hitchcock, Nicholas Ray and Anthony Mann. These approaches to film authorship – insisting that popular cinema, even studio product, could be an art form – were introduced into American film criticism largely by Andrew Sarris during the 1960s,[3] and developed in journals such as *Movie*, *Film Comment* and *Sight and Sound*. John Ford and Howard Hawks – and the ways in which their contrasting personal styles, beliefs and concerns were expressed through the Western genre – were a particular focus.

An extended essay on John Ford by Robin Wood, first published in 1971, gives a sense of this traditional auteur criticism. Wood approaches Ford very much as an *'homme du cinéma'* – a flesh-and-blood man, whose conscious and deliberate artistic choices are rooted in his personal history. 'One could argue that Ford in his old age had the right to take his previous work for granted, that no one should ask him to do again what he did in [*My Darling*] *Clementine* [1946] when he wants ... to go on to do something quite different.'[4] *The Man Who Shot Liberty Valance* (1962) is, to Wood, characterised by 'a weary, elegiac feeling of loss. What is lost for the characters is defined in concrete, dramatic terms in the film – but there is beyond this a sense that the loss is also Ford's.'[5] Wood finds parallels between Ford's cavalry films and his later *Cheyenne Autumn*: 'that Ford himself wanted us to be aware of a connection is suggested by a number of cross-references ... Ford clearly made *Cheyenne Autumn* with the deliberate intention of righting the balance of sympathies and allegiances in the earlier cavalry westerns.'[6] The contrast between *My Darling Clementine* and *Cheyenne Autumn* is, finally, rooted in 'the change in Ford's attitude to American civilisation.'[7] Even this brief sampling from a single essay captures traditional auteur theory's respect for the director as an individual whose films, for the most part consciously, express an evolving worldview and can be illuminated through a study of the artist's life and beliefs.

We should remember that, while new approaches rose to prominence, they did not simply replace this school of auteur theory, but developed alongside it, often in debate with it. David A. Gerstner observes that

> Although film, for the most part, is produced as a collaborative medium, the urge and desire to discuss theoretically and market film in relation to the auteur are striking. Years of film criticism have drawn upon issues of authorship and theoretical models of the auteur to explore an array of cinematic topics; the interest has simply not waned. Yet, if such inquiries still find momentum in film scholarship, the critical tools for analyzing the author's body of work ... have undergone important and significant rethinking during these periods.[8]

Jack Boozer's introduction to *Authorship in Film Adaptation* offers a further history of the 'disappearing author', explaining that 'the influence of the auteur theory began to wane with the academic rise of semiotics and structuralism.'[9] In the 1960s, a new tendency within film scholarship shifted focus from the creator's intentions to patterns of language (through semiologists such as Christian Metz) and patterns within narrative (through structural anthropologists such as Claude Lévi-Strauss). While more conservative and traditional auteur theory saw the film as the deliberate expression of an individual artist – a real person with a biography and background that could help to explain their intentions – semiological and structuralist studies of authorship identified patterns of repetition and opposition within a body of work, whether consciously expressed or not. Within this model, a director tells the same story repeatedly but with variations; distinct themes and preoccupations emerge from the *oeuvre* as if through recurring dreams.[10] It is this approach that led Peter Wollen, in his influential book *Signs and Meaning in the Cinema*, first published in 1969, to distinguish the structures exhibited in 'Hawks' – the oppositions evident in his adventure films and comedies alike – from the flesh and blood director, Howard Hawks.[11]

At a greater level of complexity, poststructuralist theories of intertextuality – the idea that every text merely reworks the texts that precede and surround it – further problematised the figure of the individual author. Among those who challenged the notion of unique, original creation, arguing instead that all writing was part of, and in dialogue with, an endless matrix of preexisting texts, were Julia Kristeva – who drew on the earlier work of Mikhail Bakhtin – and Jacques Derrida. We will return to them later.

One of the most celebrated contributions to this debate, intersecting with this notion of the text as a mere citation from the network of the already-said, was Roland Barthes' essay 'The Death of the Author', first published in 1968.

> We know now that a text is not a line of words releasing a single 'theological' meaning (the 'message' of the Author-God) but a multi-dimensional space in which a variety of writings, none of them original, blend and clash. The text is a tissue of quotations drawn from the innumerable centres of culture. [...] the writer can only imitate a gesture that is always anterior, never original. His only power is to mix writings ... Did he wish to *express himself,* he ought to know that the inner 'thing' he thinks to 'translate' is only a ready-formed dictionary, its words only explainable through other words, and so on indefinitely.[12]

Barthes proposes the new figure of the 'scriptor' to replace the author: more an editor and recycler than a traditional creator, the scriptor recognises that the text can only draw on the preexisting texts in an 'immense dictionary ... that can know no halt ... the book itself is only a tissue of signs, an imitation that is lost, instantly deferred.'[13] This suggestion that meaning exists as a shout in an echo chamber, or a mask in an endless hall of mirrors – always reflecting and referring to another interpretation, with no guarantee of a source, origin, truth or ultimate explanation – is key to poststructuralist theories of language and textuality, and those theories are central to this book, as will become increasingly clear as we go on.

In Barthes' terms, the author is a cultural function rather than a universal absolute: 'a modern figure, a product of our society'.

(He uses a broad sense of 'modern', to mean after the Middle Ages and the Reformation.) It is 'the epitome and culmination of capitalist ideology ... which has attached the greatest importance to the 'person' of the author'.[14] Similarly, Michel Foucault argued in his essay 'What is an Author?' (1969) that the author is merely a function, a 'means of classification' whose role is decided by its cultural context.[15] In contemporary society, Foucault suggests, an author's main purpose is to provide a label, a way of categorising and distinguishing texts in relation to each other.

The author-function, to Foucault, serves bourgeois, capitalist notions of art by identifying a creator's work as 'a form of property ... a possession caught in a circuit of property values.'[16] In short, it provides a kind of branding, a guarantee of status; and Foucault confirms that this is simply the current end point of an evolutionary process, the culmination of a model that had been developing for hundreds of years. From the seventeenth and eighteenth centuries, he notes, literary discourse had to be 'authorised' by its writer's name: 'every text of poetry or fiction was obliged to state its author and the date, place, and circumstance of its writing. The meaning and value attributed to the text depended on this information.'[17] Rather than attributing authorship to an individual, then, Foucault defines the author-function in terms of systems of ownership, classification and legitimation; and rather than asking, romantically, how a 'free subject' creates artistic meaning, he proposes that we should ask what position this author-figure occupies in discourse, what functions it exhibits, how it is produced, and how it in turn produces meaning.[18]

Boozer concludes, with particular regard to film adaptations, that these challenges 'belittled the role of all authorship by reducing source novel writers, and screenwriters and directors by implication, to invisibility or mere "author-functions" in a galaxy full of textual influences and cultural signifiers.'[19] However, note that Barthes' 'Death of the Author' is more a call for assassination than a funeral notice; he is not announcing that the death has taken place, but suggesting that this dominating figure must be overthrown, in order to give more interpretive power to the reader.[20] The reader, he argues, 'is the space on which all the quotations that make up a writing are inscribed without any of them being lost; a text's unity lies not in its origin but in its destination.'[21] The receiver of the text, in this model, becomes a kind of author, governing its meaning. However, this is not simply to shift all interpretive power from one individual to another. Barthes insists that the figure of the reader, too, 'cannot any longer be personal; he is simply that *someone* who holds together in a single field all the traces by which the written text is constituted.'[22] We might want to question his characterisation of the reader as 'destination', which seems, after presenting meaning as a transmission of endlessly-deferred energy, bouncing off reflections with 'no halt', to ground it in a final end point. Rather, we could argue that each viewer shapes and transmits, as well as receiving meaning; each reader is a switchboard, sending meaning on its way, rather than simply holding it together. Again, the next chapter will develop these ideas further.

Returning to Barthes' proposal, we should also realise that it was prompted not by the decline of the author's role but by the author's continuing power in popular culture: 'the *author* still reigns in histories of literature, biographies of writers, interviews, magazines ... the image of literature to be found in ordinary culture is tyrannically centred on the author.'[23] Foucault, similarly, concludes that 'in our day', as in previous centuries, 'literary works are totally dominated by the sovereignty of the author.'[24] These assessments from the late 1960s are equally valid in the twenty-first century. Some 25 years after the first publication of Barthes' and Foucault's essays, Janet Staiger and David A. Gerstner conceded that 'every scholar (even those who subscribe to the "death of authorship") speaks of going to a Robert Altman film.'[25]

Contemporary scholarship is inevitably shaped by these decades of contesting debate around the author, whether in literature, film or in the process of adaptation between the two; and as we shall see, these ideas have also influenced the way authors are discussed outside the academy. As noted, we will engage extensively with theories of intertextuality throughout this book: the concept of meanings operating in 'multi-dimensional space' is particularly appropriate to a cross-media matrix of stories, with hundreds of authors, about a character whose universe is split into alternate earths. However, as the commentators above all note, the more traditional, romantic model of authorship remains stubbornly embedded – presumably because it remains useful and valuable – within the popular discourse of promotion, journalism and reception among a more general, non-academic audience.

This chapter continues by looking at the ways in which 'Christopher Nolan' – his name, his brand, his oeuvre and his biography – functioned in the promotion and reception of *Batman Begins*. What we witness here, this discussion suggests, is not a fully-fledged notion of Nolan's authorship making its mark immediately on *Batman Begins* in 2005, but the evolution of that function over time; and in turn, we see other meanings competing for prominence in a fluid dynamic, while the sense of Nolan's authorial persona develops within public discourse.

Through this case study, we can identify what role, if any, traditional authorship continues to play in contemporary discussion around the director, and the extent to which the focus on the biography and psychology of a flesh-and-blood '*homme du cinéma*' has shifted, in popular conversation about cinema, to a more auteur-structuralist concern with recurring themes and motifs. We can examine the development of Nolan's author-function, and the figures and forces other than the director who are seen as potentially 'authoring' the text; particularly in the case of an adaptation, where the film is a new iteration of a familiar narrative. Finally, this extended example allows us to identify a form of authorship based in the creative collage and reediting of existing tropes, closer to Barthes' 'scriptor' than the figure of the traditional auteur.

Christopher Nolan: Evolution of an Author

Christopher Nolan came to the Batman franchise with three films to his name: the relatively obscure *Following* (1999), shot on a $6,000 shoestring; *Memento* (2000), which initially proved a hit at film festivals and was critically acclaimed, but struggled for broader distribution; and *Insomnia* (2002), a head-to-head between Al Pacino and

Robin Williams that marked Nolan's first entry into broader-canvas, bigger-budget, star-name cinema.

We can gain an initial sense of how Nolan's name operated within the promotion of *Batman Begins* by looking at the film's 'paratexts'. The term originated with Gérard Genette's 1987 discussion of the peripheral elements that shape our reception of literature, and was valuably applied to film and TV in Jonathan Gray's 2010 *Show Sold Separately: Promos, Spoilers and Other Media Paratexts*. Though known in English as *Paratexts*, the original title of Genette's book is *Seuils*, or 'thresholds', which captures his sense that these surrounding texts form a kind of entrance hall or airlock between the reader and the novel itself.

> More than a boundary or a sealed border, the paratext is, rather, a *threshold*, or ... a 'vestibule' that offers the world at large the possibility of either stepping inside or turning back. It is an 'undefined zone' between the inside and the outside ... indeed, this fringe, always the conveyor of a commentary that is authorial or more or less legitimated by the author, constitutes a zone between text and off-text, a zone not only of transition but also of *transaction*.[26]

Genette breaks down paratexts further into several subcategories. Peritexts are elements within the same volume as the primary text – the title, the preface, chapter titles and notes. Epitexts, on the other hand, circulate at greater distance, and 'are located outside the book'; they include interviews, letters and diaries. Returning to *Batman Begins*, we can see the title itself as a rich peritext: in Genette's terms, it does two jobs at once. *Batman Begins* is both 'thematic' – alluding to the subject, Batman – and 'rhematic' – referring to the text itself.[27] The title signals that this film is an origin story, but 'Begins' also positions it as a reboot and a clean slate for the franchise.

In early 2004, the first *Batman Begins* one-sheet posters were released: they featured only the main character's iconic silhouette against an ochre-tinted, smoggy sky, accompanied by the title and date.[28] The next wave of posters showed more of Batman's face and listed six of the key cast members (Bale, Caine, Neeson, Holmes,

Oldman and Freeman), but Christopher Nolan's name remained almost hidden in the small print at the lower edge of the image. Clearly, before the film's release, the director was considered far less an audience draw than any of the stars – including Katie Holmes, whose only significant role to date had been in the teen TV series *Dawson's Creek*.

The initial teaser trailer focuses on Bruce Wayne's childhood trauma and subsequent search for his identity, by Bale's gravelly voice over. 'That night my parents were murdered, I caught a glimpse of something ... something out there in the darkness ... something terrifying ... something that will not stop until it gets revenge.' With the pay-off line – '*me*' – we glimpse Batman in a split-second lightning flash. While the trailer is true to Nolan and writer David S. Goyer's intended approach to the Batman myth, with its emphasis on Wayne's journey,[29] the director's name is never mentioned; and later, lengthier trailers continue this focus on character and narrative.[30]

Although the actors' names are not flagged up in these promotional shorts, either – the only text in each is the opening Warner Bros. logo and the final title – their roles are signified visually and, in some cases, aurally: the longer trailers showcase all of the main characters, with ample space on the soundtrack for Michael Caine's distinctive nasally tones, Christian Bale's growl and Liam Neeson's calmly potent whisper. By contrast, *King Kong*, released in the same year, announces itself as 'from Academy Award winning director Peter Jackson' just over halfway through its trailer, while the preview for *Charlie and the Chocolate Factory* (also 2005) identifies the film as 'from director Tim Burton' within its first minute. These clips showcase Foucault's notion of author as a classifying function: the names are not used to refer so much to the real individuals or their biographical histories, but as an indication of brand values and a guarantee of quality and status – particularly in the case of Peter Jackson, whose own name now comes double-barrelled with 'Oscar'. Among that year's summer blockbusters, the promo for Warner Bros. *Harry Potter and the Goblet of Fire* provides a final, instructive parallel: in the riot of soundbites, star appearances and special effects, Mike Newell's name never comes up. In some cases,

then, the existing brand is a bigger 'author' than the film's director; and in 2005, this was apparently how Warner Bros. perceived
the relationship between both Harry Potter and Mike Newell, and
Batman and Christopher Nolan.

The official press kit, or 'Final Production Information', confirms the sense that, at this stage, the studio had little faith in the
brand power of Nolan's name alone. The first three pages are taken
up with a pitch about the character, his comic book origins and his
multimedia success to date. Christian Bale gets a name-check in the
second line of the document (in capital letters), followed by a mention for Batman's creator, 'artist Bob Kane' on page two, and a little
lower, Paul Levitz, 'President and Publisher of DC Comics'.

The press kit, then, sells the star, the industry spokesman, but
above all, the Batman brand before it gets round to a spotlight on the
director – and when it comes, it is a brief moment in the spotlight.

> 'What I wanted to do was tell the Batman story I'd never seen,
> the one that the fans have been waiting to see – the story of how
> Bruce Wayne becomes Batman,' says Nolan, whose taut, provoc-
> ative psychological thrillers *Memento* and *Insomnia* established
> him as a bold new talent with a keen sense of character and a
> remarkably assured directing style.[31]

Nolan is presented as a new kid, a smart guy and a fresh pair of eyes,
but certainly not as the bankable guarantor of value in this project.
Even in this short paragraph devoted to his filmmaking work, the
main character takes precedence over the director. Rather than
Nolan's author-function, this is Batman's party. Indeed, the document opens with a formal specification about the movie credits, stip-
ulating that Nolan's name should be 'not larger than 75% of title';
again, Batman is bigger, by order; and again, the peritext – the credits, framing our entryway to the film itself – help to shape our perception of the author's importance in relation to the main character.[32]

Note also the promise of fidelity to the original ('the one that
the fans have been waiting to see') with its implied distinction from
all previous Batman films, which are subtly constructed here as

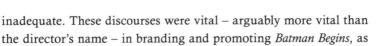

inadequate. These discourses were vital – arguably more vital than the director's name – in branding and promoting *Batman Begins*, as we will see below.

Journalism operates as a go-between in the process: it receives, filters, amplifies, adapts, edits and adds to the information from documents like the official press kit, and forms part of the relay between producers and audiences. From a study of 27 reviews and previews of *Batman Begins*, all from 2005 and drawn from British and American print and online journalism, including major news outlets and independent websites, we can gain a sense of the role these sources played in recognising and constructing Nolan as author.

We can establish one initial finding from this broad sample of journalistic discourse around Nolan in 2006: there is no focus on the director's biographical background, his upbringing, his early experience with film or his influences and their influence in turn on his work. The more traditional, romantic approach to the author that we saw in Robin Wood's essay on Ford – as an individual whose history, beliefs and life experiences are consciously expressed in a body of art – is extremely rare. I found it only in an interview published after the release of *The Dark Knight*: In Kodak.com's 'On Film', Nolan is encouraged to speak about his parents, his childhood Super 8 projects, his undergraduate studies and his wife, all in relation to his later filmmaking career.[33]

To an extent, a further exception can be found in the *Batman Begins* review by Edward Lawrenson in *Sight and Sound*. Lawrenson pays unusual attention to Nolan's 'distinctive identity' – as exhibited through his previous films, rather than through any sense of personal biography – and their relationship to this, his first major blockbuster. He observes that *Memento*'s 'fractured, wilfully elliptical narrative owed more to a tradition of modernist art cinema – which Nolan had already explored in his haunting debut *Following* – than the sleek, pacey conventions of comic book adaptations,' and worries initially that Nolan's individual style and expression will be lost in this tent-pole summer movie, but is reassured that 'Nolan's stamp is detectable throughout.'[34] *Sight and Sound* is, however, distinct from the other examples in this set because of its more serious, while not quite scholarly, focus on cinema, its assumed readership of film aficionados, and the generous space it gives to each review. It is worth noting that the magazine was publishing auteurist essays on John Ford back in 1956.[35]

The romantic sense of the director as an *'homme du cinéma'* is, therefore, entirely absent at this stage, and unusual even after the release of *The Dark Knight*. Nolan's personal stamp – what he brings to the table as a director – is established, where it is mentioned at all, entirely through reference to his earlier films, rather than his biography.

In quantitative terms, 15 of the 27 reviews mentioned *Memento*, 9 name-checked *Insomnia* and four referred to *Following*. Only one-third, then – 9 out of 27 – felt any need to situate *Batman Begins* in relation to the director's previous feature. The reviews quoted below demonstrate that, where a sense of Nolan's authorial styles and concerns is suggested, that sense is consistent; but it is invariably brief, and it should be remembered that even these brief examples are not representative of the discourse around *Batman Begins* as a whole, as almost half the reviews in the sample chose not to mention Nolan's previous films at all.

To Martyn Palmer in the London *Times*, Nolan is a 'hip young director' with 'impressive credentials [that] seem more suited to independent, edgier productions'. There is another hint here of the traditional auteurist approach, with its interest in a director's conscious exploration of recurring themes, as Nolan suggests 'I think when people see the film, if they have seen my other work, they will see a continuity of style and ideas.' However, any *Times* readers concerned that either Nolan's previous indie edginess or an undercurrent of French theory would nudge the film into an off-putting sphere of art cinema were quickly reassured through a reference to the generic pleasures of the summer action blockbuster. 'But this film is exciting and, hopefully, fun.'[36]

Sukhdev Sandhu writes in the *Telegraph* that 'the job of restoring Batman's tarnished reputation has fallen to Christopher Nolan, Anglo-American director of high-class, *noir*-tinged dramas such as *Following* and *Memento*.' His further observation that 'Nolan's previous films featured leads who had lost the ability to remember or to sleep' suggests the influence of the auteurist (and auteur-structuralist) approach on popular discourse; but this, understandably in terms of Sandhu's remit and readership, is only a remark in passing, rather than a more in-depth consideration of Nolan's underlying and recurring themes. The review concedes that Nolan is 'smart' and that the movie seeks to be 'edgy' in its 'dingy colour palette and all-pervasive downbeat ambience', but wonders why Nolan, 'a cerebral and gifted director of twisty, left-field action thrillers, felt the urge to apply his artful energies to such backwards-looking fare.'[37]

Empire magazine's review, by Kim Newman, touches briefly on the same territory. 'The Nolan who made *Memento* and *Insomnia*,' Newman suggests, 'is at home with extreme psychological states – this might complete a Three Colours Of Neurosis trilogy by following memory loss and sleeplessness with phobia.' His review, however, uses comic book continuity and the previous Batman film adaptations as its main points of reference. Like many other journalists in this sample, Newman situates *Batman Begins* in the context of the existing franchise – 'this sets out to be radically different from the series inaugurated by Tim Burton's *Batman* in 1989 and trashed by Joel Schumacher's *Batman & Robin* in 1997' – while he draws on his knowledge of comic books to compare Nolan's film favourably with the source texts. He praises it, in conclusion, for finding 'new things to do with, and say about, a character who's been around since 1938.'[38]

Variety confirms this sense of the values connoted by 'Nolan' in 2005, and also the overriding impression that this set of associations around the director played a relatively minor role in journalistic discourse around the film.

> It was a fairly gutsy bet on Warner's part to entrust the job to Nolan, a crafty young director whose *Memento* and *Insomnia* evinced storytelling smarts, visual flair and good instincts with actors. But these matters aren't at issue. Rather, it's the story that's been chosen to be told, and the degree of gravity invested in it.

Variety's Todd McCarthy shifts gear immediately – Nolan's youth, smarts and craftiness are not 'at issue' – to discuss narrative and (as the reference to 'gravity' suggests) notions of realism, and the relationship between this film and previous representations of the character. McCarthy suggests that *Batman Begins*, with its foregrounding of 'the demons that haunt and drive Bruce Wayne', is stripped of the 'sheer childlike fun' that sustained the comic books for at least part of their lengthy history.[39]

We can start to identify patterns in the process. When Nolan's authorial style is mentioned at all, the journalistic discourse echoes – quite possibly through direct influence – the structures and ideas put forward by the Warner Bros. promotional material, including the posters, trailers and press kit.[40] Nolan's distinctive values are thought to combine a sense of independence, edginess, intelligence and youth, and his previous films are remembered as psychological dramas with recurring themes, similarly troubled protagonists and unusual storytelling techniques. But these connotations are not turned up loud in the mix of meanings around *Batman Begins*; when they are discussed, they are discussed in passing, en route to a consideration of genre, narrative, realism or source material. Nolan as author is not exactly dead, but he haunts the text quietly, a ghostwriter, a trace and whisper of traditional authorship rather than a bold function.[41] That is to say that while he is appreciated as an individual artist and stylist, his name has not yet become commercially useful to the studio, or recognisable to reviewers, as a brand. A function, to Foucault, is not just a set of characteristic traits but a guarantor of value and bankability. Nolan has not yet reached this stage.

For context, 10 of the 27 reviews offer specific credit to David S. Goyer as co-writer of the screenplay, and 11 refer to Frank Miller, author of the *Dark Knight Returns* and *Batman: Year One* graphic novels. Of course, number-crunching of this kind can only give a rough impression. However, based on this tally, Nolan's previous film, *Insomnia*, with nine mentions, was judged to have less relevance to *Batman Begins* than Goyer's contribution (10 mentions) – which, given the low public visibility of screenwriters, and Goyer's own modest reputation at the time, does not imply major status – and

Miller's work on two related Batman texts, in an entirely different medium, from the 1980s (with 11 mentions). What is perhaps more striking is that, again, of these 27 reviews, 19 refer to Tim Burton, and 19 discuss Joel Schumacher.[42]

Again, the ways in which *Batman Begins* was explicitly promoted as a reboot of the franchise, and distinguished by contrast to the previous Batman movies, will be considered at greater length in the following chapters, but we can note here the key finding that when the individual author carries comparatively little voice in the discourse around a film, and has not yet become a commercially powerful 'function', other aspects rise in volume to fill that space. In this case, the discussion ranges across questions of genre, narrative and tone, but – as an adaptation of a long-established cultural icon, and the latest in a franchise – the common point of reference for *Batman Begins* is the source text, in all its previous variations. That is, the central term in these reviews is not 'Nolan', but 'Batman': the matrix of Batmen, from Kane's through Miller's to Burton's and Schumacher's.[43]

What we see here is similar to the approach proposed by Barthes, above, whereby the idea of author as creator of individual and original meaning is played down, and Nolan is viewed more as an editor of existing Batman meanings and a recycler of previous texts. Drawing on Barthes' description, we could suggest that Nolan expresses himself, according to these reviews, through 'a variety of writings, none of them original', and that 'the inner "thing" he thinks to "translate" is only a ready-formed dictionary, its words only explainable through other words.' Faced with the lack (not the death, but the marginal presence) of a distinct and familiar author, the predominant mode in these reviews becomes a 'lite' variety of poststructuralism.

To summarise, rather than the authorial name and its associations – 'Nolan' as a powerful function that classifies and guarantees a certain set of values – in 2005, with Nolan's reputation and persona relatively obscure, the relationship of the film to the main character's varied history in various media was the prime concern. More specifically, what is at stake in this discourse is *Batman Begins*' distinction from previous Batman films, and its assumed fidelity to the comic book. The main point of reference is its relationship of sameness to a specific group of Batman texts, and difference from another; and this relationship is defined primarily in terms of 'fidelity' and 'realism', as I'll explore in subsequent chapters.

As a further level in the relay between producer, text and audience, we can examine some of the other authorised texts that circulated around *Batman Begins*. As I've already suggested, any new Batman film is released into a complex network of stories and representations – far more so than, for instance, the 2005 film adaptation of Jonathan Safran Foer's novel *Everything Is Illuminated*, but also to a greater extent than the movies of *Charlie and the Chocolate Factory* or even *Harry Potter and the Half-Blood Prince*, with its relatively recent history and its smaller set of source texts. A new Batman film, as we have seen, has to position itself, through connection and contrast, in relation to a vast number of existing, ongoing and previous Batman texts. However, some of those artefacts – such as official merchandise, promotional materials and spin-offs – cluster more closely around the film itself. We have come across examples of these already in the discussion of movie posters and trailers as paratexts.

In addition to the split between peritexts and epitexts, Genette further distinguishes between paratexts in terms of their time frame, categorising those 'original' paratexts that appear at the same time as the text as separate from those which are 'later', or 'delayed'.[44] Gray, in turn, makes a distinction between 'entryway paratexts' and 'paratexts that flow between the gaps of textual exhibition, or that come to us "during" or "after" viewing, working to police certain reading strategies in medias res.'[45]

The novelisation, screenplay and comic book adaptation of *Batman Begins*, all published in 2005, could, like posters and trailers, be regarded as entryway texts – some keen fans would no doubt buy them before seeing the movie – but it seems more reasonable to group them in Gray's 'in medias res' category, as texts encountered at around the same time as the film itself. The DVD was released in October 2005, and for many viewers, would qualify as a 'later' paratext in Genette's terms, providing a repeat viewing of the movie within the new framework of bonus features and documentaries.[46]

On the whole, these paratexts firmly reinforce the patterns of discourse already identified above. The boldest, biggest text on the cover of the novelisation – aside from the title itself – is 'based on the Warner Bros. Pictures Film', associating authorship with the studio. The name of the book's author, Dennis O'Neil, appears above that of Nolan. Nolan is jointly credited here with the screenplay alone, while his collaborator David S. Goyer is referenced twice on the cover, for screenplay and story. The back cover blurb contextualises the movie only as 'the eagerly awaited new feature film', with no mention of Nolan except in minute text near the bottom of the page; instead, the book promises the "exciting origins of the ultimate crime fighter".[47] O'Neil's acknowledgements to Nolan, while no doubt meant with due respect, almost read as a snub: it is hard to imagine a more curt form of courtesy.

> By now, the Batman saga is huge. Bruce Wayne and his crime-fighting alter ego have been appearing continuously for sixty-five years, in every medium. But we should remember that it all began with 'The Case of the Chemical Syndicate' in *Detective Comics* #27, written by Bill Finger and with art by Bob Kane. I thank them both.
>
> I've never met Christopher Nolan and David Goyer, who wrote the film script that became *Batman Begins*, and probably never will, but I'd like to state for the record that they did a nifty job and it was a pleasure collaborating with them.[48]

The film's director – its ostensible author – is nodded to only as co-creator of the script, and O'Neil's faint praise ('a nifty job') feels like an obligatory, rather forced vote of thanks to someone in whom he has little personal interest. O'Neil's paratextual commentary situates the film primarily within the history of Batman stories across multiple media, and particularly in relation to the original comics.[49]

The comic book adaptation gives away its agenda through its full title, *Batman Begins: The Movie and Other Tales of the Dark Knight*. A comic book rendition of the movie – rushed in its pacing, careless in its writing and artwork – is followed by four original stories excerpted from previous Batman monthlies, including Denny O'Neil's 'The Man Who Falls' from 1989. 'You've just read how the Dark Knight came to be in the adaptation of the hit movie *Batman Begins'*, a caption explains. 'Now read the origin of Batman from the comics ...' A promotional spread inside the back cover encourages the reader to graduate towards other key titles. Some, as we will see, are chosen for their role in shaping the film (Frank Miller's *Year One* and *The Dark Knight Returns*), while others are selected for their continuity with *Batman Begins* in terms of featured characters. The connections sometimes have to be explained: *Scarecrow Tales* is straightforward enough, but *Tales of the Demon* is explicitly labelled as a Ra's al Ghul story, while *Blind Justice* is recontextualised as 'introducing Henri Ducard, the man who trained Bruce Wayne!'[50] Notably, the back cover introduces the film as 'this summer's hot action movie' and lists seven star names associated with the film. Not one of them is Christopher Nolan.

The screenplay offers another rare exception to this trend. Published by Faber and Faber, and taking a traditional approach to authorship, its introduction (by journalist James Mottram) suggests that Nolan 'uses the blockbuster framework to further his own thematic obsessions ... Nolan finds ghosts from his first three films returning for his fourth.'

> Bruce Wayne is tailor-made for Nolan's interest. As with *Memento's* Leonard, events have trapped Wayne into a cycle of violence and vengeance .... Compare Wayne also to Will Dormer, the detective at the heart of *Insomnia*, who likewise treads a delicate moral line between right and wrong. Nolan remains fascinated by the negative psychological effects of upholding law and order ... once more, Nolan centres on the notion of identity.[51]

An interview with Nolan, preceding the screenplay, continues this auteurist approach with questions about the director's personal taste in Batman texts and the film's relationship to *Insomnia* and *Memento's* questions of identity. Mottram seeks patterns and recurring themes within Nolan's work, briefly raising the issue as to whether they are consciously or unconsciously expressed.

Both Bruce Wayne and Leonard, from Memento, *are haunted by their pasts. Was that going through your mind when writing?*

Actually, at that stage, I don't think it was. Now that I look at it I think they are very similar characters, with that hollow, burned-out quality very present in both characters.[52]

As noted, though, this focus on the director's previous work and characteristic themes is unusual in the discourses circulating around *Batman Begins*. Even the Special Edition 2-Disc DVD features Nolan as a collaborator, one voice among the many included on the documentary features. Rather than being positioned as the sole creator, Nolan is a talking head alongside not just Goyer and the film's producer Emma Thomas, but DC Comics spokesmen Paul Levitz and Dan DiDio, joined by Batman writer/editor Dennis O'Neil and artist Jim Lee. The relationship they construct between *Batman Begins* and the comic books will be the subject of the following chapter, but even the fact that Nolan appears in such crowded company confirms that the director's role here is constructed more in line with Barthes' 'scriptor', an editor with the task of patching together a narrative from multiple quotations and previous references, rather than the sole creator of traditional auteur criticism. While Goyer and Nolan express careful reverence for the comic book mythos, DiDio's remark that Batman is 'a very hard character to break' as long as creators 'stay true to the origin of who he is and what he's about' almost sounds like a veiled threat, and O'Neil confirms the sense of comic book custodianship with his comment that 'we've been perfecting Batman's story for sixty-six years.'[53]

Amateur internet reviews and fan discussion from the time provide a sample of the way audiences responded to *Batman Begins*, and how they saw its authorship.[54] In the first 20 customer reviews of *Batman Begins* from Amazon.com – all posted in 2005, and in a ranking determined by 'most helpful first', indicating that these 20 most closely represent the general opinion of site visitors – there are only 10 references to Christopher Nolan.

After years of not having a Batman film and mostly due to the franchise hitting bottom thanks to Joel Schumacher's disastrous

Batman Forever and *Batman and Robin*, Christopher Nolan present us his version of the character [sic] with an impressive all star cast and a story brilliantly written by David S. Goyer.[55]

While the Tim Burton directed films ... were stylish and dark, they also suffered from plot holes. Then Joel Schumacher introduced a Day-Glo sensibility to the Dark Knight in *Batman Forever* ... fortunately, indie film director Christopher Nolan reinvigorates the franchise in *Batman Begins*, a reboot of the Batman legend. [...] This film is blessed with a solid cast that adds wonderfully to Nolan's vision. [...] The screenplay by Nolan and David Goyer (who wrote the *Blade* films) is awash with characterisation and motivation.[56]

Director Christopher Nolan has stripped away all the flash from the previous two movies ... if this movie's intent was to wipe the slate clean, and offer an apology for the previous four Batman movies, then mission accomplished.[57]

Another surprise is director Christopher Nolan of the highly acclaimed *Memento* ... suffice to say that Nolan is great with thought and suspense – but action? What an exciting risk to employ. Personally, I think these risks pay off in spades.[58]

Chris Nolan as director may have outdone himself in ways that we may never be able to estimate. Forget the old movies. They belong in the last century.[59]

So completely does writer-director Christopher Nolan reinvent, reimagine and reinvigorate this franchise, you may well entirely forget about the campy casting ... leaden dialogue, and nonexist plotting [sic] that Joel Schumacher used to try to kill off the series in the 1990s ... Nolan, the auteur behind *Memento* and *Insomnia*, likes his thrillers dark and twisted, and this one is no exception.[60]

Nolan is more than an auteur – he is an artist, and this will be the pivotal moment in his career, much as *Jaws* was for Spielberg

... Nolan effortlessly pulled the whole thing together, turning in the film on time and on budget, as though already he had years of experience directing big budget epics. Clearly his confidence and lack of pretentiousness allowed the actors to deliver pitch-perfect performances.[61]

One further contribution refers to 'Christopher Nolan and his co-screenwriter, David Goyer'[62] but makes no comment about Nolan's further shaping influence on the film; another credits Nolan and Goyer with 'a great script ... an incredibly touching and suspenseful plot',[63] while the final post praises Nolan for capturing 'with crystal clarity, and for the first time on screen, the dual aspects of the Batman character.' ... [64] In total, then, only half of the top-ranked 20 comments mention Nolan at all. Of those, only two mention his previous films.

We can see that Nolan's persona, such as it is, is constructed here in much the same way as it was in the press kit and in professional journalism: 'indie' and assured, with a proven talent for thoughtful, suspenseful, plot-twisting thrillers, and an ability with actors. Yet while two of the commentators actually use the word 'auteur', even these brief moments of recognition and contemplation around Nolan's role in the film are extremely rare, in the context of twenty lengthy reviews. That context includes praise for Hans Zimmer's composition, Goyer's writing and 'the design people'[65], and choruses of comments about the cast, from credit to Katie Holmes for 'shedding her *Dawson's Creek* image'[66] to the confession 'Christian Bale is handsome as Bruce Wayne/Batman, and I feel guilty because I had never previously cared to see something which he was playing in before now.'[67]

Note that other possible authors, besides Nolan, are suggested throughout this discourse. We have already seen, for instance, that Goyer is frequently co-credited with Nolan, as writer/author of *Batman Begins*. There is also a distinct sense in which Christian Bale is identified as an 'authoring' presence: his interpretation of Batman's voice dominates the first teaser trailer, while his physical embodiment as Batman overshadows the posters. It is Bale's name that tops the billing on paratexts like the comic book adaptation, and Bale's face, or an approximation of it, which distinguishes the *Batman Begins* line of toys from previous Batman action figures. (See for example the 'Batman Dark Knight Movie Master Deluxe Action Figure Batman from *Batman Begins* (Crime Scene Evidence)', which is praised by a customer for a 'genius' sculpt that 'has Bale's likeness'.[68]) While Nolan's evolving authorship is my main focus here, the star persona of Christian Bale (and later of Heath Ledger) as author-function within the discourses around *Batman Begins* and *Dark Knight* is worthy of further study, and will be discussed later in this chapter.

Above all, though, in this audience response as elsewhere, the frame of reference is to the surrounding texts of Batman – the comic book and the previous movie franchise – and again, *Batman Begins* is positioned in terms of sameness and difference. It is praised for its distinction from both Burton and Schumacher – Schumacher's films are reviled, whereas Burton's are more apologetically criticised – and for its fidelity to the comic book tradition. To offer just a few examples:

> The story uses the two villains exactly as they would act in the comic book ... Gary Oldman looks exactly as Jim in the comic.[69]

> This is THE definitive comic book movie of all time. It stays true to the source material, and is as true to reality as possible.[70]

> Not as cartoonish as past *Batman* movies, void of any influence of the old TV series starring Adam West, what started out as a comic book character so long ago ... has returned with a true essence of what Batman, and Bruce Wayne, are really all about.[71]

> This movie returned Batman to his dark roots, and don't get me wrong, I like *Batman* with Michael Keaton ... but that doesn't even come close to touching *Batman Begins*. It makes reference to [Frank Miller's] *Batman: Year One*. *Batman Begins* is the Batman film I've been waiting for.[72]

Let's all take a moment and try to remember (or forget) just how bad the last two Batman movies (*Batman Forever* and *Batman and Robin*) actually were. They were horrible ... it has haunted us true and loyal comic book fans for a long time. [...] Now comes *Batman Begins* ... it is dark, gritty, emotional and everything a *Batman* movie SHOULD be.[73]

At last, you can forget Joel Schumacher's Batman flops, and you can even lay aside Tim Burton's efforts at bringing the Batman to the screen. Finally, in *Batman Begins*, we have a film that treats the Batman as he should be treated.[74]

Across each stage of meaning-making, then – from posters, previews and press kits through the professional reviews of journalists to the amateur, but no less informed and arguably more invested, public responses of audience members – the story is the same. If the idea of Christopher Nolan as auteur can be identified throughout as a distinct but faint signal, it is almost drowned by the noise of other competing discourses; and these, whether they are concerned with fidelity to the comic book or contrast to the previous films, almost invariably centre on the history, continuity and variety that is 'Batman'. The sheer scale of the 66 year mythos, at this stage, overwhelms the relatively unknown director.

But after *Batman Begins*, that started to change.

The Prestige was released in 2006, one year after *Batman Begins*. Here the 'noise' was tuned way down – the film was adapted from a 1995 novel by Christopher Priest, but its source text obviously had nowhere near the public recognition of Batman – and so Nolan's brand, bolstered by the success of *Batman Begins*, rose to prominence without the interference of existing, competing discourses. There was no 66 year history of *The Prestige*, no previous adaptations by Tim Burton and Joel Schumacher, no campy 1960s *Prestige* TV show, and no dedicated fanbase of the *Prestige* comic. Now, in the absence of other associations, Nolan's name began to come into its own as a signifier of quality and a guarantor of certain values: as a function, in Foucault's terminology.

The *Prestige* poster announces, above the names of its cast, that it is 'from the director of *Batman Begins* and *Memento*.' The trailer makes the same announcement, just over a minute into its 2.30 running time – notable when we recall that Nolan was never mentioned on the posters or in the trailers for *Batman Begins* – while the press kit echoes and expands upon this sense of authorial branding. 'From acclaimed filmmaker Christopher Nolan (*Memento, Batman Begins*) comes a thriller woven out of the stuff of illusions.' It is worth examining the entire passage, and remembering, by contrast, the brief account of Nolan's previous work and authorial persona given in the *Batman Begins* production notes.

> Nolan, has already, with just a handful of films, established himself as one of filmmaking's most creative minds, and one with a striking ability to evoke the mysterious and disorienting, whether in independent classics or major action blockbusters. He first came to prominence after his promising debut *Following*, with *Memento*, the ingenious, backwards-moving thriller about a desperate man trying to avenge his wife's murder while suffering from the loss of all short-term memory. Lauded as a cinematic masterpiece that played with notions of time, space and subjective reality, *Memento* continues to confound audiences and is now studied by film students. Nolan went on to cut his teeth on a bigger thriller, a remake of the Norwegian noir film *Insomnia*, in a fresh version starring Al Pacino, Robin Williams and Hilary Swank, which once again took the audience on a dizzying journey into crime and fear. He then made another leap, this time into superhero territory, tackling *Batman Begins*, which unveiled the untold origins of the Dark Knight's emergence as the savior of Gotham City. The film was hailed as one of the most original and engaging of all superhero movies and went on to worldwide acclaim, the rare summer box-office blockbuster that met with equal critical success. Now, it seemed that Nolan was the perfect person to tackle material as intricate and unconventionally entertaining as *The Prestige*.[75]

The evolution of Nolan's author-function here is dramatic; while the key terms and ideas have not changed, those modest seeds from the previous press kit have grown into a towering presence. Nolan's talent for indie provocation now has a proven crossover success into the mainstream commercial market; his previous films are now positioned retroactively as stepping stones in his apprenticeship, with *Insomnia* as a form of training before *Batman Begins*. Indeed, Nolan's career is (perhaps unconsciously) constructed as an echo of Bruce Wayne's path towards becoming Batman, described in a language of rigorous, physical struggle – cutting teeth, a leap, a tackle, a dizzying journey – while equally subtle associations (disoriented and confounded audiences, evocations of the mysterious, play with reality) portray the director as a magician, like the protagonists of *The Prestige*. Nolan's authorial interest in psychological drama, his recurring themes of fear and memory and his characteristic experiments with narrative have now become established traits, validated by academic study and critical acclaim: his earlier work, *Memento,* is now confirmed, with hindsight, as a classic and masterpiece.

Of 21 reviews of *The Prestige* examined for this chapter, 14 give significant attention to Nolan's authorial style in relation to his previous films. These are more than passing mentions, and a detailed consideration of Nolan's characteristic approach is, in contrast to the reviews of *Batman Begins*, no longer exceptional. Even though Nolan's previous oeuvre is occasionally brought up in unfavourable contrast to *The Prestige* – the film received 75 per cent on the review aggregate site *Rotten Tomatoes*, compared to 93 per cent for *Memento*, 92 per cent for *Insomnia* and 84 per cent for *Batman Begins*[76] – there is a shared impression, throughout these reviews, of an artist with identifiable traits. For instance, when Peter Bradshaw, in the *Guardian*, laments the loss of the 'vital elements of wit, of insolence, of light-footedness and light-headedness that make magic so compelling – and incidentally, also made Christopher Nolan's first two films so compelling,'[77] he reinforces the sense of Nolan's typical approach even while recognising its absence.

Elsewhere, the pattern we saw in the *Prestige* press kit continues, with the 'signal' established around Nolan's authorship of *Batman Begins* amplified but otherwise unaltered. Matt Stevens, writing for *E! Online*, warns the viewer that '*The Prestige* presents a convoluted setup, with jumps in time, different locations and multiple characters.

Hey, this is *Memento* director Christopher Nolan's show, so the plot's not gonna be straightforward.'[78] Kenneth Turan's *Los Angeles Times* review asserts that 'Nolan, as is often the case (think *Batman Returns*, [sic] *Insomnia*, *Memento*), is concerned here with questions of identity, with what is hidden and what is not.'[79] Stephanie Zacharek, in *Salon*, guesses that Nolan was attracted to the project for 'its magnificent plot-twist potential' and 'the tortured manhood of the two main characters',[80] while Dana Stevens, in *Slate*, compares the film to *Memento* in its 'intricate, time-shifting story that never stops turning the tables on the viewer.'[81]

As a final example, consider the lengthy discussion of the director's perceived concerns and characteristics that opens Ben Walters' review in London's *Time Out*. Walters observes that *The Prestige* 'shares the fractured chronology common to [Nolan's] earlier work', and usefully summarises the 2006 Nolan brand:

> With *Following*, *Memento*, *Insomnia* and the uncommonly smart blockbuster *Batman Begins*, Christopher Nolan has established himself as a filmmaker fascinated by the fluid, tricksy contingencies of memory, identity, narrative and time: the way we depend on the stories we tell ourselves about who we are, and the little slips and dodges, ignorant or willed, that allow us to keep those stories straight – at least for a while. Selfhood emerges from these films as a rickety trick, an illusion dependent on misdirection and oversight. Apt, then, that the director's latest is a story about magicians.[82]

The consensus around Nolan's traits and themes remains remarkably consistent throughout these reviews. It is impossible to be sure whether they shaped each other, in a self-fulfilling process of rebounding, reinforcing meanings – the US reviews appeared before those in UK publications, due to staggered release dates[83] – or to assess the extent to which this journalistic discussion of Nolan was influenced by the Warner Bros. production notes.[84]

What we can identify for certain is that, following *Batman Begins* and *The Prestige*, Nolan's author-function has become far more established.[85] Although there is still no investigation here of Nolan's biography, or the ways in which his personal experiences and beliefs might have influenced his body of films – that is, this engagement is not the romantic, individualised *homme du cinéma* approach epitomised by Wood's discussion of Ford – these reviews, like the *Prestige* production notes, carry a strong sense of the director's deliberate agency and active creation. Nolan is 'concerned with questions of identity', picks projects for their correspondence with his favourite themes, has a fascination with ideas of narrative and time, and turns the tables on the audience. He is a conjuror, consciously in control, rather than expressing meanings as if through the recurring structures of repeated dreams.

With the release of *The Dark Knight* in 2008, we see a further shift in the dynamic. 'Batman', obviously, returns to the mix; but 'Nolan' is now a stronger voice, and his 2005 reboot has been judged successful in wiping the slate clean of previous traces. Recall that of the *Batman Begins* reviews, 19 out of 27 referred to Burton, and a distinct but overlapping set of 19 used Schumacher as a reference point. By contrast, from 44 reviews and previews of *The Dark Knight* – again, drawn from UK, US and online sources – only four mention Joel Schumacher's Batman films. Although 17 of the reviews touch on Burton's *Batman*, this is easily explained in terms of Nolan's reuse of the Joker as villain: the references are almost invariably a comparison between Heath Ledger's performance and Jack Nicholson's hammier act of 1989.

Overall, the matrix of references is far more complex and varied in this set of reviews. With *Batman Begins* successfully distinguished from Burton and Schumacher's interpretations, Nolan's *The Dark Knight* had fewer ties to the previous films in the franchise, and was free to circulate among a broader, more diverse and arguably more distinguished group of cultural texts.[86] Jonathan Romney, in the British *Independent*, muses revealingly:

The franchise received a radical overhaul in Christopher Nolan's *Batman Begins* (2005): sombre and portentous, it stripped away the previous films' gothic expressionism and their cartoonishness [...] Still, if you think that film burned the Bat-bridges, it was nothing compared with Nolan's follow-up. Note that the word Batman doesn't appear in the title. This is possibly because that might have attracted a pre-pubescent audience, and *The Dark Knight* is absolutely not a children's film. For that matter, I'm not sure it's strictly a Batman film.[87]

Romney goes on to compare *The Dark Knight* to the films of Michael Mann, John Woo and Sidney Lumet, with a further nod to *The Wire*. His points of reference are typical within these reviews: other critics identify the influence of *The French Connection*,[88] *Heat* and *The Godfather*.[89] The London *Times*' James Christopher aims even higher, discussing the film in relation to Greek tragedy and Shakespearean drama, while *The Washington Post* compares Ledger's patter to Molly Bloom's soliloquy in *Ulysses*.[90] Further parallels are drawn between Nolan's *Dark Knight* and two Oscar-nominated films of the same year, Paul Thomas Anderson's *There Will Be Blood*[91] and the Cohen brothers' *No Country for Old Men*.[92]

There are continued mentions of the comic book throughout this sample, and some context is provided through other superhero films of the same year such as *Iron Man* (Jon Favreau, 2008), *The Incredible Hulk* (Louis Leterrier, 2008), *Hancock* (Peter Berg, 2008) and *Hellboy II* (Guillermo del Toro, 2008) – often in terms of *The Dark Knight*'s more sophisticated and pessimistic take on vigilantism and villainy.[93] Roger Ebert's opening remark is telling. '*Batman* isn't a comic book anymore. Christopher Nolan's *The Dark Knight* is a haunted film that leaps beyond its origins and becomes an engrossing tragedy.' Sonny Bunch in *The Washington Times* confirms this sense of the film's distinction:

> To say that *The Dark Knight* is the finest comic book movie of all time sounds tinny — relegating this movie to the ghetto of mediocrity inhabited by films like *Wanted* or *Hellboy II* is insulting. *The Dark Knight* transcends its genre: it is an amazing movie, an epic tragedy in the Grecian sense.

The film achieves this transcendence, for Bunch and other critics, partly through its engagement with broader political issues. '*The Dark Knight*,' he concludes, 'is a masterpiece of the first order, and the first

great post-Sept. 11 film.'[94] Similarly, Dana Stevens in *Slate* credits
Nolan with turning 'the Manichean morality of comic books—pure
good vs. pure evil—into a bleak post-9/11 allegory.'[95]

The relationship between Nolan's Batman and post-9/11 issues
will be explored at greater length in Chapter Five; so let us return here
to the way that Nolan's brand now functions in discussions around
The Dark Knight. The director's name features more prominently on
the posters for this film than it did for *Batman Begins* – alone above
the title in a small font, rather than relegated to the group credits
on the bottom margin – but it remains a modest credit, dominated
by the images of Bale and Ledger, and the cast names. The primary
theatrical trailer runs without naming a director; the closest here to
an authorial presence is the Warner Bros. logo, closely followed by
that of DC Comics. Institutional and studio ownership continue to
trump Nolan's individual style and vision, in this case, as the thun-
der of the 'Batman' brand drowns out Nolan's voice.

In the production notes, too, Nolan has been demoted from his
previous lead role in the authorship of *The Prestige*, though this nevertheless constitutes a promotion from his cameo in the *Batman
Begins* press kit. Here, Nolan is effectively positioned as co-star
alongside his main actor and the central character, whose name
again resonates with history and myth. '*The Dark Knight* reunites
director Christopher Nolan and star Christian Bale, who reprises
the role of Bruce Wayne/Batman ... with *Batman Begins*, writer/
director Christopher Nolan opened a new chapter in the Batman
film franchise by taking the legendary character back to his
origins.'[96]

However – despite the still-powerful Batman brand, and the
broader network of cross-references now circulating around *The
Dark Knight* in journalistic discourse – there exists a far more distinct
and developed sense of Nolan as auteur in the reviews, both amateur
and professional, of 2008, compared to those that circulated around
Batman Begins three years earlier. Anthony Quinn of the *Independent*
and Bill Gibron from *Popmatters* agree closely about Nolan's key
themes, with Quinn remarking that the director is 'obsessively concerned with doubleness and duplicity'[97] and Gibron observing that

'from *Memento*'s Leonard to *The Prestige*'s duelling magicians, the split personality within all of us has become this filmmaker's aesthetic playground.'[98]

Stephanie Zacharek (*Salon*) and Jonathan Romney (*The Independent*) both give a sense of Nolan's career trajectory, from 'DIY tyro to Hollywood gun' in Romney's words. Romney tracks the director's rise from the 'resourceful' *Following* through the 'ingenious' *Memento* to his current A-list status[99], while Zacharek, with presumably deliberate repetition, lists the 'tricky backwards teaser *Memento*' and the 'tricky duelling-magicians teaser' *The Prestige* as evidence that Nolan 'takes delight in tricking and teasing his audience'.[100]

Nolan's associations with crafty play and psychological complexity remain intact, but as Romney suggests, a central question now emerges around the potential contradiction between the independent edginess of his earlier career, and the demands of Hollywood genre blockbusters. Peter Bradshaw worries, for instance, that the Batman franchise 'may be a bit of a career blind-alley for the talented director who gave us brilliant and disquieting movies like *Following* and *Memento*, whose inventions still linger in the mind.'[101] Anthony Quinn sees the director confidently handling this shift, but nevertheless highlights its potential tensions:

> Nolan, whose key film is the fractured amnesiac thriller *Memento*, touches on areas of psychological dread and doubt that hardly seem containable within a blockbuster. Yet, also to his credit, he never forgets that a blockbuster is what he has been hired to deliver.[102]

Bill Gibron notes that Nolan's more introspective approach could have undermined the action franchise – 'When he first revamped the Batman mythos for his 2005 blockbuster, fans were worried that future instalments in the series would be more psychological than spectacle'[103] – while Sukhdev Sandhu, who was alone in raising this issue around *Batman Begins*, expresses concerns from the opposite angle about the waste of Nolan's independent talent: 'shouldn't Nolan, marvellous as his directing here is, be creating original films rather than rebooting and retooling franchise fare?'[104]

'Nolan' has, by this point, become a distinct, recognisable term, carrying an agreed set of traits: a 'function' with enough presence to hold its own in this dynamic of meanings, and strong enough to establish a perceived tension between the impulses of authorial style and the generic demands of a Batman narrative. Indeed, of the amateur *Dark Knight* reviews on Amazon.com, the most significant trend is from commentators who, like Ebert, Bunch and Stevens above, agree that Nolan has transcended the genre and source material. One reviewer, Justin Heath, announces that 'Christopher Nolan has a vision' and sees *The Dark Knight* as

> A film that re-defines 'comic-book-flicks'... Christopher Nolan has opened a new door in cinema: allowing action flicks to become more serious, capable of intelligence. He has transformed this into a piece of artwork, full of beauty, terror, moral conundrums. This movie has changed things ... forever.[105]

This critic frames Nolan not in terms of Bruce Wayne's energetic training or the audience-confounding conjuring of *The Prestige*, but – through the quotation in the final line – as *Dark Knight*'s trickster and transformer, the Joker. Another reviewer suggests that Nolan and his brother, co-writer of the screenplay, have

> taken the Batman mythos and ... turned it into their own. [...] The director has abandoned the idea that 'Batman' has to have a comic book feel. Comic book fans have a reason to rejoice, the director has taken the Batman myth to new heights.[106]

A third comments that

> Most directors would have given this movie a distinctly comic-book, slick pop-culture feel. But no matter how hard you search, there's not a single hint in *The Dark Knight* that anything kitschy or campy came before it, or that it was originally a comic book.[107]

Finally, a contributor states simply that 'Nolan's vision of Batman has transcended the genre of superhero film.'[108]

While of course, this is a selective sample, it is representative of a broader community – Justin Heath's review above was approved as 'helpful' by 469 site visitors – and as such suggests a distinct and significant shift from the Amazon reviews of *Batman Begins*. In 2005, the amateur reviewers praised Nolan's film only for respecting and resembling the comic book; now they praise it not just for matching the original, but for going beyond it, even to the point of leaving the source material behind. There is no longer any need to compare Nolan's interpretation favourably to the low standard set by Schumacher: that slate is now judged to be clean, with 'not a single hint' remaining. The main point of reference here is the superhero genre itself, and the overriding sense is that Nolan's individual artistry has not just met expectations but exceeded them, pushing the boundaries and raising the bar.

Christopher Nolan's next film was *Inception*, released in 2010. The posters and trailers declared, unequivocally, 'From the Director of *The Dark Knight*.' Nolan's author-function had arrived: it had evolved into a powerful, unambiguous stamp of quality and a guarantee of values. Paradoxically, it was by managing to make his voice heard clearly and distinctly against the competing dialogue of other Batman 'authors', and by imprinting his style successfully on such a diverse network of meanings, that Nolan's authorial approach had been proven and his brand recognised: he had effectively wrestled his own interpretation from the matrix. It was, at least in part, through the struggle of retaining this personal interpretation and coherent identity in the process of adapting an overdetermined cultural icon that Nolan's author-function had emerged so strongly.[109]

We have seen that in both professional and amateur reviews, Nolan's authorial function was seen to transcend the structures and conventions of the source material, both in terms of the superhero genre movie and the comic book original. However, despite these shifts, *The Dark Knight* was not simply and unambiguously 'a Christopher Nolan film'; while Nolan had become a far more powerful player between 2005 and 2008, *The Dark Knight* was still, to one key audience group, first and foremost a Batman film.

That group was made up of Batman fans; people with a deep-seated investment in the character, and to whom Nolan was simply the latest interpreter of a larger myth. How were Nolan's increased status and authorial interpretation received by these committed fans? If 'Batman' remains the most important term to a dedicated audience, how were the director's increasingly powerful individual style and stamp reconciled with their long-standing investment in Batman as a broader cultural icon across multiple texts?

To answer this question, I surveyed 75 individuals in June 2010, using an online questionnaire that I promoted through *Batman on Film: The Dark Knight Fansite*. Established by 'Jett' in 1998 to lobby for a new instalment of the film franchise, the website now, in addition to movie news, includes comic book, game and merchandise reviews and has 'evolved to cover all things Batman'.[110] Sixty-eight per cent of respondents were aged between 20 and 30, while 93 per cent were male. Most were from the United States, though the questionnaire also attracted British, Canadian and Australian respondents, and scattered replies from nations such as Poland, Norway and Holland. One-hundred per cent identified themselves as Batman fans.

At the end of my survey, I asked an open-ended question: 'explain what Batman means to you.' A sample of the responses gives a sense of these fans' long-term, heartfelt investment.[111]

Batman is everything I want to be: a hero, a vigilante, an athlete, an expert fighter, an expert in many sciences, a playboy, and wealthy.[112]

Batman is just a big a part of my life as my family. I try to live by his values. To stand up to injustice. To live by a code, and to help people in any way that I can with no questions asked.[113]

In my 20s, I amassed a huge collection: the biggest prize was a Batman stuntman's costume from the Tim Burton 1989 movie. My wife, who looked very similar to Michelle Pfeiffer, would dress as the *Batman Returns* Catwoman. Now in my 40s, I have sourced and purchased a *Dark Knight* Batman suit. My middle son has followed my passion and now, in his late teens, he dresses as the adult Dick Grayson Nightwing character. My girlfriend is very supportive and dresses up as a very sexy female Robin.[114]

When it comes to Batman I still am, and always will be, that five-year old boy who got his first Batman mask and cape, put it on and truly lived for everything that the Caped Crusader did.[115]

We've all felt like the outsider at some points in our lives and have also felt like there's more within us than our social façade ('Inside I am ... I am more', Bruce Wayne; *Batman Begins*). Anytime I've been afraid of growing up and losing the comfort of my surroundings, I've looked to Batman. He is inspiring and has helped motivate me to embrace the unknown with confidence.[116]

All of these respondents were primarily Batman fans, rather than fans of Christopher Nolan's movies. Asked which Batman films and TV shows they remembered, almost all the responses hit the 90 per cent mark or above – 93 per cent had seen the 1960s TV series, 99 per cent Tim Burton's movie of 1989, 96 per cent had sat through Schumacher's *Batman & Robin*, and 100 per cent had seen *Batman Begins* – while only 17 per cent had seen Nolan's debut *Following* and 65 per cent *Insomnia*.[117]

However, when asked whether they thought Nolan's films had common themes, ideas or visual style, those who felt qualified to respond – having seen enough of Nolan's work to judge – closely echoed the sense of 'brand' we saw above, with a focus on psychological themes and non-linear storytelling.[118]

His use of psychological disorders (amnesia in *Memento*, voyeurism in *Following*, insomnia in *Insomnia*) has been prevalent throughout his work.[119]

Nolan's films so far feature a central character who has to overcome an obstacle of the mind – *Memento* followed a character that tried desperately to remember aspects of his life, *Insomnia* featured a character who was guilt-stricken and unravelling mentally, and Nolan's Batman is not only full of guilt but has been severely traumatised.[120]

They have stories that can twist in directions that you don't see coming ... the story is often not chronological.[121]

I believe the mind is a running theme throughout his movies – in *Memento* it was a character trying to regain his memory, in *Insomnia* it was the effect the lack of sleep had on the Al Pacino character ... in *Batman Begins* the Scarecrow used hallucinogens to affect people's minds, and in *The Dark Knight* there was schizophrenia. Even *Inception* will be about the mind. Duality, fear and guilt are also prevalent themes in his movies. Another common theme is his non-linear method – meaning the films jump back and forth via flashbacks. It is rumoured that *Inception* will also play out in a non-linear way.[122]

The fan approval of Nolan's Batman had clearly spilled over into or, in some cases, overlapped with an interest in the director's other films: this last respondent typified the 89 per cent who now planned to see Christopher Nolan's *Inception* (released the following month).

Asked to select as many options as they liked to explain their primary motivation in buying a *Dark Knight* ticket, 97 per cent opted for 'because it's a Batman movie' as opposed to 59 per cent who were positively influenced by Nolan's previous films. It is interesting to note further that only about one-third claimed to be encouraged by reviews (37 per cent) or interviews (33 per cent).[123] Although the discourses surrounding Nolan, discussed throughout this chapter, seemed consistent from promotion through journalism to audience response, with the same terms and ideas recurring at each stage, magazine and newspaper reports apparently played a fairly minor role in persuading these fans. With Batman proving such a strong draw for this group – bringing them in dutifully even to Schumacher's second film, despite its critical mauling[124] – it could be suggested that journalism's response, which I posited as a middle-term in the process of meaning-making around Nolan, is less relevant to fans who already have a loyal commitment to the central character. However, over two-thirds of this group admitted that they were swayed towards *The Dark Knight* by its trailers, and over half by its posters alone.[125] Official promotional materials are therefore a more important stage in the relay, directly confirming the style and tone of a new Batman adaptation, and reassuring comic book fans of the studio and director's approach.[126]

Traditional notions of authorship were still identifiable in this group's response. Given the choice to select as many possible 'authors' of *The Dark Knight* as they wanted, from a list including the stars, director, cinematographer, producer, production designer and others, 97 per cent picked Christopher Nolan. One respondent, who selected Nolan alone in this category, expanded on his reasons:

> whilst many people are responsible for the success of *The Dark Knight*, I would argue that the director ... is most worthy of the title 'author'. All the actors, producers, writers, cinematographers, designers and composers portray their own talented and varied skills; however, all take their cue from Nolan's direction.[127]

Despite the visual impact of Christian Bale and Heath Ledger in trailers and posters, the role of their image in branding the films across merchandise lines, and the particular prominence of Ledger in media discourse – his unsettling performance as Joker seemed even more resonant and haunting in the context of his sudden death in January 2008 – only one third of these fans were drawn to the film because of Bale, and the same proportion for Ledger.[128] However, Ledger's creative contribution to the film was recognised by the 43 per cent of respondents who chose him as a possible 'author' (compared to 33 per cent for Bale). One commented that

> ... once I found out Heath Ledger was the Joker I was instantly hooked. I had been a big fan of his and loved all his movies from *Ten Things I Hate About You* to *Brokeback Mountain*. If anyone could portray the sinister Joker it had to be Ledger. Christopher Nolan said it best when describing Ledger: he said he was 'fearless'.[129]

Another, who picked only Ledger and Nolan for the 'author' category, explained that 'Ledger should get an author credit as his performance surprised even Nolan himself – I'm not sure another actor could have brought the Joker to life in the same way.'[130] Note though, that while this fan gives Ledger a 'credit', he still lists Nolan first as 'the author of *The Dark Knight*, as it was his vision and story that brought it to life' – and both he and the previous respondent bring in the director's approval as part of their argument for the star's contribution.

Finally, while the 87 per cent selecting Goyer and 88 per cent selecting Jonathan Nolan confirms a traditional view of writing as authorship, almost half of this group (48 per cent) credited Bob Kane, who died a decade prior to the film's release, as an 'author' of *The Dark Knight*. To these Batman fans, comic book origins were so important that the character's creation in 1939 could still qualify as a direct authoring influence on a film from 2008, almost 70 years later.

We saw above a change in the popular conception of Nolan as author, as he rose in prominence and as a sense of his personal motifs and themes clustered about his name. Between 2005 and 2008, he evolved from a ghostwriter whose own individual approach and sense of direction carried little weight in popular discourse – and whose interpretation of Batman was defined more in terms of what it was not (Burton and Schumacher) and what it was close to (a vague sense of the 'original' comics) than what he brought to it himself in relation to his previous work – to a more visible and active agent.

To mainstream reviewers, whether amateur or professional, we saw that the Nolan of 2008 transcended genre and source material. The Batman fans see the relationship slightly differently. There remains a tension between this sense of personal auteurist vision and the continuing fan perception of Nolan, even in 2008, as a kind of editor, negotiating the encyclopaedic existing versions of Batman continuity and selecting certain aspects for his compilation.[131] However, we can also see how they resolved this tension and overcame this apparent contradiction. The answer lies in their listing of Nolan alongside favoured interpreters of the myth, when asked which particular version of Batman they preferred.

One respondent explained his fandom in terms of being 'torn between Nolan's version of the character and Grant Morrison's comic book version.'[132] Another bluntly stated 'Nolan's + Grant Morrison's + Dennis O'Neil's + Frank Miller's Batman.'[133] A third chose *Year*

One because 'Miller hadn't lost it completely back then';[134] another explained 'I will always have a soft spot for the Denny O'Neil, Neal Adams version, but Frank changed the character back to what he was always meant to be and turned the entire comics industry on its head.'[135] Another fan listed the *Animated Series* alongside Nolan's films, adding 'the recent *Batman: Arkham Asylum* video game also gets on the list ... it draws influences from all areas of Batman to create the character for the game.'[136]

What these responses demonstrate is threefold. Firstly, despite the fact that 100 per cent of the respondents identified as Batman fans, each individual prefers different texts, which in turn offer quite distinct versions of Batman; in these answers alone, they range from the 1970s comic books of O'Neil and Adams through 1980s graphic novels to the films and video games of the 2000s. Secondly, each individual fan is able to embrace different interpretations, some of which involve contrasting, even contradictory takes and personal styles: Grant Morrison and Frank Miller's versions of the Batman, as I'll explore in the following chapters, are quite distinct, though they share common features. Thirdly, and most importantly, fans recognise and value these texts as a balance between individual 'vision' and the existing mythos: Miller is seen as an auteur who actively revised the character (then 'lost it'), yet his achievement is seen in terms of a return to earlier versions, while the *Arkham Asylum* video game Batman is praised as a distinct character even as it is described as a composite.

Another respondent confirmed Kane's importance, while also crediting Nolan as a creative focus. His response, tellingly, combines a romantic sense of the auteur as a visionary individual with the scriptor of Barthes' account, who filters, selects and rearranges aspects of the already-said. 'Bob Kane remains the creator of the Batman universe and many vital characters ... it is through Nolan's vision that these elements are reimagined and presented to a contemporary audience.'[137] In this model, Nolan continues to filter and edits the existing Batman texts, but does so through his own identifiable 'vision': fidelity to the source is balanced with a sense of individual authorship, which lies not in original creation, but in creative selection, arranging and representation. That is, the process of editing can itself be both 'faithful' and a form of 'authorship'; it can strike a successful and respectful balance between the old and the new, the collective myth and the individual retelling, the familiar tale and the new take.

In this context, the notion of Nolan's recycling and assembly of existing texts into a new amalgam fits into an established model of comic book authorship, whereby 'authorship' lies in the skill of the recycling: the fresh twist on old material, the originality of the selection, and the talent with which the familiar pieces are combined in a new arrangement.[138]

This dynamic between familiarity and novelty is inherent to comic book storytelling, as Umberto Eco observed with regard to Superman stories,[139] and is not just accepted and readily negotiated, but welcomed by fans. Richard Reynolds points out, for instance, that while 'John Byrne's arrival at *Superman* or Moore's scripting of *Swamp Thing* are decisive events in the evolution of those particular characters,' and that 'we can legitimately speak of Byrne's Superman or Messner-Loeb's Flash as being different from other writer's [*sic*] conceptions of those characters', this sense of distinct authorship confirms rather than disrupts the continuity – the sense of sameness and narrative coherence – that holds the character together. 'There always remains plenty of room for the reinvention of consistent facts within the style of a particular creative team.'[140]

As further confirmation, consider the celebrated Alan Moore introduction to Frank Miller's *The Dark Knight Returns*:

> ... how are comic books to reinterpret their traditional icons so as to interest an audience growing progressively further away from them? [...] In deciding to apply his style and sensibilities to The Batman, Frank Miller has come up with a solution to the difficulties outlined above that is as impressive and elegant as any I've seen.
>
> [...] He has taken a character whose every trivial and incidental detail is graven in stone on the hearts and minds of the comic fans that make up his audience and managed to dramatically redefine

that character without contradicting one jot of the character's mythology. ... everything is exactly the same, except for the fact that it's all totally different.[141]

Nineteen years later, Joss Whedon introduced Brad Meltzer's DC superhero graphic novel *Identity Crisis* in almost identical terms.

The nature of epiphany is that it changes the universe without moving a hair. Everything before you is cast in a new light, a light so revealing it sometimes hurts. So it is with great mainstream comic writing. Mainstream comics ... are a universe, one that is as established and often unfathomable as the real one. A great novel or film might take you to a new world, but books like *Identity Crisis* have a much more complex criterion. They have to make you feel you're seeing something different without destroying the familiar.[142]

Finally, in 2007, Bob Schreck praised Grant Morrison's ability to respect and retain the character's heritage while bringing a fresh twist to his *All-Star Superman* as 'magic. Pure and simple.'

Common sense tells us that every possible tale that could ever have been told with these amazing players must already have *been* told at least ten times over by now. And yet, with the craftiest sleight of hand, Grant breathes new life into each and every one of the characters while never straying from the purity of their creators' original intention.[143]

The established tradition of authorship within comic books then, involves a complex negotiation whereby novelty is wrought from tradition; where the trick is to do something new with something old, to add sympathetically to the mythos without undermining its integrity, to respect the 'original' while revealing it from new angles.[144] It is within this tradition that Nolan's Batman films were successfully positioned and ultimately received by fans of the comic book character; not, as Whedon notes, as auteurist creations that stood stubbornly alone as idiosyncratic expressions, or as unauthored compilations of clips and quotations, with no guiding hand or shaping vision, but as a dialogue between novelty and continuity, between respect for the myth and individual interpretation.

As such, we can recognise in Nolan's role neither the death of the conventional author nor its triumphant return, but instead its evolution into a different type of creative authorship: from the auteur as sole provider of meaning to the scriptor as, in Barthes' words, 'a compiler or arranger of pre-existing possibilities within the language system',[145] a role that involves individual agency, creativity and vision through the editing process. This model also corresponds with Foucault's concept of the author-function which, as Jonathan Gray suggests, 'allows a middle ground, wherein the author is denied outright authority, but exists as a discursive entity that channels and networks notions of value, identity, coherence, skill and unity.'[146]

We have followed the evolution of the director from a quiet voice in the hubbub of meanings, almost overwhelmed by the source text, into a figure whose distinctive stamp lies not in the creation of entirely original art, but in the selection and collage of elements into a new arrangement. My case study focused on Nolan alone, but its findings have broader relevance, with particular significance to film adaptations: we could test this model against Peter Jackson and *The Lord of the Rings*, Mike Newell and *Harry Potter*, J. J. Abrams and *Star Trek* (2010) and Tim Burton's selected oeuvre from *Pee-Wee's Big Adventure* (1985) through his *Batman* films to *Planet of the Apes* (2001), *Charlie and the Chocolate Factory* (2005) and *Alice in Wonderland* (2010), all of which engage with a familiar source text while imprinting it with an identifiable style.

The study of adaptation has become an academic discipline in itself. We saw above that 'Nolan's Batman' could now qualify to be listed alongside Miller's Batman, Grant Morrison's Batman, O'Neil's Batman, even Kane's Batman, in the eyes of these comic book fans.[147] The details of how this relationship was constructed – how Nolan's interpretation was deliberately associated with the comic book authorship tradition, distanced from the previous film adaptations, and expanded to encompass not just the films, but a sub-brand of cross-platform spin-offs – are explored in the next chapter.

THE BATMAN MATRIX:
ADAPTATION

Adaptation Theory: A Very Short Introduction

The previous chapter noted that traditional notions of the individual auteur persist despite, or alongside and in tension with, the challenges of poststructuralism and concepts of intertextuality. Much the same pattern can be seen within the field of adaptation studies. In this case, the traditional model that clings on stubbornly – despite attempts to demonstrate that the process of artistic creation involves a complex mosaic of meanings – is based not around the idea of individual authorship, but the equally romantic notion of 'fidelity'. Just as Staiger and Gerstner wryly observed that 'every scholar (even those who subscribe to the "death of authorship") speaks of going to a Robert Altman film,' so Deborah Cartmell and Imelda Whelehan noted in 2010 that

> Even now and in spite of what are overgeneralised as 'poststructuralist' approaches to adaptation, regarded as having marginalised or theorised the concerns of fidelity-seekers in adaptation, the study of adaptations can still bring out the nascent prejudices in the most acute critic.[1]

We should further remember that, as was the case with authorship, an approach can become outmoded and discredited within academia, but still retain its currency within popular discourse: 'Fidelity,' Cartmell and Whelehan continue, 'remains at the fringes in the study of adaptations, but it dominates popular reviews and fan sites alike.'[2] Yet even a marginal fringe can be persistent and influential. Thomas Leitch's essay in the first issue of the journal *Adaptation* summarises the state of play in 2008, agreeing that 'despite the best efforts of Cartmell and Whelehan … the field is still haunted by the notion that adaptations ought to be faithful to their ostensible sourcetexts.' He finds even recent collections of adaptation studies perpetuating stale questions founded in traditional cultural hierarchies, such as 'does the movie in question betray its literary source?'[3]

One key tendency of adaptation studies is its invention of ever-more complex systems of classification to describe the process of translation from literature to cinema. Cartmell and Whelehan identify this '*will to taxonomize*' as 'symptomatic of how the field has tried to mark out its own territory',[4] and list a diverse variety of categories, from Jack Jorgen's modest 'theatrical, realist and filmic' of 1977 through Dudley Andrew's 1984 model of 'borrowing', 'intersecting' and 'transforming' to Kamilla Elliott's division of adaptation into six rather baroque types (psychic, international, ventriloquist, decomposing, genetic and trumping).[5] Leitch observes that while these terms need not involve value judgements, a sense that one type is better than another is allowed to 'sneak in under its cover, as if the will to taxonomise were only a mask for the will to evaluate.' He further suggests that all such categorisations explore the same relationship in the same terms, examining the film adaptation 'with primary reference to its closeness to literature',[6] and declares in frustration:

> Of all the ways to classify adaptations, surely the decision to classify them as more or less faithful to their putative sources, especially by critics who insist that Julia Kristeva, Mikhail Bakhtin and Robert Stam have persuaded them that there is no such thing as a single source for any adaptation, is one of the most fruitless.[7]

We saw in the previous chapter that the figure of the author is far from dead, though the discussion identified a stage when Nolan was relegated into the marginal role of spectral ghostwriter. Leitch sees the field of adaptation as similarly 'haunted' by fidelity; its relationship with literature is, in his vividly sustained metaphors, a 'dead hand' and an 'un-dead spirit' with which the discipline has to wrestle.[8]

We can also see that the challenges to this traditional approach came from the same direction as those that disrupted the idea of the author as individual creator. The intervention of poststructuralist theory into adaptation studies is largely credited to the work of Robert Stam in 2005,[9] and the opening up of what Stam called the 'dyadic source/adaptation model'[10] – a simple pairing of original and copy – into a network of intertextuality.

Stam's goal, set out in the introduction to his co-edited volume *Literature and Film*, is to overturn the notion, implied by terms like 'fidelity' and its common opposites such as betrayal, violation and bastardisation, that, in the process of adaptation, 'cinema has somehow done a disservice to literature.'[11] The conventional rhetoric around adaptation, says Stam, laments what has been lost in transition, rather than what has been gained; his goal is to challenge this implicit hierarchy that constructs the film version of a text as 'subaltern' to its literary source,[12] and move beyond the 'the moralistic and judgemental ideal of "fidelity."'[13]

In place of this romantic notion of adaptations that struggle in vain to faithfully copy their original, Stam presents adaptation as a promiscuous orgy of exchange – 'transfers of energy'[14] or, in the even racier term he borrows from Jacques Derrida, 'mutual invagination'.[15] 'Any text that has 'slept with' another text ... has also slept with all the other texts that that other text has slept with,'[16] he proposes, later suggesting that 'adaptations redistribute energies and intensities ... in an amorous exchange of textual fluids.'[17]

To complicate the process further, Stam suggests that the 'original' or source text[18] is not a single entity but merely a set of signals and signifiers that trigger different possible meanings in different readers at different historical moments: so even the sense of a stable core at the 'source' is split into multiples. Any purist idea of the spirit or essence of a text, Stam points out, usually comes down simply to the critical consensus of what it means to most people (or to the most vocal people) at any particular time;[19] and this consensus can also shift. 'Batman' does not carry the same dominant meanings now as he did in 1998, or 1967, or 1945.

'Adaptation,' Stam concludes, 'is a work of reaccentuation, whereby a source work is reinterpreted through new grids and discourses.' In place of the hierarchy between a high-status original and its copy, Stam sees 'an open structure, constantly reworked and reinterpreted by a boundless context', within which 'the text feeds on and is fed into an infinitely permutating intertext, seen through ever-shifting grids of interpretation.'[20]

Stam's provocative shake-up of the traditional and limited 'dyadic' model of original/adaptation draws, as we have seen, on key concepts from poststructuralist theory: specifically from the work of Mikhail Bakhtin, who as a Russian theorist writing in the 1920s was, strictly speaking, a 'proto-poststructuralist',[21] *avant la lettre* and ahead of his time, and Julia Kristeva, whose work from the 1960s – itself an early example of poststructuralism – reanimated and entered into a dynamic dialogue with Bakhtin's relatively unknown ideas of 40 years previously.

At the heart of this discussion is Bakhtin's concept of 'dialogism': the notion that no word, text or utterance speaks for itself, and that its meaning is only created in a kind of conversation, through the dynamic between speaker and listener, and in the context of what has been said before and what can be said in future. Meaning is therefore defined by relationships: not just along a horizontal axis, in the dialogue between author and reader – whose relative status and control over meaning is also open to debate – but also vertically, in the relationship between the text and other texts. Each text reads what has gone before and replies to it; in Bakhtin's phrase, the text 'lives and takes shape'[22] through conversation and conflict with other texts, always in process rather than stasis. 'The living utterance,' Bakhtin argues, 'having taken meaning and shape at a particular historical moment in a socially specific environment, cannot fail to brush up against thousands of living dialogic threads ... it cannot fail to become an active participant in social dialogue.'[23] Kristeva, writing in 1966, proposed in her summary of Bakhtin's insights that 'any text is constructed as a mosaic of quotations; any text is the absorption and transformation of another.'[24]

This interchange between Bakhtin, Kristeva and, in turn, Robert Stam – and at a further modest level, my citation of all three within this chapter – provides a meta-example of what it describes: a process whereby the meaning of a text is not found within the text itself, but in constant communication with and relation to other meanings within a network, like stations on a multidimensional subway map. As a further link within that system, we can connect back to Barthes' 'Death of the Author', with its similar proposal that a text is not a source of authoritative meaning, but a 'tissue of quotations', a space in which 'a variety of writings, none of them original, blend and clash.' Rather than an isolated station down a branch line, Barthes' essay was itself an important contribution to this circuit, and in keeping with the dialogic model, it entered into an intertextual conversation with Kristeva's writing at the same historical moment, with Bakhtin's of the 1920s, and indeed with the multiple uses of 'The Death of the Author' that continued after Barthes' death in 1980; like all texts, it entered a dialogue with speakers and listeners of the past, present and future.

The Batman Matrix

There are four clear differences between Nolan's *Batman* films and more conventional adaptations. Firstly, the cultural hierarchies are reversed. Film may stand in a subordinate relationship to literature, as Stam suggests, but comic books are even lower down the ladder than movies. Luca Somigli comments that 'when drawing from canonized texts (in particular, so called literary texts), from works firmly enshrined within the cultural tradition, the prime concern is faithfulness to the original ... however, when the source is a work of "popular culture", the integrity of the original is not an issue.' Somigli points out that the pitch for the 1978 *Superman* movie had to play down its source, 'so that the film could be cleansed of the unfavourable association that the source medium, the comics, carries with it.'[25]

Following the brief respectability of graphic novels during the 1980s and early 1990s, the comic book has long since fallen back into a cultural ghetto, and the industry, as Derek Johnson observes, is economically dwarfed by cinema. '*Batman*, the top selling comic in July 2003, sold only 146, 601 issues. ... calling the validity of the comic book form as "popular" culture into serious question.'[26]

> While none of the multiple *X-Men* comic books published in 2003 ... regularly sold significantly more than 100,000 issues a month, the *X2* film that same year made $85.6 million at the box office in its first weekend alone. [...] As popular texts, a clear discrepancy exists between the cultural status of comic books and their filmic counterparts, one that certainly contributes to the subordination of the former at the industrial level.[27]

Johnson explores this two-pronged 'subordination of the comic book to more profitable media' in terms of Marvel's rebranding 'not as a comic book publisher, but as a repository of licensable superhero characters'; over at DC Comics, Dennis O'Neil agreed with a 2003 report that comics had become the 'R&D division of the entertainment industry', a 'hidden asset' of Warner Bros, rather than an autonomous narrative medium in its own right.[28] *Batman Begins*' promotion as a faithful adaptation of the 'comic book original' has to be examined in this context.

Secondly, although a Batman film could in theory adapt a single specific text – along the lines of *300* (2007) or *Watchmen* (2009) – none of the ten Batman movies released in theatres since 1943[29] have done so. Even the aborted Batman film and television projects between Joel Schumacher's final attempt in 1997 and Christopher Nolan's reboot of 2005, including two draft scripts based on Miller's *Year One*, veered wildly away from direct translation; bizarrely, Miller's own script, with Alfred as a large middle-aged African American called Little Al, is less faithful to his original comic book than Nolan's later version.[30] Nolan, while less perversely creative with the source material than Miller, made no attempt to adapt a particular text; while there are many tales of Ra's al Ghul, stories of the Scarecrow, and retellings of Thomas and Martha Wayne's murder, *Batman Begins* is not, in itself, a rearticulation of any single comic. Rather, it recycles from a wealth of existing material – and invents new scenes and characters of its own – to narrate Bruce Wayne's journey from the loss of his parents through his training and transformation to the moment when his greatest adversary, the Joker, first leaves a calling card.

A film of 'Batman' – even of Batman's origins and early career – is, then, a quite different project from the majority of adaptations, which usually settle for the more modest task of translating one text into a different medium. For comparison, George Orwell's novel *Coming Up for Air* was first published in June 1939, about a month after *Detective Comics* #27 introduced Batman to the public; for the two to be equivalent now, the story of *Coming Up for Air* would have to have continued in several monthly formats since that date, with its protagonist George 'Tubby' Bowling appearing in a wartime serial, a campy TV show, various merchandising lines and video games, and a series of recent blockbuster movies.

There are, of course, examples from the middle ground between these two extremes, and the influence of intertextual theory on adaptation studies has prompted the recognition that many adaptations – even those ostensibly based on a single text – in fact draw, to various degrees, on multiple sources. Linda Hutcheon's *A Theory of Adaptation* offers a range of examples:

> For instance, when later writers reworked – for radio, stage, and even screen – John Buchan's 1914 novel, *The Thirty-Nine Steps*, they often adapted Alfred Hitchcock's dark and cynical 1935 film adaptation along with the novel ... and films about Dracula today are often seen as adaptations of other earlier films as they are [sic] of Bram Stoker's novel.[31]

Hutcheon further suggests that many viewers will have seen Kenneth Branagh's *Henry V* of 1989 'as much as an adaptation of Laurence Olivier's famous 1944 film as of one of Shakespeare's play'[32], and on a more literal level, she reminds us that Neil Jordan's *The Company of Wolves* (1984) is based not just on Angela Carter's story of that title, but also on two other chapters from her collection *The Bloody Chamber.*[33]

Cartmell and Whelehan observe, similarly, that 'it is obvious how the 1994 adaptation of *Little Women* pays homage to and borrows from' earlier adaptations of the Louisa May Alcott novel, and that each version of *Little Women* on screen tugs at cultural strings to other texts of its time: Susan Sarandon's casting in the 1994 film carries 'baggage from the likes of *The Witches of Eastwick,* 1987 and *Thelma and Louise,* 1991'[34] while the 1949 movie carries 'an intertextual reference to LeRoy's earlier film, *The Wizard of Oz.*'[35] Further examples could include Kevin Reynolds' 1991 *Robin Hood: Prince of Thieves,* which in Dan Georgakas' phrase, was 'aware of its illustrious 1938 predecessor and a number of other *Robin Hoods* in between",[36] and the many adaptations of *Oliver Twist,* which Christine Geraghty argues 'find their inspiration and source as much in previous versions as in the original source.'[37]

Roger Sabin and Martin Barker's monograph on the mosaic of texts that surrounds James Fenimore Cooper's *The Last of the Mohicans* also suggests a poststructuralist perspective in its conclusion that 'our myths have become more and more like a shattered mirror. A million fragments of story-glass, each refracting small elements back into our lives.'[38] The authors trace the passage of the novel through books, films, television and comics, and confirm the notion that many later adaptations refer back to earlier versions, as well as to the original text. The 1957 television series of *Mohicans* 'opens with a series of shots culled from the 1936 film',[39] while 1994's *Hawkeye: The First Frontier* 'uses clips from three different parts of Michael Mann's film.'[40] At an even more complex level of intertextuality, Kamilla Elliott's article on Tim Burton's 2010 *Alice in Wonderland* sees the film not as a conventional adaptation but a compendium, which 'adapts so much *besides* the Alice books': the film is a collage of references to video games, *The Chronicles of Narnia, The Lord of the Rings, Blackadder, The Muppets,* TV chef Nigella Lawson and Burton's 'own prior work'.[41]

Even films that define themselves explicitly against earlier adaptations inevitably imply a relationship with those texts: Zefirelli's 1966 *Taming of the Shrew*, Hutcheon argues, aims to displace the earlier Mary Pickford and Douglas Fairbanks film,[42] while Rebecca Bell-Metereau reports that the creative team behind Adrian Lyne's 1997 *Lolita* 'actually looked upon the Kubrick version as a kind of "what not to do."'[43] Nolan's Batman, as we have already seen, occupies a similar relationship with Schumacher's, and to a lesser extent Burton's earlier movies; in the process of cutting ties with the previous version, these protestations of difference tend to make the earlier text visible.

However – although these case studies argue convincingly that all adaptations occupy a network rather than a simple pairing – the set of *Little Women* intertexts, while more extensive than that of *Coming Up for Air*, remains a modest and contained system compared to the vast Batman universe. Even *The Last of the Mohicans* and *Alice in Wonderland,* with their complex cultural lives, involve a central source and satellites of various sizes: even if, as Stam argues, the meaning of that source depends on a contemporary consensus, we can still lay our hands on the core text of *Alice*, a book published in 1865. Batman has no such centre – the first story of 1939 is not the last word of the myth, but its first, its starting point – and its body of stories increases every month. For Nolan to attempt an adaptation of an ever-expanding mythos with no definitive ur-text remains a challenge quite different from engaging with a conventional novel.

Thirdly, while adapting prose text to cinema presents its own challenges, the process of adapting comic books to cinema poses a specific set of difficulties. John Fowles said of his novel *The French Lieutenant's Woman* that it depends on 'word things the camera will never photograph nor actors ever speak'; indeed, the twentieth-century novel as a whole, to Fowles, 'has been more and more concerned with all those aspects of life and modes of feeling that can *never* be represented visually.'[44] R. Barton Palmer's article on the 1981 Karel Reisz adaptation observes that the 'characteristically literary' device of Fowles' obtrusive narration was translated not into a voice over but into the more characteristically cinematic language of cross-cutting; some aspects of the novel (any novel) 'can never be pictured or dramatised.'[45]

Although adaptation from the largely visual form of comics to the screen may seem a smaller and more straightforward step than expressing 'word-things' through shots and editing, Pascal Lefèvre's article on the 'incompatible visual ontologies' of the two media lists a number of obstacles.

> ... panels are arranged on a page, panels are static drawings and a comic does not make noise or sound. Film is quite different. First, there is a screen frame, second, the film images are moving and photographic, third, film has a soundtrack. These characteristic differences of the two media become enacted as the four adaptation problems of (1) the deletion/addition process ... (2) the unique characteristics of page layout and film screen; and (3) the dilemmas of translating drawings to photography'; and (4) the importance of sound in film compared to the 'silence' of comics.[46]

Various adaptations have tried in different ways to capture or at least suggest a comic book aesthetic – from *Dick Tracy*'s deliberately flat colour scheme and *mise-en-scène*[47] to *The Hulk*'s (2003) innovative editing and framing devices[48] and *300*'s (2007) extensive use of blue screen and 'digital backlot' technology. While *Batman Begins* aims for a 'realist' aesthetic, and locates itself more in relation to the conventions of the crime movie than the ultra-faithful comic book translation such as *Sin City* and *Watchmen*, its paratexts attempt to bridge the gap between print and screen media.

Finally, just as most literary adaptations focus on a single text, they also, for the most part, result in a single text. The 2005 adaptation of *Pride and Prejudice*, directed by Joe Wright, carries its own paratexts – posters and trailers, of course, but also a relaunch of the original novel with a new cover, a soundtrack album and DVD/Blu-ray release.[49] However, compared to the texts that surrounded and circulated in the wake of 2005's *Batman Begins*, including a range of toys, a novelisation and published screenplay, a video game, several rereleased comic books, the *Gotham Knight* DVD, the viral marketing for *The Dark Knight* and, arguably, *The Dark Knight* itself, Austen's spin-offs are relatively conservative and uncomplicated. In addition to drawing on a range of sources, then, the story that started in *Batman Begins* continued across multiple platforms and over several years, and the relationship between Nolan's extended cross-media text – from *Batman Begins* in 2005 to *The Dark Knight Rises* in 2012 – and the existing, ongoing and subsequent Batman narratives also needs to be examined.

The rest of this chapter addresses those four key issues: the questions raised by the relative status of comic books and cinema, the challenges of adapting not a single source but a vast archive, the translation across media from the comic page to film, and the implications of an adaptation that produces not one text, but many.

The reverence and respect with which the creative team behind *Batman Begins* treated the comic book – evidenced, for instance, in the press notes that paved the way for the film's release, and the DVD documentaries that framed its entry into the home – are surprising in the general context of comic books' subordinate cultural role, and more specifically, previous Batman directors' indifference to comic book continuity and its associated fandom. Although the producer of 1989's *Batman*, Jon Peters, was reportedly shaken by a *Wall Street Journal* article that questioned the film's financial prospects in the face of fan disillusionment, and responded by cutting together a reassuringly 'dark' preview,[50] Tim Burton kept his eye stubbornly on the mainstream audience, rather than the comic-reading minority. 'There might be something that's sacrilege in the movie ... But I can't care about it ... This is too big a budget movie to worry about what a fan of a comic would say.'[51]

Burton's *Batman* was, ultimately, far more Burton than *Batman*; this was a case of director firmly in place as author, making another eerily comic film about gothic outsiders, freaks and clowns,[52] rather than humbly taking the role of scriptor and trying to cut, edit and stitch together a short, coherent film story from the vast tapestry of 'Batman'. However, the fact that producers had to respond to fans at all seems to have nudged the balance of power and prompted a new attitude towards the minority audience. Ian Gordon, Mark

Jancovich and Matthew P. McAllister report that, the year after the *Wall Street Journal*'s Batman scare, 'Walt Disney Pictures made sure to preview its film *Dick Tracy* to comic fans at the San Diego comic conference'[53]. By the 2000s, this courtship had become routine:

> Short rough-cut previews of films debut at comics conventions in an attempt to generate early buzz, such as an eighteen-minute version of *Constantine* at the 2004 San Diego Comic-Con international (in fact, seventeen other comics-related films were teased there).[54]

The authors cite *Sin City* as a particularly reverent example of adaptation – 'as close to a frame-by-frame, panel-by-panel visual recreation of the comic as you could imagine'[55] – though Zach Snyder's 2009 movie of the graphic novel *Watchmen* arguably went further. Bob Rehak describes it as 'fanservice with a $120 million budget ... *Watchmen* simply takes faithfulness and fidelity to a cosmic degree.'[56]

As should already be clear, *Batman Begins* was not a 'faithful adaptation' even in the limited, formal sense attempted by *Sin City* and *Watchmen;* it chose not to adapt a single text, so could not boast that it had painstakingly translated the artwork and dialogue of a specific comic to a new medium. However, discourses of fidelity, and sensitivity to the preferences of comic book fans, played an important role in the film's promotion. A 2005 interview with Nolan in the *Guardian* confirms the increasing importance and influence of fandom – particularly online – and suggests that Warner Bros., burned by the response to Schumacher's instalments, had become particularly cautious.

> First and foremost, Nolan has had to grapple with the legacy of the Joel Schumacher Batman films, the last of which, *Batman & Robin*, was famously torpedoed by streams of abuse on internet fan sites. Not only did this episode alert Hollywood to the influence, baleful or otherwise, of the chatroom nerd, it also induced a climate of fear around the Batman movies themselves. One attempt after another to resuscitate the profitable franchise has

failed to get off the ground. By the time Nolan came into the picture, around two and a half years ago, he says, he was looking at a blank slate. [57]

'Warner Bros,' the article goes on, 'mindful of the *Batman & Robin* fiasco, went to considerable lengths to keep a lid on their plans'; as Nolan explains, 'The last thing we wanted was for any early ideas to get out there and be rejected by the fans and the internet guys.'[58] While the comic book industry may be the poor cousin to cinema in terms of cultural status and economic returns, film producers know that comic fans have a voice and a power disproportionate to their number. There may not be many of them, but they're loud, and they can kick up a stink. Despite the supposed relegation of comics to the 'R&D' department of blockbuster movies, the fans are respected, and courted, as a small but vocal pressure group.[59]

As we saw in the last chapter, the studio was only partially successful in its attempt at a clean reboot. Rather than assessing it on its own merits, 19 of the 27 reviews surveyed above compared Nolan's film to Schumacher and Burton's Batman movies; although the comparisons favoured Nolan, the traces of previous Batmen were still clearly visible. This notion of Batman as a palimpsest rather than a blank slate – always bearing the marks of other stories and incarnations, and impossible to wipe completely clean – is central to my argument in this book, and will inform this and later chapters.

However, the promotional push behind *Batman Begins* did result in foregrounding comic books as a key reference point in the discussion; we saw that eleven of the reviews mentioned Frank Miller's graphic novels, and that the amateur reviews on Amazon frequently praised *Batman Begins* for its close relationship to 'the source material'.

As noted, the idea that the 2005 Batman would mark an unprecedented return to the 'original' was put on the agenda by the press notes, and kept there by subsequent paratexts like the DVD documentaries. The previous chapter discussed the authorship ranking implied by the production document, with 'artist Bob Kane' given the first mention, followed by an interpretation of Batman from DC Comics executive Paul Levitz before Nolan earns his brief turn under the spotlight. A quotation from Batman's comic book origin – 'Criminals are a cowardly, superstitious lot …' – provides the document's epigraph, while lines from *Year One* literally frame the discussion, with subheadings such as 'He will become the greatest crimefighter the world has ever known. It won't be easy' taken directly from Frank Miller's 1987 series.

The opening pages involve various members of the production crew paying their respects to the comic books, as if taking the microphone at a tribute ceremony. Nolan claims he wanted the movie to be 'the cinematic equivalent of reading a great graphic novel',[60] while Christian Bale 'discovered the Dark Knight several years ago at a comic book store in Santa Monica', and enthuses that 'graphic novels like *Arkham Asylum* presented a Batman that I had never seen before. He was dark and dangerous and more interesting than any other comic book hero or villain.'[61] Producer Emma Thomas notes that 'Gary's performance captures the essence of Gordon from the comic books. He very much looks the way the character does in [Frank Miller's] *Batman: Year One*',[62] and Gary Oldman dutifully agrees: 'Chris wanted me to look as much like Gordon does in the comic as I realistically could'.[63] Even references to the Scarecrow and his alter ego Jonathan Crane are supported by reminders that these 'are important characters in Batman's comic book mythology'.[64]

While Nolan has admitted that 'I've always been more of a movie person than a comic person',[65] and Goyer is, as we'll see, presented as the comic book expert of the pair, the director's diligent research, and again, his respect for the source material, are heavily foregrounded here.

> I looked at the great comics and graphic novels through the history of Batman to try and distil the essence of what those extraordinary pictures and drawings were saying about what Batman should look like. Each artist interprets the costume differently, but there are these common aspects that define the essence of the character.

Bale, too – presumably guided by Nolan – undertook a similar process of research, and according to the director 'spent a long time looking at graphic novels and illustrations of Batman, to form his own sense of how he should move and communicate with the other characters.'[66]

The bonus features that supplement *Batman Begins* on DVD work hard to reassure the viewer of the film's loyalty to its source material. Even the menu is an animated comic book – a Bale-like Batman investigating the Scarecrow's lair, as heavy rain cycles on the soundtrack – with clickable elements in each frame cueing individual documentary films. As I'll discuss, features like this help bridge the gap between comics and film, but clearly, the idea is also to insert Bale/ Nolan's Batman into the comic book mythos, blurring boundaries into a smooth continuity.

The documentaries that launch from this menu replay the sense of reverence we saw in the press notes. Nolan again modestly admits 'I've always been a big fan of the character, but I am by no means any kind of comic book expert,' and explains that he called in Goyer for his expertise. 'I felt I needed a writer on the project who really knew the character inside out, really knew the comic world.'[67] Goyer, in turn, had 'always wanted to write a Batman movie … in a way I'd been waiting my whole life for this call.' 'I guess he's just such a big fan of the character, he couldn't resist,' Nolan smiles. This set-up – the writer as lifelong fan, and the director modestly deferring to that expertise – could hardly be more different from Burton's professed indifference to fan opinion. Nolan, by contrast, seems deliberately and humbly to be playing down his own authorial role, and portraying himself – in keeping with the findings of the last chapter – more as the editor of a Bat-encyclopaedia.

'David Goyer and myself drew very heavily on this great history of this character,'[68] Nolan claims, again suggesting that *Batman Begins* is a composite and condensation of the 66-year mythos. Yet the visuals tell a different story; and now the documentary starts to clarify, very subtly, what 'adaptation' actually means in this case. While Nolan and Goyer speak, the camera slides tightly over comic book images, exploring artwork in close-up. Those images, cut with clips from the film to suggest a relationship of influence, are from Frank Miller and David Mazzucchelli's 1987 *Year One,* Jeph Loeb and Jim Lee's *Hush* (2003), Miller's *Dark Knight Returns* (1986), Tim Sale and Jeph Loeb's *The Long Halloween* (1996) and a Brian Bolland cover from October 2002. Gary Oldman's resemblance in the film to the Jim Gordon of 'the comic' is again made clear, but again, 'the comic' is narrowed down to a very specific text, Miller's *Year One*. The source for *Batman Begins* is – contrary to what the interviews suggest – not the entire, unwieldy mythos of the character from 1939–2005, but a far more selective tradition.

This sleight of hand continues in the disc's final documentary. The title itself, 'Genesis of the Bat', suggests a look back at Batman's origins in the 1930s and development to the present day, which Nolan confirms with a reiteration of his previous speech – 'David Goyer and myself drew very heavily on the history and the mythology of Batman ... there is this great, you know, seventy-year history of the character.'[69] Dennis O'Neil, the next talking head, adjusts the time frame but reaffirms the sense of history: 'Batman has ... attracted more good writers and artists over the sixty-plus years than almost any other character.'

But again, the illustrations almost subliminally shrink 'history' to a narrow window. O'Neil is interviewed in front of a movie poster and a painted portrait of Batman by Alex Ross, a fan favourite since 1996's *Kingdom Come*. When O'Neil describes Batman as the 'crown jewel of the comic book world', his comment is illustrated with a 2002 cover by Brian Bolland; and just as the Ross painting is linked visually with the movie poster, so the documentary cuts from the drawing to a similar image from *Batman Begins*, suggesting a direct translation from print to screen. (There is no such connection; Bolland's cover to *Gotham Knights* #29 shows Batman attacked by zombies.) When O'Neil first mentions Batman's 60-year heritage, we see the cover of Frank Miller and Jim Lee's *All Star Batman and Robin The Boy Wonder* from 2005, and his claim that 'we've been perfecting Batman's story for sixty-six years' is illustrated with a Mike Mignola cover from 1988.

The documentary reaches furthest back into the archive with its brief display of O'Neil and Neal Adams' 'Daughter of the Demon' story from June 1971 – the first appearance of Ra's al Ghul – which is followed swiftly by Miller and Mazzucchelli's *Year One* and a 2003 cover from Jeph Loeb and Jim Lee's *Hush*. Again, in a disjuncture that only the comic book pedant with a finger on the pause control would consciously notice, this montage is accompanied by Nolan's declaration that 'I felt that everything we were going to do in terms of translating the character's story onto film was going to have to be extremely reverent to the history of the character and the mythology of Batman.'[70]

So, rather than distilling an essence of Batman from the vast reservoir of stories gestured to by both O'Neil and Nolan, the visual subtext of the documentary suggests spear-fishing from within a small pool; and that pool of stories in turn suggests a particular aesthetic, a particular set of authors, and a particular period. The tone, the mood and the type of Batman that operates within this tighter framework – not a free-ranging and diverse myth, but the more consistent and inevitably limited figure of the 'dark', modern tradition – will be discussed the next chapter. The time period, as we have seen, begins not with 1939, despite the talk of respecting origins and mythology, but in 1970, when O'Neil and Adams were tasked with rebooting the character from his campy television incarnation.[71] Bob Schreck, DC Comics' Batman editor, confirms this revisionist historical perspective with his praise for the way that Nolan and Goyer 'really, really cared about the source material ... they went through tons and tons of different graphic novels and comics. They definitely culled from the last thirty-some-odd years, and they got the character ... they got it.'[72]

As for the writers and artists who have been perfecting and guarding the character – before, it's implied, passing him temporarily into Nolan's hands – further scenes in the documentary make their influence, already suggested by the illustrations, fully explicit. Again, the list is short. Indeed, the interview with Paul Levitz suggests that DC Comics may have carefully shaped the selection process; culling the canon down to key works, gently educating Nolan's crew, and drawing the boundaries around the 'Batman' they were to adapt.

What we tried to do was to provide the best resources for the filmmakers. So we went back and did everything from finding the most interesting versions of the Batman origin ... the most interesting treatments of a particular villain ... here's the classic arc that introduced Ra's al Ghul. Here's the two or three best Scarecrow stories that were done. And you really let the film-makers draw their inspiration where they may.[73]

For Levitz to recommend Ra's al Ghul's origin was, of course, entirely sensible, and as a relatively recent addition to the mythos, the character has only a modest library of stories to his name; but Scarecrow made his first appearance in 1941. To hand over only two or three 'best' stories from 64 years of continuity clearly involves a rigorous selection process, and far less creative choice for the film-makers than Levitz implies.

Although Goyer has been presented as a lifelong fan who 'knew the character inside out' and could presumably have written Batman without this heavy-handed guidance, he seems – perhaps with an air of self-conscious apology – to accept DC's restricted playing field.

There were three pieces of work, or eras of Batman, that were somewhat influential to Chris and I when we were working. *The Long Halloween* was a piece of work that influenced us ... there are elements of that, Carmine Falcone, who's one of the mob bosses in Gotham. It's a very sober, serious approach to Batman, and we really liked that. And then we were also influenced by some of the '70s Batman comic books.[74]

The task of adapting 'Batman' in his 66 year complexity has been cut down to adapting Batman since the early 1970s; and even that archive has been whittled further to a handful of specific books by specific creators. *The Long Halloween*, Loeb and Sale's maxi-series from 1996–1997, is joined by O'Neil's Ra's al Ghul tales from 1971 – which, in Goyer's words, opened out the Batman mythos beyond Gotham to a broader, global scope – and then by another O'Neil title, 'The Man Who Falls' from 1989, which Nolan names as his 'jumping-off point' for the idea that Wayne travels the world, is mentored and tutored, and then returns to Gotham.[75] The third key influence named by Goyer is Miller's *Year One*, for its focus on Batman's origins, its relationship between Batman and Gordon, and because 'the approach was very no-nonsense and very tough'.[76] The 'three eras' of Batman turn out to be 1971 (O'Neil and Adams) 1987–1989 (Miller and Mazzucchelli/O'Neil), and 1996–1997 (Loeb and Sale): four years out of the 66 then available in the character's history.[77]

So, while the production materials and documentaries suggest a broad and holistic sense of the 'source' – the entire 'history of Batman' – this vast range is narrowed down to a manageable group of texts: a small constellation of stars (O'Neil, Adams, Miller, Loeb) rather than a universe. However, even within this group there remains no single source; these are multiple, contradictory 'originals' of equal status circulating on their own distinct orbits, rather than a central, luminous ur-text and its satellites.

Therefore, although the production notes and documentaries stress romantic notions of loyalty, reverence and fidelity in an attempt firmly to position Nolan's Batman as distinct from Schumacher's and win the approval of the fan audience, the process of adaptation even from a relatively small set of source texts still fits the more promiscuous poststructuralist model, with the film occupying one node in an interlinked network, rather than a more traditional view of 'original' and 'copy'. Rather than the faithful pairing implied by both the film crew and the comic book creators, *Batman Begins* entered a matrix.

What, then, does *Batman Begins* actually adapt? On the simplest level, it transfers aspects of character faithfully from these comics to the screen. Batman is Bruce Wayne, whose parents were murdered and who now fights crime in Gotham City, aided by his trained mind and physique, and supported by his wealth and ingenuity rather than any superpowers. Moreover – while these fundamental character traits are common to almost every version of Batman, past and present[78] – Bruce/Batman's demeanour and behaviour are consistent with the 'darker', more troubled and more brutal comic book representations of the 1970s onwards, rather than, for instance, the lighter touch of the 1960s TV show. The supporting cast is also true to the source materials, with various degrees of fidelity. Gary Oldman's Gordon, as we've seen, closely resembles Mazzucchelli's depiction from *Year*

One, and operates within the established character template of good cop and family man who forges a tentative friendship with Batman; Alfred is written with the compassion and dry wit familiar from Miller and O'Neil's stories, and Jonathan Crane/Scarecrow's modus operandi is grounded in chemicals and psychology rather than the supernatural. Even at this level there are deviations – Bruce's childhood friend Rachel Dawes was invented by Goyer and Nolan, while the Lieutenant Flass of the film is a greasy, dishevelled wreck rather than the stocky, clean-cut blond of *Year One* – but in its depiction of character, *Batman Begins* nevertheless ticks most of the boxes.

However, with a conventional literary adaptation, we would hope for more than the appearance and generally familiar behaviour of, say, Mr Darcy or Oliver Twist;[79] to further state the obvious, we would expect a rough translation of the plot, at least in its key scenes. Yet the mythology of 'Batman' – even when reduced to the handful of texts suggested by the documentary – offers no such thing as a single plot. The stories named by Nolan and Goyer as particular influences take place at different times within Batman continuity, defying a clear linear narrative. *Year One*, as the title suggests, narrates Bruce Wayne's first attempts at crime-fighting, prior to the appearance of his costumed rogues gallery,[80] while *The Long Halloween* is set during the second year of Batman's career, by which point Gotham City is home to the whole roster of masks, clowns and freaks, but before the introduction of Robin. 'Daughter of the Demon', the first O'Neil and Adams' Ra's al Ghul story, begins with Dick Grayson at Hudson University, which locates it significantly later in Batman history – long after Dick's recruitment as Robin, and following his graduation to 'Teen' rather than 'Boy' Wonder. Finally, 'The Man Who Falls' is an extended flashback to Bruce's education and training, framed by a sequence featuring the mature Batman of the 1980s.

Nolan and Goyer's narrative is a selective collage of these sources, stuck together and filled out with original, connecting material. Some of the influences can be clearly identified. Wayne's sojourn in Asia, where his martial arts training is combined with psychological tests, is lifted from 'The Man Who Falls',[81] along with several other briefly mentioned details such as Bruce's aborted university education and his dalliance on the wrong side of the law. The movie's final scene, with Batman and Gordon discussing the new threat posed by the Joker, closely parallels, but does not replicate, the end of *Year One*. Young Bruce's fall down the disused well – the opening sequence of *Batman Begins* – also appears in 'The Man Who Falls', though this scene in the comic is itself a quotation from *Dark Knight Returns*. The tank-like 'Tumbler' is far more similar to the military vehicle of *Dark Knight Returns* than any other Batmobile, while *The Long Halloween* and O'Neil's Ra's al Ghul stories lend supporting characters and locations – the Falcone gangster family, the Himalayan mountains – rather than narrative structure or continuity.[82] As noted, *The Long Halloween* pits Batman against a broad cast of costumed villains, rather than just Two-Face and Joker, whereas 'Daughter of the Demon' has Ra's al Ghul first encountering Batman as a seasoned crimefighter, rather than as the neophyte Bruce Wayne.

Some moments from the film, such as the ultrasonic transponder calling a storm of bats, owe a clear debt to *Year One*; others, such as Batman hanging a criminal upside down for interrogation, have a more obvious source in *Dark Knight Returns*. More broadly, Bruce Wayne's initial amateurishness in *Batman Begins* – he almost falls from a fire escape during a dramatic exit from his meeting with Gordon – recalls his first, disastrous attempt at patrolling Gotham in *Year One*, while his first public appearance as Batman in the film – more a dark force than a person, visible only through his razor-sharp missiles and a trail of terrified criminals – echoes the partial glimpses of an urban legend in the first chapter of *Dark Knight Returns*. However, none of these examples constitute adaptation, in the conventional sense: they all lift a visual motif, a narrative device, or simply an idea from the comic book and use it in a new context, rather than transposing the entire scene. In *Batman Begins*, to give just one example, the corrupt cop Flass is suspended from a building and interrogated about a drugs operation, while in *Dark Knight Returns*, the unlucky perp is a teenage gang member involved in gun running; the individual shot may look superficially similar to the corresponding frame in the graphic novel, but its context is entirely different.

In story terms, then, *Batman Begins* is built around brief quotations from some of these texts; the start and end points, loosely inspired by 'The Man Who Falls' and *Year One* respectively, are joined up to other dots through Nolan and Goyer's own invention, and dressed with aspects such as character (the Falcones), design (the Batmobile) and location (the Himalayas) from within (and also beyond) the named set of comic books. Goyer and Nolan are open about their own contribution, which they claim to balance with their respect for the source material. In the director's words,

> The origin story had never been addressed on film, or really even in the comics. That is to say, there isn't really a single, defini-tive account of the journey of Bruce Wayne into Batman. There's these key events in Bruce Wayne's life that we know of, and then a lot of very interesting gaps that we were able to interpret our-selves ... [83]

An adaptation of Bruce Wayne's evolution into Batman, then, even when drawn from a manageable set of texts, is more akin to a new film of Robin Hood's adventures than to a film of Jane Austen's *Emma*; that is, its source is closer to folklore than to a literary novel.[84] Rather than a coherent and detailed sequence of actions and consequences, Goyer and Nolan based their narrative on independently-authored episodes which often overlap but do not necessarily connect, and sometimes even contradict each other. The key story arc – Bruce Wayne is orphaned, trains and fights urban crime in a costume – is an adaptation not so much of an individual story, but of Batman's funda-mental character; what the selected canon of O'Neil, Miller and Loeb provides is more a guide to the protagonist and his milieu's tone and appearance – that is, dark, grim, gritty – than any specific plot points or dialogue.

However, in a sense this unusual process of adaptation is extremely faithful to the comics; not to any individual title or story, but to the way comic book narratives work. *Batman Begins* takes familiar elements and rearranges them in a novel way, just as Miller did in *Dark Knight Returns*, as Morrison did in *Arkham Asylum*, and Loeb and Sale did in *Long Halloween*. O'Neil's 'The Man Who Falls' provides the most obvious example of the process, with its direct lifts and quotations from previous stories, but each of the 'source' texts discussed above are already reliant on other sources. Even the first ever Batman story was itself a clever compilation and reordering of existing tropes from the pulps, the cinema and *Superman*. Comic book 'authorship', especially with a long-established character, is inherently a form of editing and creative collage.[85]

Nolan and Goyer, as suggested at the end of Chapter One, were therefore entering into this model of authorship, which is itself a process of adaptation. That is, every new Batman story is always already an adaptation of existing elements and earlier stories, combined in a new order with a twist and a handful of innovations. Authorial expression, and the pleasure of these texts for the reader, lies neither in the reassuring repetition of entirely familiar patterns and motifs or in the surprise of entirely new inventions, but in the dynamic between the two. As Alan Moore said of Miller's *Dark Knight Returns* – and the observation was meant as high praise – 'Everything is exactly the same, except for the fact that it's all totally different.' Julian Darius agrees that this process, whereby creators 'appropriated past stories, expanding upon them according to the standards of the times, often improving them, and filling in gaps or accounting for retroactive addictions to the mythos ... is a longstanding feature of American comics.'

> But *Batman Begins*, in turn, participates in the same process of appropriation, borrowing bits and pieces from various stories in order to make something that is, in turn, longer, larger in scope, more internally logical, and more coherent as a single narrative.[86]

My account of *Batman Begins*' debt to its source material is not meant as a final word on the matter: it can't be. Recall that, within the poststructuralist model, one of the key axes across which meaning is made lies between the speaker and the listener, the author and reader, the producer and viewer. My list of which Batman stories were quoted in Nolan's films, and in which way, is inevitably subjective, and depends on my knowledge and interpretation of the movie and the comic books. Linda Hutcheon's suggestion that some audiences will see Branagh's 1989 *Henry V* as an adaptation of Olivier's 1944 film was dependent on that particular audience: in her example, 'film buffs' who 'likely see new movies through the lenses of other ones.'[87] Similarly, Neil Rae and Jonathan Gray's study, focusing on *Spider-Man* audiences, proposes that

> The viewer's experience of a film that has been adapted from a favorite comic book will involve, and rely upon, significantly more intertextual ties and connections here to that comic ... than it would for a non-comic-book reader, who is more likely to approach the text as an individual text, not as a number in a series.[88]

'Differently knowing audiences,' as Hutcheon suggests, 'bring different information to their interpretations of adaptations'; and the relationship between the film and its source text(s) is inevitably seen through, or even created by, that particular filter. To the viewer who knows nothing of *Year One*, *The Dark Knight Returns*, *The Long Halloween* and 'The Man Who Falls', *Batman Begins* may scarcely qualify as an adaptation at all. Eleven of the 27 reviews in my sample referred to Frank Miller; but that leaves more than half that discussed the film with no mention of his influence. Although the film's paratexts, such as the documentaries discussed above, work hard to frame *Batman Begins* in relation to key comic book texts, it could just as easily be interpreted, and enjoyed, as a Nolan film in the context of *Insomnia* and *Memento*, or a generic superhero film in the style of the recent *Spider-Man* (2002) and *Hulk* (2003), or even a gritty, urban crime film like *The French Connection* (1971) and *Serpico* (1973).

'We experience adaptations (*as adaptations*),' Hutcheon goes on,

> ... as palimpsests through our memory of other works that resonate through repetition with variation. For the right audience, then, the novelisation by Yvonne Navarro of a film like *Hellboy* (2004) may echo not only with Guillermo del Toro's film but also with the Dark Horse Comics series from which the latter was adapted.[89]

The multiplicity of a text like *Batman Begins,* then, lies not just in the text itself, but also in its reception. However, while Hutcheon offers the useful reminder – echoed by Rae and Gray – that the network of texts in which an adaptation operates depends on the interpretive community that views it, whether 'film buffs' or *Hellboy* fans,[90] we can drill deeper within this community. Not all Batman fans will identify exactly the same matrix of relationships and influences between *Batman Begins* and its source texts: Julian Darius, for instance, draws many parallels that I ignored above, seeing echoes between the escaping criminals in *Batman Begins* and the graphic novel *Arkham Asylum,*[91] and linking Batman's fall in flames to a similar moment in Jeph Loeb and Jim Lee's *Hush.*[92] Similarly, while the majority of my survey respondents mentioned *Year One* and *The Long Halloween* as clear influences on the film, some individuals made their own connections to sources such as the 1990s animated series,[93] the 1939 origin story[94] and again, *Arkham Asylum.*[95]

That said, these variations operate within a clear framework. They may quibble over the precise source texts, and on the extent of the borrowing, but they broadly agree that *Batman Begins* is influenced by stories of the 'darker' Batman. As such, variations between individual readings do not fully endorse Barthes' provocative argument that all meaning resides in the person receiving the text: 'the reader is the space on which all the quotations that make up a writing are inscribed without any of them being lost; a text's unity lies not in its origin but in its destination.'[96] While we can agree that the text of *Batman Begins*, to borrow Barthes' words again, 'is made of multiple writings, drawn from many cultures and entering into mutual relations of dialogue', and that in theory, there may be infinite possible readings of the film, in practice those readings – the transition of meaning horizontally from director to viewer – are structured by vertical terms such as context (an awareness of recent Batman comic books) and paratexts (the promotional materials' insistence on their fidelity to those comics).

None of my respondents saw *Batman Begins* as an adaptation of Adam West's *Batman;* none of them saw it as a disguised version of Punisher or Wolverine; none of them saw it as a riff on the operetta

Die Fledermaus. While, as noted, reviewers outside the comics fan continuity may be more likely to read the film in terms of genre, director, or even with regard to Christian Bale's previous work, their interpretations are nevertheless structured by existing contexts, and are unlikely to be wildly and idiosyncratically rogue. It is possible, as we will see later in the book, to read the Batman of *The Dark Knight* as an avatar of Vice-President Dick Cheney, but I have not come across a single review that sees Batman as a more violent Mickey Mouse. The meaning of the text may be ultimately formed only at its destination in the reader's consciousness, but that meaning will have been filtered, guided and shaped along the way.

That *Batman Begins* does not adapt a specific comic book text immediately distinguishes it from films like *Sin City*, *300* or *Watchmen* in terms of its visual style. As Lefèvre points out, 'in contrast to an average photographic image, a drawing is literally and figuratively "signed"... every drawing is by its style a visual interpretation of the world ... a drawn image offers a specific view on reality and the creator's subjectivity of this reality is built into the work, and a fairly obvious part of this work.'[97] *Sin City* tries deliberately to capture the distinctive worldview and visual expression of Frank Miller's *noir* saga through a range of techniques, from digital effects – to closely reproduce the lighting and colour– and prosthetic makeup to transform Mickey Rourke into Miller's grotesque anti-hero Marv, while Zach Snyder's *Watchmen* closely imitated the composition and the detailed mise-en-scéne of Dave Gibbons' original artwork. In both cases, online commentators were able to hold panels up side by side with screen grabs to demonstrate the similarities. Apart from the resemblance between Mazzucchelli's Gordon and Gary Oldman's interpretation of the character, *Batman Begins* makes no such attempt to reproduce an artist's individual style; and as the film takes selective inspirations from various sources, this approach would be inappropriate, even impossible. Tim Sale's Batman is a hulking mass of muscle wrapped in shadow, his cloak and ears forming dark points like curls of smoke; Mazzucchelli's is a humbler, more human figure, down to the visible folds and creases in his grey bodysuit. To adapt the visual interpretation of both artists would be incoherent;

the main character would change size, shape and costume between scenes, even before the distinctive art styles of Neal Adams (for the Ra's al Ghul scenes) and Dick Giordiano (flashbacks from 'The Man Who Falls') were factored in.

While 'page to screen' online comparisons suggest that the comic book panel and cinema shot are equivalent units – a supposition encouraged by their shared use of the term 'frame' – Lefèvre and Somigli both highlight a significant difference between the two media, in that cinematic frames supplant one another, while comic book frames coexist as part of a larger unit, and convey meaning not only through their individual panels, but through the arrangement of those panels on the page. Somigli therefore identifies both a syntagmatic relationship between comic panels, usually read from top left to bottom right, and a paradigmatic relationship among images on the same page,[98] while Lefèvre observes that 'the interplay of the various panels (their relative dimensions and their location) is a constitutive aspect of the comics medium.' Somigli's analysis is in turn indebted to Jim Collins' study of *Dark Knight Returns,* which identifies both the 'chronological succession of narrative incident producing a sequential processing of the images', and a second, simultaneous way of seeing whereby 'the entire page becomes the narrative unit, and the conflictive relationship among the individual images becomes a primary feature of the "narration" of the text.'

> The end result is a narration that proceeds syntagmatically across and down the page, but also forces a paradigmatic reading of interrelationships among images on the same page or adjacent pages, so that the tableaux moves the plot forward but encourages the eye to move in continually shifting trajectories as it tries to make sense of the overall pattern of fragmentary images.[99]

'Cinema with its moving images and standardized screen formats is not well equipped to imitate the page layouts of comics, although attempts are made.'[100] Ang Lee's *Hulk* remains the prime example of a superhero movie that tries to evoke its source medium through 'cinematic devices inspired by those dynamic pages', such as split-screen.[101]

Batman Begins, despite the discourses of fidelity to the original that surround it, makes no such attempt. Instead, its paratexts help to link it to the comic book source and bridge the two media. As discussed above, the DVD bonus disc menu opens with a clip from the film, which then segues into an animated comic book page, with Batman drawn to resemble Bale, and the costume of course matching the film's particular design rather than the quite different interpretations of Sale, Mazzucchelli, Miller or Adams. The images from *Hush, Long Halloween, Year One* and other recent titles that illustrate Nolan and Goyer's interviews – coupled with the reverential attitude of the interviews themselves – obviously suggest a clear line of influence between the comic book and the film. However, some moments in the documentary go further, and imply a direct translation between individual panels and shots, promising a level of fidelity on the level of *Sin City* which is, in fact, entirely absent from *Batman Begins*.

I have already noted the cut between a shot of Batman in the Narrows, mobbed by victims of the Scarecrow's fear toxin, and the visually similar but unrelated Brian Bolland image of Batman being attacked by zombies. When O'Neil proposes that 'we've been perfecting Batman's story for sixty-six years … the movie carries that one step further', the documentary alternates between comic book and cinematic images of Alfred, Lucius Fox, Gordon and Batman, suggesting a direct translation that is not always convincing; the comic book Alfred is consistently depicted as taller and slimmer than Michael Caine, while Lucius Fox – as drawn by Tim Sale in *Haunted Knight*, for instance – is significantly younger than Morgan Freeman. When a Tim Sale image of Scarecrow on a rearing horse is coupled with a soundtrack of hooves and neighing, then cuts into a brief but similar shot of Scarecrow from the film, the implication is clearly that the movie 'brings the comic to life'. The documentary's final sequence hammers this relationship home in a fast-moving montage of shots interspersed with comic panels: so the Tumbler, for instance, cuts to *Dark Knight Returns'* tank-like Batmobile. Sometimes the connection between the two is particularly tenuous – a Tim Sale drawing of a shirtless Bruce Wayne cuts to Bale in his pyjama bottoms, as if the idea of Wayne getting out of bed is adapted directly from a comic book – and on other occasions, interestingly, the film image is presented alongside the very different visual interpretations of two artists, as though suggesting that Nolan merged Tim Sale and Dave McKean's Scarecrow into the amalgam figure played by Cillian Murphy.

In a very brief paratext, the opening seconds of the film itself also confirm the source material and convey a sense of bringing it to life; the Warner Bros. logo is followed by a CGI sequence that flicks through Jim Lee images animated with speed lines and dotted patterns that, as Julian Darius notes, evoke both digital pixels and the Ben Day dots of classic comic book printing.[102] Darius describes the inclusion of Lee's artwork as 'a remarkable little bit of synergy', as the artist's regular title with Frank Miller, *All Star Batman and Robin the Boy Wonder*, debuted the month after the film's release; the DVD documentaries also promote the series as a new take on the character that, it is implied, parallels and complements Nolan's film not so much in its details as in their shared project to reinterpret the existing mythos through a distinctive creative vision.

Other paratexts take a similar approach, linking *Batman Begins* to the range of existing Batman narratives while preserving a sense of authorship and distinction between texts; as such, they confirm the integration of 'Nolan's Batman' into the tradition I discussed at the end of Chapter 1, where it coexists alongside various other authors' individual interpretations. Thus the comic book of the film is packaged with 'The Man Who Falls' and a story from each of the three main monthly titles of the time (*Detective Comics, Batman* and *Legends of the Dark Knight*) while adverts at the back promote Loeb and Sale's *Long Halloween, Dark Victory* and *Haunted Knight*, Miller's *Dark Knight Returns* and *Dark Knight Strikes Again*, and, as noted above, collected stories featuring the Scarecrow, Ducard and Ra's al Ghul.

Of course, the adaptation of the film back into a comic book closes the circuit, effectively translating a translation back into its original language. However, what could be an interesting exercise is undermined by over-hasty execution, with panels apparently imagined from the script and pre-production images rather than from

either the film or the comic books that inspired it.[103] In theory, the
scene where young Bruce falls down the well should closely resemble
the pages that influenced Nolan and Goyer, but this sequence in the
adaptation by Scott Beatty, Kilian Plunkett and Serge LaPointe is,
unfortunately, less imaginative in its use of comic book panels and,
ironically, less 'cinematic' than either Miller's original *Dark Knight
Returns* or O'Neil's take on the same moment in 'The Man Who
Falls'.

O'Neil's version shows the sequence in a series of frames, which
grow larger from left to right as Bruce tumbles through the air and
past the broken planks of the well until he hits the floor; Miller has
Bruce as a small figure suspended in a narrow, vertical, black frame
the height of the page, with the panel itself representing the sheer
drop. The sound-word 'skree', repeated in overlapping clusters of
orange at the base of the frame, suggests both the noise and the
shape of the waiting bats. The next frame reverses Bruce's position,
placing him near the bottom of the tall, black rectangle, with the
bat-sounds circling above his head; and the next two images give an
illusion of movement as our point of view remains static, and Bruce
twists, his hands up for protection, from one frame to the next.[104]
By contrast, Beatty, Plunkett and LaPointe simply depict the fall
in one image. To their credit, it fills most of the page, so that Bruce
and the shattered planks of the well tumble into an unbounded black
space that reaches to the corners; but while it makes use of the paradigmatic relationship between the artwork and the page itself, by
showing the fall in a single picture their interpretation involves little
sense of sequential, syntagmatic progression from one frame to the
next.

Collins warns against the label 'cinematic' for Miller's work,
precisely because it ignores the paradigmatic aspect – such analo-
gies 'fail to do justice to the juxtaposition of the disparate images
that appear within the single page'[105] – but by creating movement
through the dynamic between panels, both O'Neil and Miller's versions are more similar to the film's storyboard, reproduced in the
official published screenplay, than they are to Beatty's comic book
adaptation. In fact, the storyboard follows its own unique sequence,

with its own angles and rhythm, so that while it, like O'Neil and Miller's comics, shows the fall in a series of panels rather than a single image, what we actually have are four different visual interpretations of the same scene: five, if we include the film.[106] Despite the differences between these four versions, though, the echoes between them – with O'Neil's included in the same volume as the Beatty adaptation, and Miller's promoted on its back pages – help to confirm the sense of a matrix whereby the film becomes linked, via the hybrid forms of comic book adaptation and storyboard, into a group of related texts that includes Miller and O'Neil's comic book originals.

The Batman Brand

Recall from the Prologue that, after only 50 years of Batman continuity, *The Many Lives of the Batman*'s contributors saw the various incarnations of the character as 'a deluge of material', 'a complex web of cross references', 'seemingly endless re-articulations', 'multiple narrativizations', 'the most divergent set of refractions'. They describe the matrix of Batman texts, even in 1989, as 'complicated'; Pearson and Uricchio suggest that different iterations struggle for visibility and market share, and that 'the contradictions among them may threaten both the integrity of the commodity form and the coherence of the fans' lived experience of the character necessary to the Batman's continued success.'[107]

Clearly, the authors' fears were unfounded: the fragmentation of the 'Batman' character in 1989 did not threaten the brand's commercial success or undermine its fan following. The complex web Eileen Meehan identified, where meanings ricochet from Burton's *Batman* through the 1960s TV show and *Dark Knight Returns* to Bob Kane, and back again, did not seem to confuse consumers; the diffusion of the character across various diverse platforms, from breakfast cereal to the *Arkham Asylum* graphic novel, did not, as Pearson and Uricchio suggest, 'threaten his function as the series hero of an ongoing line of comics'[108] or 'result in tensions … which act as potential time-bombs'.[109] On the contrary, the success of Burton's *Batman* and its

1992 sequel led to a further diffusion in the comic book series, with *Legends of the Dark Knight* launching in November 1989, followed by *Shadow of the Bat* in June 1992. September 1992 saw the pilot episode of the *Batman* animated TV series, which in turn spawned its own comic book title and two feature-length films, all of which operated in the slightly different continuity of the 'animated universe'. The big-screen Batman was fragmented still further when 1995's *Batman Forever* – ostensibly the third instalment of the series begun in 1989, rather than a reboot – diverged from Burton's two films in terms of style, tone, costume design, director and lead actor.

Yet Pearson and Uricchio's concerns were in no way based on naïve assumptions or incomplete research. They shrewdly identify strategies of containment intended to control and limit Batman both as a character – such as Denny O'Neil's editorial 'Bat-Bible' – and as a commercial product. They accurately note a creative tension whereby creators such as Frank Miller and Alan Moore were encouraged towards 'maximum differentiation within the standardization imposed by the key components of the Batman character'[110] – an approach towards authorship that, as discussed in Chapter One, continues to the present day. Their observation that 'the challenging of the Batman's identity ... threatens DC with the loss of a profit-maker' seems well-founded in relation to other, similar franchises. Kerry Gough, for instance, stresses the importance of consistency between the Alien comic book series and film franchise, with 'faithfulness and coherence to the visual style of the films'[111] a priority for the comics; the creators aimed to 'provide a seamless intervention'[112] between media forms.

Similarly, Derek Johnson's case study of *Wolverine* branding in the context of the *X-Men* films, comic books and video games argues that fan cultures 'depend on the unity, coherence and "ontological security"' of texts[113]. While he observes that Marvel's attempt to 'blend all the various Wolverines into a single, uniform entity more like the Hugh Jackman Wolverine'[114] was not always smooth, he identifies the continuing presence of alternate Wolverines as evidence of the struggle to combine many into one, rather than a deliberate embracing of difference. Marvel's temporary categorisation of the Wolverine character into labelled 'sub-brands' – classic, Ultimate and film versions, all 'subordinate to 'the overall Wolverine character/range brand' – implies a controlled, limited form of fragmentation, rather than a free-for-all, and Johnson suggests that even this was a 'stop-gap measure'.[115] As Marvel's Editor-in-Chief, Joe Quesada, put it, the company worked towards 'a single [design] to appease licensees … you need consistency … we came up with a look that was similar across all fields.'[116] Johnson's article therefore documents 'a slow, gradual, embattled process of bringing the character under control', based around the trajectory towards a 'much more homogeneous look' and the creation of a kind of über-Wolverine, a master-brand who would 'encompass and amalgamate all the Wolverines of the present and the past.'[117]

Wolverine provides the case study for Johnson's chapter, but this character's forced mutations towards uniformity are symptomatic of a broader process. 'Marvel found it necessary to eliminate the inconsistencies and contradictions between incarnations of its characters,' Johnson explains:

> A range brand like the Spider-Man character had toys, comics and television shows all based upon it, but if each synergistic aspect of the character presented Peter Parker/Spider-Man in a different way, there was no way for 'Spider-Man' as a brand to cohere into any one single identity. Because a subbrand character like *Ultimate Spider-Man*'s Peter Parker, a teenager, existed alongside the Peter Parker from the 'classic' continuity – then a divorced school teacher – 'Spider-Man' as a (range) brand remained discontinuous and nebulous.[118]

Why, then, has the Batman brand developed neither the level of corporate control and cross-platform conformity discussed by Johnson and Gough, nor the dispersed, confusing fragmentation warned against by Uricchio and Pearson? Twenty years since the publication of *The Many Lives of the Batman*, we can identify neither an über-Batman who unites every Bat-product across multiple media, nor a chaos of signifiers that diffuse Batman's meaning into splinters so small that DC has nothing coherent to sell and fans have nothing solid to follow.

Instead, artefacts related specifically to Nolan's Batman – DVDs, posters, toys, websites, ongoing journalistic rumours and fan debate about *The Dark Knight Rises* – coexist with a range of distinct Batman texts, each of which presents a slightly different interpretation of the main character and his mythos. In the second half of the 2000s alone, these included the televised cartoon *The Batman* (2004–2008) – aimed at younger viewers, with its continuity quite separate from both the previous animated series and mainstream comics – and its spin-off comic, *The Batman Strikes*; the entirely different animated series *Batman: The Brave and the Bold* (2008–present), with its own spin-off video game and monthly comic book (2010–present); the adult-oriented video game *Arkham Asylum* (2009) and its sequel *Arkham City* (2011), in addition, of course, to the mainstream continuity of the comic book.[119]

Yet even the Batman of contemporary comic books is far from a unified, coherent character. One-shot graphic novels like Brian Azzarello and Lee Bermejo's *Joker* (2008) stand outside all other continuity, while Frank Miller and Jim Lee's *All Star Batman and Robin The Boy Wonder* (2005–2008) gave the creators *carte blanche* to produce their own distinctive take on Batman's first meeting with his sidekick, in a series meant to provide an accessible entry-point for new readers. As such, its depiction of events clashes radically with another recent series by equally high-status DC creators. Jeph Loeb and Tim Sale's *Dark Victory* (2000) also shows Batman and Robin's first encounter, but in an entirely different way: the two books are not just alternate retellings of the same narrative, but distinct in their depictions of events, dialogue, character and the developing relationship between the two protagonists.

Miller and Lee have a growling, stubbled Batman kidnapping Dick Grayson after a date at the circus with Vicky Vale: "Sleep tight, PUNK. Sleep TIGHT, my WARD,' the Dark Knight grins as he drives his new protégé back to the Bat-cave. The journey itself takes three chapters, as Batman torches pursuing cops, rockets the car into the air and then plunges it into a secret lake. Once at the cave, he leaves Dick to forage for rats, snarling to himself 'this little brat is going to ruin EVERYTHING.'[120] By contrast, Loeb and Sale's

Bruce goes alone to the circus, having recently ended a relationship with Selina 'Catwoman' Kyle. When Dick crouches over his parents' fallen bodies, Bruce is a solitary, silent witness. Without further dialogue, he abandons Dick to Alfred and the cold expanses of Wayne Manor; the relationship between the two is explored through parallel flashbacks to Bruce's childhood, rather than through conversation.[121] Needless to say, Sale and Lee's artwork presents different takes on the same characters; although both play on the visual contrast between hulking vigilante and circus scamp, their interpretations of details such as Dick's circus costume have nothing in common. More fundamentally, Loeb and Sale's story has a subdued, noir, 1940s mood, while Miller and Lee's, though set at precisely the same moment in Batman's career, feels high-tech, bright, shiny and contemporary.

If we discount the 'All Star' line as an exception, much like the 'Ultimate' category within Marvel – which, in Johnson's words, 'recalled the origins of its superhero characters while at the same time reworking them for modern youth audiences'[122] – and set aside, equally, the three distinct comic book continuities spun off from the various animated series, we are still left with a range of different interpretations within what should be the stable core of Batman narratives, the monthly comic book titles. While this central generator of stories is bounded by rules of continuity, and aims for consistency at a micro level – if Robin dislocates his arm in one issue, it should remain dislocated in all monthly episodes until fixed[123] – the regular titles are still deliberately distinguished from each other, with variations that go beyond the inevitable differences in creative interpretation between writing and art teams.

This is not a recent development. Legends of the Dark Knight was initially launched in 1989 to tell stories only from Batman's first year, and retained a focus on the character's early career; its successor, Batman Confidential (2006–2011) had the even more specific remit of presenting first meetings between Batman, his villains and allies, and capturing key developments in the mythos. Shadow of the Bat (1992–2000) took a psychological slant on Batman's then-contemporary continuity, and Gotham Knights (2000–2006) was intended to focus on Batman's extended cast. The regular titles *Detective Comics* and *Batman* continue monthly publication as the most consistent Batman hub, as they have since 1939 and 1940 respectively, but are supplemented by dedicated vehicles for key supporting characters such as, at various times, *Robin, Nightwing, Batgirl, Batwoman, Azrael, Red Robin* and the police of *Gotham Central*. A new monthly title launched in 2011, *The Dark Knight*, aims to recapture the street-level, O'Neil and Adams aesthetic, mixed with Nolan-style gritty 'realism'; it coexists with *Batman and Robin*, pitched as 'David Lynch meets the Adam West *Batman* TV show',[124] with Dick Grayson and Damian Wayne in the title roles, and *Batman Incorporated*, which follows Bruce Wayne on a globetrotting mission to establish a worldwide corporation of crime fighters.

This last title provides the key to understanding how Batman can apparently sustain consistency and coherence despite such diversity; and the solution is also already suggested by Uricchio and Pearson's closing focus on the bat-logo, which in their words 'floats untouched, above criticism' as 'that expression of the character which has the widest cultural currency ... unthreatened either by textual challenges to the Batman's role ... or by the centrifugal forces of commodification.'[125] The answer lies in the power of that logo, both inside and outside the fiction.

Batman is a 'range brand', not just in our world but in his own. Bruce Wayne/Batman is not just a superlative detective and martial artist, but a businessman, in both his public and private lives. As owner of Wayne Enterprises, he fully understands the power of branding: but Batman is also the head of a crime-fighting corporation. The 'W' logo that adorns Wayne Tower in Nolan's films is echoed as the Bat-symbol across Batman's costume, gadgets, vehicle, environment and associates.[126] Everything Batman makes carries his brand, from the biggest tank in his garage to the smallest of the bespoke *shuriken* he carries on his belt. The 1960s show pushed this trend to comic extremes, where a pole was always a Bat-pole, a computer always a Bat-computer, and the Caped Crusader even carried his own dedicated brand of shark repellent; but a recent episode of the gritty, contemporary comic *The Dark Knight* shows that

Batman's throwing rope is still weighted at one end with a precisely-shaped black bat. He would never carry a generic bola, even now; it must always be a Bat-bola. The brand carries such power within the fiction that others adapt it, paying tribute to or perverting it: Joker occasionally constructs parodic variants such as Jokercopters, while the largest Bat-symbol in Gotham, the searchlight symbol, was built not by Batman but the police department. Unlike Wolverine, unlike Superman; unlike Thor, Green Lantern and even the entrepreneur Iron Man, Batman is a business leader not just in his civilian identity, but as a crimefighter.

The Bat-symbol functions so flexibly yet potently across diverse titles because it plays the same role inside and outside the fiction: the logo, whether it appears on an armoured chest, a book cover, a rooftop or a black vehicle, clearly identifies and fixes character, genre, location and props, and carries an unchanging set of meanings across a range of diverse creative interpretations. Miller and Lee's *All Star Batman* may seem a world away from *Dark Victory*, but the Bat-symbol remains a stable signifier across both texts, branding the two stories as variants, however wildly divergent, of the same fundamental narrative: these are very different takes on the character, but the protagonist of both remains, unambiguously, Batman. Despite their considerable differences, these, like virtually every Batman story ever written, call on the same fundamental set of rules, history and conventions. The logo is a guarantee that this is a story of Batman, who fights crime in Gotham City, aided by his trained mind and physique, and supported by his wealth and ingenuity rather than any superpowers. Those basics are sacred, except in rare circumstances. Whatever their aesthetic disagreements, Jeph Loeb and Frank Miller, Tim Sale and Jim Lee all share that understanding.

Within the diegesis, too, Batman has proved adept at sub-branding. From his recruitment of Robin in 1940 to his corporate mission in 2011 to gather an international community of crime fighters under the 'Batman Incorporated' banner, Batman has effectively licensed out his logo for decades. Robin, of course, has his own design, but Nightwing's mask is a variant on the Bat-symbol, and his colour-scheme pays tribute, consciously or not, to Batman's black and blue. The extended

'Batman family' also fits an industry model – the various Batgirls are temporary franchise-holders, Bat-Mite is a copycat fanboy, and Ace the Bat-Hound a corporate mascot. Recent continuity has confirmed that the 'Batman' brand can exist independently of Bruce Wayne: Dick Grayson currently performs the role in the monthly *Batman and Robin*, while *Batman* #700 showed Bruce's son, Damian Wayne, as his successor, and suggested a dynasty of Batmen – including Terry McGinnis, from the animated *Batman Beyond* – that could be sustained long after the original's death. The fictional 'Batman' is, increasingly, not about a single man, but a concept, a corporation; Bruce Wayne still plays a central role, but 'Batman', the idea he created, has become something bigger. 'Batman and Robin will never die' is the opening line to *Batman RIP*, which we later realise is spoken not by Bruce at all but by Dick Grayson, wearing his mentor's costume.

'Starting today, we fight IDEAS with BETTER IDEAS,' Bruce declares in *Batman: The Return*. 'The idea of CRIME with the idea of BATMAN'.[127] In *Batman and Robin* #16, he announces his new, global franchise, Batman Incorporated: the logo glowing from his lectern doubles as an advertisement for a new monthly title of the same name, and the similar but distinct logos for the other ongoing titles (such as *Batman and Robin*) appear beneath it. Again, the brand functions both textually and extratextually, diegetically and non-diegetically: Bruce Wayne is in effect launching and advertising his own comic books.

Because branding is such a long-standing and integral motif within the fictional world of Batman, spin-offs like the Burger King 'Dark Whopper' and Domino's 'Gotham City Pizza' arguably work more successfully than – or at least, in a different way to – ostensibly similar promotions such as the Burger King campaign around *Thor* in 2011. Jonathan Gray suggests that the Gotham City Pizza contributes nothing meaningful to the film except for signalling its scale ('it even has a pizza named after it') and even diminishes the movie, 'making it seem, well, cheesy.'[128] Gray's argument that the pizza adds nothing substantive to the story-world is persuasive, but his criticism that it fails to even 'sample that world for would-be viewers' and undermines the film's 'dark aesthetic' can be disputed.

The pizza box, with the promise 'Cloaked in Pepperoni: Deliciously Mysterious', is clearly tongue-in-cheek, but its white-on-black design, with a moody, monochrome cityscape photograph, echoes the film's subdued 'realism' (and contrasts to the brand's usual blue and red, subtly echoing *The Dark Knight*'s distinction from both earlier Pop Batman incarnations and the brighter colours of Superman), while the slogan 'You Got Thirty Minutes' ties in neatly with the movie's ticking-bomb scenarios. Moreover, this particular spin-off was supported by a dedicated 'Gotham City Pizzeria' website, discreetly 'powered by Domino's' but otherwise entirely immersed in the story-world, offering support for Batman and self-defence classes for its customers. Even without this extensive online presence – tied in, as Gray notes, to the Alternate Reality Game – a Batman pizza already functions differently to a Thor 'Asgardian Gleamin' Bracelet' in Burger King, simply because Batman, a successful businessman and head of a crime-fighting organisation, extensively brands products within his own narratives, whereas Thor, a Norse God, has no such diegetic corporate presence. Although the idea of Batman launching his own Italian food range remains far-fetched (or campy, like Adam West ordering a 'Batman Special' at a bar) Nolan's films show that the cops and citizens of Gotham take up his logo and costume in their own ways: as noted, the Bat-Signal is owned by the police force, and *The Dark Knight* witnesses a wave of copycat vigilantes. A Batman-themed pizza arguably works within the same terms, as a sign of this urban legend's influence on, and integration within, his city's culture.[129]

If Wayne Enterprises is the DC Universe equivalent of the Trump Organisation, or Richard Branson's Virgin Group – it includes Wayne Foods, Wayne Biotech, Wayne Steels, Wayne Yards and Wayne Aerospace, among several other departments and foundations – Batman is as much a corporate industry and icon, in his own fictional world, as Coca-Cola. Within the range brand are variations for distinct tastes, generations and genders, each subtly differentiated while retaining a family resemblance. Dick Grayson is a younger, lither Batman lite, with a slightly different logo and livery from the bulky head honcho Bruce Wayne: Coke Zero, perhaps, to Bruce's old-school Classic Coke.[130] Within this model, Batgirl, a slimline feminine version, is Diet Coke; a short-lived novelty variant like Red Robin is Batman's equivalent of Cherry Coke.

The parallel may seem facetious, but this long-established tradition of breaking the larger range brand down into subcategories within the Batman diegesis consolidates and supports the same process in real-world, industry terms. Batman readers have long been comfortable with the idea of Batman's fictional sub-brands and franchisees: if Robin grows up, becomes his own man and rebrands himself as Nightwing, it makes perfect sense for that character to spin off into his own title. Within Batman continuity, characters frequently pass on a name, logo or costume to a new generation, and effectively reboot themselves: during recent years, as noted, Nightwing has become Batman and Damian Wayne has taken the role of Robin, prompting the previous Boy Wonder – Tim Drake – to relaunch himself as Red Robin, a twist on the established Robin sub-brand. Again, the announcement of a new monthly comic with that name in August 2009 was motivated and supported by changes within the diegesis: the new brand was already introduced within the narrative world.[131]

Put simply, then, Batman – the character, the concept, the cultural icon – is about strategic branding at every level, in a way and to an extent that escapes all other major superheroes. The Bat-logo is a powerful enough symbol, as Pearson and Uricchio note, to float above and hold together a diverse range of texts, just as it brands people, weapons and vehicles within the fiction; but it is also powerful enough to be split into diverse subcategories, in a dynamic of similarity and distinction. While Pearson and Uricchio accurately recognise the unifying status of the symbol, they do not take its variations into account. The 1989 Bat-logo, a rich, glossy black and gold, was not the same as the flatter, canary-yellow comic book logo of the time; and both were different again from the 1960s TV logo, ludicrously topped with a masked face.[132] *Batman Begins* was launched with a symbol that, while recognisably a bat, was significantly different both from previous film logos and the comic books of the same period: rather than the costume chest-plate, it represented Batman's *shuriken*, or Batarang, and the movie carried an appropriate rusty orange colour scheme on all its associated merchandise. *The Dark Knight* retained that knifelike shape, but blasted it with blue-white light; a tonal reprise of the shift between the 1989 *Batman*'s gold symbol and the frost-crusted version of *Batman Returns*. At the level of monthly comic books, *Batman Incorporated* reduces the symbol to its bare minimum of black curves on yellow, while *The Dark Knight* monthly uses only its top half, like a moon rising over the horizon.[133] Again, though, the concept of different Batman brands for different tastes and moods – each subtly differentiated while belonging to the same family – was already long-established within the fiction through the Batman/Robin/Batgirl/Nightwing network, and has been reinforced in the recent stories that confirm the status of 'Batman' as a label rather than, necessarily, a single individual.

Batman Begins therefore entered a matrix of difference and sameness, variation and familiarity, which runs through both diegetic representation of 'Batman' as corporate concept and the real-world circulation of the character as a commercial property, and allows for a great deal of diversity within the broad boundaries of its unified brand, in our lived reality as in the fiction.

That fans were able clearly to understand and locate its role in this matrix, as a distinct sub-brand, anchored by the author's name ('Nolan's Batman') within a larger concept ('Batman'), was confirmed by my survey results. One question presented respondents with a choice of 29 texts or groups of texts, and asked them how those texts related to the broader narrative of *The Dark Knight*: absolutely, closely, slightly or not at all.

They agreed almost unanimously (97 per cent) that *Batman Begins* was absolutely part of the same narrative of *The Dark Knight*, and felt strongly that the official soundtrack albums also belonged to this story (86 per cent for *Batman Begins*, 90 per cent for the *Dark Knight* score). The majority placed the published screenplays in this category;[134] just over half felt the same way about the novelisations, and exactly half grouped paratexts such as the comic book adaptation, junior novels and *Art of Batman Begins* books closely with the movies.[135] Over half saw viral marketing and the Alternate Reality Game 'Why So Serious' as absolutely integral to the film's narrative.[136]

These respondents were equally clear about texts that did not belong to the 'Nolan Batman': almost 50 per cent voted that the monthly comic books were 'not related to the *Dark Knight* story', and just over half said the same of the video game *Arkham Asylum*.[137] Most stated firmly that the animated series *The Batman* and *The Brave and the Bold* were entirely unrelated to Nolan's films (70 per cent and 76 per cent respectively); perhaps the clear line being drawn here was between Nolan's 'darker' and more adult cinema version and the lighter, more child-friendly cartoon series.

While all these texts bear a form of the Batman logo, then, the *shuriken* bat of Nolan's sub-brand, coupled with the distinctive colour-scheme consistent across the two films' merchandise, successfully grouped all the related texts together, while allowing a further division into the subcategories of *Batman Begins* (rusty ochre) and *The Dark Knight* (ice blue). The diffusion of the Batman brand during the first decade of the twenty-first century clearly presented no threat to fan comprehension or commercial success – again, I suggest that the process was consolidated by the long-established themes of branding and sub-branding within the Batman diegesis.

That said, the distinctions were not always clear-cut. Only one in four respondents saw *Gotham Knight*, the DVD collection of animated shorts that links the two Nolan movies, as 'absolutely' related to the films.[138] By comparison, a significant minority (just over 10 per cent) felt that the Domino's 'Gotham City Pizza' – which obviously carries no narrative in itself – was firmly part of the *Dark Knight* story. The response here can, again, be explained through branding. The 'Gotham City Pizza' clearly bears the *Dark Knight* logo and a photograph of an urban cityscape, while *Gotham Knight*'s cover is dominated by a cartoonish Batman and a DC Universe logo, linking it most obviously to the continuity of the comic books.[139] The Nolan-style, sharp-edged bat is part of the design, but reduced in size and easily missed; at a glance, it is the pizza box that seems more clearly to belong to the Nolan aesthetic, although closer examination of *Gotham Knight* shows that it was meant to provide a transmedia bridge in the tradition of *The Animatrix* (2003).[140]

There were other ambiguities in the responses. Over half felt that the video game *Arkham Asylum* was entirely unrelated to the films, but one in four felt it was 'slightly related'. Fifty per cent of respondents distinguished the monthly comic books firmly from the films, but again, 20 per cent felt that the comics were 'slightly related'. This uncertainty is, in fact, well-founded, and has a long-standing historical basis. While varieties of Batman such as the Adam West TV show, the animated series of the 1990s, the All Star line and mainstream comic book continuity are distinct sub-brands that run along separate lines, those lines have also been known to intersect. In any network, there will be borrowing, influence and cross-reference: and sometimes those borrowings are unexpected.[141]

It was the 1960s TV show, for instance, that introduced Barbara Gordon as Batgirl to the comics; a role she played until 1988's *The Killing Joke* shattered her spine, though she remains a key character in contemporary continuity as Oracle.[142] The animated series, in turn, created Harley Quinn, a psychiatrist whose crush on Joker turned her to crime; she crossed over into mainstream continuity in the late 1990s. Tim Burton's auteurist take on the Penguin as a deformed, Dickensian character, rather than a dapper gentleman, was taken up in the animated series, and then by mainstream texts such as *The Long Halloween and Dark Victory*; again, the 'gritty' and realistic 2011 monthly *The Dark Knight* follows this representation. Burton's 1989 movie popularised Batman's use of a grappling gun in comics as well as in subsequent films, and shaped the mainstream representation of his outfit as armoured rather than spandex.[143] While the *Arkham Asylum* game may seem to take place in its own universe, its voice casting – Kevin Conroy as Batman, Arleen Sorkin as Harley and Mark Hamill as Joker – blurs the boundaries between this sub-brand and the animated series, which consistently used the same cast. As the parallel continuity of the animated series has overlapped with and influenced the regular comics, which in turn shape the films, it is perhaps unsurprising that one in four of my respondents were reluctant to draw an absolute line between the video game and Nolan's movies. While ostensibly separate, these sub-brands frequently and unpredictably intersect; they operate as neighbours in an intertextual conversation, rather than a clearly structured hierarchy.

Moreover, while we have seen that Nolan's films clearly draw on comic book texts, they have also started to feed back, sometimes via other media. *Batman Begins* introduced a cape made of 'memory cloth', which snaps instantly into rigid glider wings. *Arkham Asylum* and its sequel *Arkham City* gave the player the same technology, while *Batman and Robin* #1 (2009) has the Dynamic Duo hang-gliding from the sky with 'paracapes'. *The Dark Knight* shows Bruce relocating from Wayne Manor and the Bat-cave to a central Gotham penthouse; the idea has a precedent in 1970s comic book continuity, but again, *Batman and Robin* reincorporated it in 2009 with a cutaway splash page showing Batman's new skyscraper. Around the time of Heath Ledger's performance as Joker, whether by coincidence or not, comics began to show the character with a crudely-sliced and scarred mouth.[144]

Grant Morrison's *Batman: The Return*, a one-shot from 2011, defines the Dark Knight in contemporary mainstream continuity as a heavy-duty, military figure whose appearance, manner and accessories combine aspects of Nolan's films with existing conventions. This is not a simple insertion of Christian Bale into the comic books, like the animated menu for *Batman Begins*; but the Tumbler, or a Batmobile very much like it, is clearly visible in the cave, and Lucius Fox is clearly both written and drawn to recall the stately presence of Morgan Freeman, rather than the younger man of *Haunted Knight*.

'What else have you got for me?' Bruce asks him, eyeing the hardware in his own R&D department.

'Right this way, Mister Wayne,' Fox replies smoothly. 'Jet-suits increase human strength and endurance as well as providing short-range flight capability. Again, considered too costly and too risky for operational use.'

'How quickly can you modify two of these?'

'A day? Twelve hours. In black, I take it.'

The scene is firmly grounded within comic book continuity – Bruce has just held a meeting with Robin, Batgirl, Red Robin, Oracle and the Dick Grayson variant of Batman – but at the same time, the conversation playfully continues Christian Bale and Morgan

Freeman's conversations in Nolan's movies.[145] Again, this is not a simple matter of bringing the comic book into line with the films to create a unified brand, as in Johnson's Wolverine case study. Robin is firmly in place at Batman's side, Joker and Two-Face are still active, Alfred looks nothing like Michael Caine, and Ra's al Ghul has been supernaturally reanimated through a Lazarus Pit, a pseudo-scientific device Nolan chose to omit from his story. Rather, Morrison embraces the idea that Batman texts are an interactive network, with different continuities lending to, learning from and even arguing with each other: his own ongoing *Batman* titles engaged in an intertextual dialogue with Miller's *All Star Batman and Robin* about whether Robin should wear a hood.

So, finally, despite the insistence on fidelity in the film's promotion, *Batman Begins* operates in a relationship far more complex and fascinating than the traditional source/adaptation dyad. Rather than a one-to-one translation, the film was always a collage from many sources; and in turn, as we have seen, it entered a matrix within which it, too, became a source for other stories and translations to other media. Its 'fidelity' was to the comic book model of authorship as adaptation and creative editing, rather than to any single story, or even a group of stories.

The traditional fidelity discourse, however, served a purpose. It reassured fans of the film's distinction from previous Batman adaptations, and Schumacher's films in particular. As such, it positioned itself within a specific, selective tradition – through concepts of fidelity, but also through 'darkness' and 'realism' – that carries specific values and defines itself against another tradition within the Batman mythos. The next chapter further examines how this was done, and why, and what was at stake. Chapter Four, subsequently, returns to the idea of the matrix to suggest that, however hard producers, authors and fans try to repress one aspect of Batman history, there is a sense within which those stories are always there, always connected, always influential – and however thoroughly they are repressed, they always tend to come back.

DARK KNIGHT LOCKDOWN: REALISM AND REPRESSION

Discourses of Realism

While the idea of 'realism' was central to the promotion and reception of Nolan's Batman – particularly *Batman Begins* – the notion of
'discourse' is at least as important to this chapter. Rather than simply
examining what was said about the film – what terms were used to
describe it and what words were associated with it – we must also
explore why those words were chosen, what purpose they served,
what work they did, and for whom. As Michel Foucault proposed
in *The History of Sexuality,* our task is to analyse 'not only these discourses but also the will that sustains them and the strategic intention that supports them.'[1] The central issue, he suggested, was not
to identify what was said, but 'to discover who does the speaking,
the positions and viewpoints from which they speak, the institutions
which prompt people to speak ... and which store and distribute the
things that are said [...] my main concern will be to locate the forms
of power, the channels it takes, and the discourses it permeates ...'[2]

The previous chapters looked at the ways in which Nolan's Batman
was positioned – though the relays of promotion and reception, from

advertising to fan response – in terms of its authorship and its relationship to the comic-book 'source'. This chapter further explores the processes through which Nolan's Batman was constructed not just through ideas of sameness – fidelity to a specific comic book tradition – but also through difference from and contrast to previous films in the Batman franchise, particularly Joel Schumacher's, and what ideas were at stake in that opposition.

'One of Chris' mantras when we were working on the script was *it has to be real, it has to be real*,' Goyer reports in the production notes.[3] But what did realism mean in this context? Goyer and Nolan seem to associate it initially with Batman's status within the superhero universe; his self-made, earthbound powers in contrast to the aliens and deities who surround him. 'Batman is human, he's flawed,' Nolan comments, and Goyer agrees: 'What distinguishes Batman from his counterparts is that he's a hero anyone can aspire to be. You could never be Superman, you could never be the Incredible Hulk, but anybody could conceivably become Batman.' The press notes emphasise this point, describing the protagonist as 'a superhero with no superpowers' whose 'ambitious quest to forge his mind and body into a living, breathing weapon against injustice inspires both fear and admiration.'[4]

In the published screenplay, Goyer again identifies these qualities in Batman's fundamental character, and connects them explicitly to 'realism'.

> What I like about Batman is that he is the most realistic of the super heroes. There is a grittiness and grimness to him … in the pantheon of DC Comics heroes, Batman is the only one who's really conflicted. Superman and Wonder Woman are effectively gods. Green Lantern isn't tortured or tormented, and nor is the Flash. But Batman is. Conflicted heroes are more interesting to watch because they're more human – we can relate to them.[5]

An online interview with Nolan echoes and elaborates on this reading.

> In taking on a realistic telling of the story, I needed someone who could play Bruce Wayne; somebody whose eyes the audience can relate to and believe that there is this absolute dedication and

discipline and drive to making himself an extraordinary icon. He has no superpower. He's just a human being. He has this rage inside himself and desire to do something emotionally and extraordinary. I can't think of anyone but Christian who [has] this fire in his eyes to be this character. [6]

Already, though, Goyer and Nolan are both expanding their previous use of 'realism' to include a slightly different concept. The notion that Batman has no superpowers and works within the conceivable bounds of human potential is not the same as being a flawed and tormented character, driven by rage and fire, with a grimness and grittiness about him. So the interviews perform a barely perceptible segue from the 'realism' of Batman's lack of supernatural abilities to a set of more specific values; Batman is not just a person, but an angry, conflicted, serious, committed person. The discourse has shifted, very subtly, from identifying Batman's essential humanity to associating him with a certain type of masculinity.

Goyer goes on to contrast *Batman Begins* with one of his previous screenplay adaptations. Again, the word 'realism' comes into play, but here – while it retains similar associations of down-to-earth toughness – it is extended to also imply a style of filming. 'There's nothing realistic about *Blade*. The film vernacular is much more extreme in *Blade* – speed-ups and things like that.'[7] Nolan, similarly, describes his Gotham as 'gritty. It's not glamorous. In so far as it has a *noir*-ish quality to it, it's not a caricatured version of that. We tried to shoot it in the same way as you'd shoot any contemporary thriller.' He explicitly contrasts this approach to Burton's, which was 'hyper-real, hyper-stylised,'[8] and explains that 'the philosophy behind everything, from design to photography to acting, was grounding it in reality. With great actors, that naturally manifests itself in a more realistic, naturalistic and low-key style.'[9]

This aesthetic – based in the conventions of the crime film, rather than the over-the-top styling of other comic-book movies – also informs Nolan's insistence on a rational explanation for all the props and gadgets of Batman's paraphernalia, which again he explicitly contrasts to previous superhero adaptations.

When you're telling the origin story of the character, if you're going to do it in a realistic fashion you have to take on that challenge and it's incredibly different. I really enjoyed the first forty-five minutes of *Spider-Man*, and it got to the bit with the costume and I just thought it was a complete sidestep. ... I felt that because we were determined to tell the story in a realistic way we had to bite the bullet. We got everything in place and the one thing I couldn't figure out was the mask; then I suddenly thought – you pull it apart and you have the ears separate from the head shape and you order it through different companies. David Goyer came up with this idea about ordering the boots through this company in Malaysia – though I said you'd have to order tons of them. I've never seen that done before, explaining the origins of the costume. They make a joke about it in one of the Batman films where someone says, 'I like your tailor', implying that Alfred has made the costume. And it's this latex thing and that's ludicrous. It was not good enough.[10]

Once more, Nolan firmly distinguishes his approach from that of the earlier Batman directors, in this case rebuking Joel Schumacher. His attitude towards Burton is more respectful and generous – 'he had the challenge of convincing a cinema audience that you could have a "cool" Batman film. And he did it, he succeeded'[11] – echoing the pattern we saw in the fan response of Chapter One, where Burton's Batman was politely appreciated for its vision but seen with hindsight as distinct from and inferior to Nolan's, while Schumacher's was openly reviled as disastrous. Note that Nolan praises Burton for 'convincing an audience who remembers that the TV show was ridiculous', suggesting an opposition between his own approach (and, to some extent, Burton's) on one side, and the 'ridiculous' TV show, grouped with Schumacher's 'ludicrous' movies, on the other. This opposition, as we'll see, was important in distinguishing *Batman Begins* from its predecessors in the franchise.

The 'tailor' scene Nolan mentions was particularly rich in homoerotic potential, as critics recognised at the time. '*Batman Forever* isn't as innocent as it looks,' observed Peter Travers in the

Rolling Stone. "Who's your tailor?" asks Batman, eyeing the Robin costume's built-in nipples and outsize crotch pouch that match his own.'[12] While Nolan is, no doubt, not intending to express a homophobic distaste for Schumacher's movie, by defining his own Batman in terms of rationality, challenge and rigour and contrasting it with 'ludicrous' latex, a pantomime lack of logic and, implicitly, homoeroticism, he nevertheless confirms the contrast between stripped-down toughness and a swishy, showy form of camp that structures the distinction between *Batman Begins* and the Schumacher films that preceded it.

So while these uses of the term 'realism' imply specific approaches to performance, editing, characterisation and narrative, they also express a broader and more significant meaning of no-nonsense masculinity. Nolan's determination to adhere to the 'realistic' explanations and logic of the thriller, and his stress on Batman as a 'real person' with credible abilities, converge with the identification of psychological 'realism' in terms of torment, anger and conflict – he describes Batman as 'a very complex character who lives on the razor's edge'[13] – to suggest an attitude of tough machismo underlying the production.

We have already seen Nolan conflate the protagonist with the principal actor, suggesting that Bruce Wayne's fire, rage and desire were uniquely inherent in Christian Bale. However, the language used by Nolan and his team also associates the production crew with a Batman-like commitment and resilience. Nolan describes himself, in his account of rationalising the mask and costume issue, as biting the bullet, facing a challenge, figuring out a puzzle and doing a job the hard way, rather than opting out as Schumacher did. 'If you trained hard enough, if you tried hard enough,' says Goyer, 'maybe, *just maybe*, you could become Batman.' Nolan, perhaps without realising it, is describing how he became a little bit like Batman;[14] that is, how he fits his own interpretation of Batman as driven and determined, rather than the latex-clad camp crusader of Schumacher's films.

The implications are subtle, but they build through repetition. When Nolan justifies the 'more theatrical ... a bit more gothic ...

more exotic' hallucinogenic scenes of *Batman Begins* through the claim that they are 'rooted in science',[15] the reasoning suits his preference for thriller logic rather than superhero fantasy, but it also underlines the opposition between his own down-to-earth rationality and its over-the-top alternative. 'The gothic' recalls Burton's distinctive vision, but it was Schumacher's Batman that was consistently labelled in terms of camp, pantomime and exotic theatricality, with reviews describing it as 'the most flamboyant Broadway musical ever staged', 'circus tent shenanigans', 'swirls of mayhem and art direction', and 'outlandishly garish.'[16] When Nolan's film strays briefly into this territory, he pulls it back by grounding it firmly in the traditionally masculine discipline of 'science'.

Similarly, while Nolan's insistence on physical stunt work and old-school effects rather than CGI makes sense in terms of his crime thriller approach to genre, it also becomes associated in the promotional materials with both muscular effort and intellectual challenge, and further cements the link between the main character and the creators; not just Nolan and Bale, in this case, but the entire production crew. 'I was determined not to use a digital Batmobile,' declares cinematographer Wally Pfister. 'Chris really wanted the chase to have a loose, raw feel ... something with the raw, gritty feeling of *The French Connection*.'[17] At this point, the production notes rev up the testosterone with a paragraph of technical specs, rattled off with a staccato precision that recalls Lucius Fox's exchanges with Bruce Wayne ('Pneumatic. Magnetic grapple. Monofilament tested to 350 pounds ... Kevlar bi-weave, reinforced joints ...')

> The Batmobile is equipped with a 5.7 liter, 350 cubic inch, 340-horsepower engine with approximately 400 pounds of torque. 9 feet, 4 inches at its widest point, the vehicle is 15 feet long and weighs 2.5 tons. It ... can jump 4–6 feet in height, up to a distance of 60 feet, and then peel off as soon as it hits the ground.[18]

Again, the emphasis is on Nolan's use of a 'real' vehicle rather than a digital version; its specifications and powers are genuine, just as Bale's increase in muscle was solid and worked-for, rather than bulked up with a costume. The camera car is described in very similar terms– 'the AMG Mercedes ML tracking vehicle, outfitted with a device called the Ultimate Arm and Lev Head, a gyro-stabilized head on a robotically controlled arm that is controlled by joysticks inside the vehicle' – which further blurs the boundaries between 'real' and 'fiction',[19] and in doing so flatters both sides. The gritty 'reality' of Batman's world is emphasised, while the film production in turn is given a sense of Batman-like, heavy-duty technological innovation.

According to the production notes, the Tumbler was designed 'in accordance with director Nolan's credo that every aspect of the film be firmly rooted in reality ... following Nolan's mantra of realism, it was important that every aspect of the Batmobile have a clear purpose.'[20] Nathan Crowley, the production designer, 'set up a little machine shop ... Chris would take a break from writing and come into the garage, where I'd be with my car concepts, covered in glue.'[21] These accounts of messy, manly, hands-on work, with a dedicated team following Nolan's inspiring direction and strict code, are interspersed with descriptions of Batman as 'an ordinary man who has made himself extraordinary, through sheer determination and self-discipline',[22] and the reminder that 'it's the fact that it's possible to be him – if you have the strength, stamina and selflessness to actually *become* him – that makes Batman so compelling and so enduring.'[23] Short of showing Nolan himself wearing the Bat-costume, the connection could hardly be clearer.

The production notes then complete the link with a description of Batman himself taking 'a gritty, do-it-yourself approach to developing his tools, including spray painting his suit matte black and grinding his own Batarangs.'[24] The director and crew, getting their hands dirty with hardware, become a little like Batman; and in turn, they create Batman in their own image as a DIY guy, prepared to design and construct his own props and costume.[25]

It is this aspect of *Batman Begins* – Nolan's determination to build as much as possible, from sets through vehicles to costumes, as functional items – that overlaps most closely with established scholarly theories of cinematic realism; or rather one theory, for 'realism' in film studies constitutes a series of debates, rather than a clear definition.

André Bazin, who co-founded the journal *Cahiers du Cinéma* and was a major influence on director-critics like Truffaut, advocated a cinematic aesthetic where the filmmaking process itself was effaced and became as transparent as possible. One of Bazin's key examples is Vittorio de Sica's *Ladri di Biciclette* (*Bicycle Thieves*) (1948), which he praises for having 'not one scene shot in a studio. Everything was filmed in the streets.'[26] By using non-professional actors, De Sica also achieved a naturalism and freshness that seemed to transcend performance: 'the question here is not one of playing a part but of getting away from the very notion of doing any such thing.'[27] 'With the disappearance of the concept of the actor into a transparency seemingly as natural as life itself,' Bazin continues, 'comes the disappearance of the set'[28] and in turn 'the disappearance of a story.'[29] The whole project 'must tend in the direction of the most neutral kind of transparency',[30] towards 'supreme naturalness, the sense of events observed haphazardly as the hours roll by';[31] the ideal of 'pure cinema'.[32]

Bazin is under no illusion that *Bicycle Thieves* genuinely records real life, without organisation or structure. 'I know of course that there is a story,' he explains, 'but of a different kind from those we ordinarily see on the screen.'[33]

> De Sica's film took a long time to prepare, and everything was as minutely planned as for a studio super-production … the numbering and titling of shots does not noticeably distinguish *Ladri di Biciclette* from any ordinary film. But their selection has been made with a view to raising the limpidity of the event to a maximum, while keeping the index of refraction from the style to a minimum. […] If the event is sufficient unto itself without the direction having to shed any further light on it by means of camera angles, purposely chosen camera positions, it is because it has reached that stage of perfect luminosity which makes it possible for an art to unmask a nature which in the end resembles it. That is why the impression made on us by *Ladri di Biciclette* is unfailingly that of truth.[34]

The film is not simply a recording of people, places and props that just happen to be there, but it gives the impression of an unpremeditated 'truth' by avoiding unnecessary artifice and avoiding tricks such as showy editing, visual effects and camera angles that draw attention to the process of filmmaking. Cinema should keep 'the index of refraction ... to a minimum', aiming to provide a pure, clean window on life, rather than a flashy lens.

While the editing of *Batman Begins* is typified by conventional Hollywood continuity, rapid action montage and Nolan's characteristic flashbacks rather than the long takes and deep focus that Bazin praised,[35] Nolan's approach has in common with Bazin's favoured techniques a desire to, if not record reality without interference, then to give the impression of doing so. His team built 'amazing things that can actually work in the real world ... once I set that all in motion it was really just a question of filming it'; and despite his reliance on quick-cutting montage, Nolan makes clear in the DVD documentaries that he shot fewer takes than would be usual for expensive stunt sequences, relying on multiple camera positions and editing as little as possible to show the action transparently, without unnecessary trickery.[36]

While of course, Nolan cast established actors rather than non-professionals, his repeated descriptions of Bale as a ready-made Batman underline this approach. Again, Nolan suggests that he simply had to find an actor who already had the qualities of the character, and record what was already there ('it was really just a question of filming it').

> ... when you're sitting down to write Bruce Wayne, that character already exists in the comics, so you know what his essence is. So when we set out to cast the film, we were looking for that essence. So when we found it, as we did with Christian, it fits and it's necessary.

> I felt that you would be able to look into Christian's eyes and believe he had the determination and self-discipline to recreate himself as a super hero, which is what Bruce Wayne does. I mean, Bruce Wayne is just a guy who does a lot of push-ups really! But that's a hell of a leap into being Batman, so whoever

was going to play him, you'd have to be able to look into his eyes and see that fire. And Christian has that in real life.[37]

So, just as the Batmobile was a 'real life', concrete, solid vehicle, Bale embodies Batman; but although he had the emotional energy and fire from the start, the production materials also stress the tough process of physical transformation that Bale went through, with extensive details of his 'rigorous physical training to prepare for the demanding role'. Again, the language emphasises rough-edged authenticity and downplays the more 'theatrical' aspects of cinema such as rehearsal, performance and choreography. Discussing the filming of an early scene, for instance, Bale's trainer explains that he devised 'a series of crude movements' for the 'down-and-dirty confrontation with seven prisoners in a Bhutanese jail'. 'This is where we see Bruce Wayne at his rawest. He's got a lot of inner anger, so his fighting has to come from pure brutality.'[38]

'It was clear to me, looking in his eyes,' says Nolan of Bale in the DVD documentary, over shots of Bale, stripped to the waist, 'that this is someone who can make you believe in the possibility of somebody devoting their life to something so extreme. Christian had a very controlled and specific approach to how he wanted to portray the aggression of this character ... the animal-like quality. He talked a lot about having Batman crouching in the shadows.' 'You just couldn't pull it off properly,' Bale adds, 'unless you were a beast when you were inside of that suit.'[39]

Of course, these interviews work to further blur the boundaries between actor and character. Bale was never a career bodybuilder like Schwarzenegger, but a man who, like Bruce Wayne, changed his body type through sheer determination and an inherent sense of drive. Bale, unsurprisingly, supports this view of himself as a focused, driven hard-ass. The mask, he confesses, 'induced headaches and would send me into a foul mood after half an hour.'[40]

But I wasn't going to be some little acting ninny who says *I can't deal with it anymore, take it off.* I used the pain as fuel for the character's anger. Batman's meant to be fierce, and you become a beast in that suit, as Batman should be – not a man in a suit, but a different creature.

Again, note the distinction Bale creates here between becoming a beast and channelling genuine pain into real anger, as opposed to merely acting the role ('a man in a suit') which is downgraded further into a whining 'ninny'. The raw, masculine 'realism' these interviews associate with *Batman Begins* is, once more, subtly contrasted with a sense of effeminate theatricality.

Bale built himself into Bruce Wayne, and the costume, in turn, transformed Wayne/Bale into Batman; again, we are given the consistent impression that Nolan constructed a real-world version of the fiction, from environments to characters, then simply recorded what was directly before the camera. In the Iceland scenes, for instance, producer Charles Roven confirms, 'you'll see a raging storm. It's not a pretend storm. It's not a CGI storm. We filmed in 75 mile-an-hour winds. But with Chris, you never stop shooting.'[41] Nolan, in turn, praises the 'the authenticity and intensity' that Bale and Liam Neeson brought to their sword-fight on a frozen lake. 'The ice was cracking in the way it's supposed to in the film.'[42]

'It was beautifully dangerous and quite daunting,' Neeson agrees. 'Every so often between set-ups we'd see ice crumbling away at the head of this glacier and bits of rock and muck falling off, and we knew this thing was a big living force that was moving towards us.'[43] 'Gradually the whole thing was falling apart, as we filmed,' confirms Bale.[44] As the stunt coordinator says of Wayne and Ra's al Ghul's tumble down an icy slope, 'It looks dangerous, it is dangerous, because anything could go wrong ... an accident could happen at any time, so yes, it's very scary.[45] Again, the descriptions combine a Bazinian approach to authenticity – the frozen lake, the heights, the threat and the physical exertion are all genuine, and the camera simply records the 'truth' – with a macho guarantee of actual danger, actual combat and actual muscle. 'Realism' does double-duty in this case, operating as a signifier of stripped-down, back-to-basics, hands-on toughness, rather than simply the purity, naturalism and freshness that could equally be connoted by a Bazinian approach to filmmaking.

This discourse of realism around *Batman Begins,* with its implied distinction from previous screen versions of Batman, was picked up by journalists, presumably in exactly the way the creators intended. Martyn Palmer's article in the *Sunday Times,* from June 2005, provides a rich example, and is worth examining in some detail.

Palmer foregrounds the grounded rationality of Nolan's project – 'With every aspect of Batman, from the Batmobile that we've designed to his costume, we have tried to explain the reality of how this guy could exist and why he would doing this' – and showcases the story of Bale's transformation, stressing the combination of emotional drive and physical training to suggest that Bale effectively brought his own 'real life' character traits to the screen.[46]

> Nolan saw just about every young actor in Hollywood for the leading role, and Bale was physically the least impressive — he had just shed 5st (31.75kg) for *The Machinist* so Nolan told him to bulk up fast for a screen test.

> 'Several weeks later he had put on the weight and blew everybody away. The significance of all that isn't about weight loss and gain, it's about the intensity and self-discipline of the guy and that was what we needed for Bruce Wayne.'[47]

Palmer's language picks up on and promotes the no-nonsense, guys-together tone we saw in the production notes. Nolan comes across in this account not as a cerebral British auteur but as a sports coach, giving Bale some tough talk – 'bulk up fast' – about getting into shape.

> With more than a year of intense preparations, including honing designs and building a vast Gotham City set at Cardington Studios (a former aircraft hangar near Watford), Nolan is confident that his vision of the Dark Knight will restore one of contemporary culture's icons to his rightful place.

'Batman,' Palmer concludes, 'is definitely back.'[48] This coolly decisive final line – recalling the deep voice-over of an action movie trailer – is significant, as the very notion of a 'rightful place' suggests a pure, accurate, 'real', authentic Batman. The franchise was 'all but extinguished by the woeful *Batman and Robin*,' Palmer explains, and the article goes on to distance Nolan's interpretation from both the TV show and the Burton films.

> Nolan, who grew up watching reruns of the 1960s TV series, promised that his would be Batman without frills — it's back to the beginning, a prequel in all but name. Although he is an admirer of Tim Burton's Batman, his film, he promises, will be different, with Christian Bale as an emotionally scarred, vengeful Bruce Wayne.[49]

The pattern here is familiar from both the fan responses in Chapter One and Nolan's interviews above: Burton's Batman is constructed as worthy but distinct and generally inferior, whereas Schumacher's contribution to the franchise is unapologetically slated, and Adam West's 1960s series consigned to the nostalgic past.[50] Once more, a subtle opposition is set up between Nolan's interpretation and its alternative; and again, its terms are familiar, as the 'realism' of Bale's character is explained in terms of scarring, torment and rage, and contrasted to 'frills'. In fact, Bale's Batman has more frills, in the sense of emotional complications, psychological complexity and baggage, than any previous screen Batman, but clearly, the implication here is of fancy frippery. Finally, note that the 'pure', stripped-down Batman is associated with going 'back to the beginning'. Literally, of course, Nolan's film is an origin story, but there is also a connection suggested between this back-to-basics approach and a return to the character's roots.

As proposed in Chapter One, film journalism is part of a complex relay; Palmer's article joins the matrix of texts that circulated around *Batman Begins* in the Summer of 2005, and it is impossible to be sure how his piece was influenced by the press notes, or how in turn his article may have shaped the subsequent discourse about the film. However, the relationships and oppositions he sketches around *Batman Begins* clearly echo and reinforce those of the production materials, and other articles from the same period fall into a very similar pattern.

'When Joel Schumacher turned the Dark Knight into the Crap Crusader,' *Empire* proclaims, 'the hopes of millions were smashed into tiny bat-shaped pieces. Gone was the gothic fairytale of Tim Burton's vision, replaced by a live-action cartoon.' From the trailer alone, the magazine confirms that 'Nolan has taken a very different approach to the character, delivering on his promise to make the story more "real" than its predecessors', and it concludes, with a hard-man tone that recalls Martyn Palmer's final line, 'Chris Nolan isn't messing about.'[51]

Total Film describes Schumacher's movies as 'bloated, camp disasters', reinforcing the sense of Nolan's interpretation as a muscular riposte to theatrical swishiness, and again making a firm, though less damning, distinction between *Batman Begins* and Burton's films. Once more, the hands-on, back-to-basics approach is emphasised, and the account of Wayne's tough, independent labour could just as easily describe Nolan and his crew, building props in Crowley's machine-shop garage.

> So, no more glitz. But no gothic, either. Nolan hasn't defaulted to Burton's original vision – remarkable in 1989, enjoyable but rather empty now behind Jack's sneer and swagger. Rather, he trusts in the inherent allure of Batman's dark heart and lets him loose on our world. Gotham here is a barely tweaked NYC, its suited and re-booted hero imposing but realistic – the logical result of a justice-seeking vigilante with limitless resources. From Wayne Enterprises' prototype body armour spray-painted black to the Bat-winged throwing stars he grinds out himself, Wayne harnesses bleeding edge technology to create an alter ego that's 'something elemental. Something terrifying.'[52]

Film4.com states plainly that it was 'camp incarnations' such as *Batman & Robin* 'that killed off Warner Brothers' once lucrative superhero franchise in 1997. Having started strongly with Tim Burton's dark fairytale vision of *Batman*, the superhero became a soft-drink peddling, Day-Glo nightmare in the hands of director Joel Schumacher.'[53] Kenneth Turan, in the *Los Angeles Times*, uses similar terms, though he dismisses Burton and Schumacher's films together as equally bad in different ways, deriding their 'mindless camp and compulsive weirdness' respectively; Nolan's intention, by contrast, is to create 'a myth grounded, as much as myth can be, in plain reality. He wants his story to be as plausible as possible, a human drama set in a believable world.'[54] Turan underlines the idea of Batman as an 'unlikely comic-book hero who does without super powers, someone, the director has said, who "really is just a guy that does a lot of push-ups"'. He repeats the story about Bale's weight training in relation to the 'sense of purpose about his performance', and implicitly associates Nolan with a Batman-like determination, drive and physical commitment.

> Nolan also did without a second unit, preferring the tonal unity he felt would come from directing everything himself ... Bringing an auteur sensibility to blockbuster material may sound next door to impossible, but *Batman Begins* shows it can be done. If you're willing to do the push-ups.

Sukhdev Sandhu describes Schumacher's *Batman & Robin* as 'camper than a field at Glastonbury', and confirms that Nolan 'has junked the campy theatrics' for a 'grindingly dark ... grim affair'.[55] Note that even when reviewers use 'grim' as a complaint about Nolan's relatively humourless film – *Variety*, similarly, bemoans the lack of 'theatricality, a sense of showmanship' and describes the film as 'terribly sober, afraid to make grand gestures'[56] – the terms of the opposition are unchanged. Nolan's 'realism' is consistently associated with toughness, grittiness, rawness and masculinity, and contrasted to an extent with the gothic stylings of Burton, but more significantly, with the camp theatricality of Schumacher. Schumacher's efforts are regarded as unmitigated disasters, brought into discussion primarily as the bad object against which Nolan's can be favourably compared.

As we saw, Palmer's review also suggested a good object, beyond Nolan's; a pure, original, accurate Batman to which Nolan's interpretation faithfully returns. This implied ideal is, ultimately, associated with the comic-book source. We saw in Chapter Two how assiduously the production paratexts tried to establish a discourse of fidelity to the comics, but I also noted the ways in which decades of diverse, contradictory source material were narrowed down into a far more limited, manageable group of texts, which in turn carry a distinct set of values and promote a specific interpretation of Batman. I will examine this 'selective tradition' more closely below.

While such extensive use of 'realism' to distinguish an interpretive approach to Batman and associate it with qualities of rawness, rigour and tough masculinity is a phenomenon unique to Nolan's reboot,[57] the underlying discourse of oppositions between a 'dark', serious Batman and a 'camp', light Batman has a long-established history. The same distinctions were used to distinguish Tim Burton's 1989 *Batman*, Frank Miller's 1986 *Dark Knight Returns* and Denny O'Neil's early 70s 'darknight detective' stories from the previous bad Bat-object, the 1960s TV show.[58] Schumacher's two films have largely replaced the Adam West series as the dominant, and most recent, example of camp's supposedly ruinous effect on the character, but the key terms in the opposition have structured Batman's meanings for decades.[59] If we follow through the implied link from Schumacher's camp to homoerotic interpretations – at which Sandhu hints, for instance, with the reference to Batman 'sporting stretch Lycra and showing off his tight nipples'[60] – we can trace this debate back at least to the 1950s and the attendant controversy over, followed by the containment and censorship of, potential gay readings in Batman comic books.[61] It was 1954 when Dr. Fredric Wertham first described Batman and Robin's relationship as 'a wish dream of two homosexuals living together',[62] prompting decades of furious denial and repeated attempts to introduce heterosexual love interests for both characters, but also encouraging endless nudge-nudge insinuations, enabling gay interpretations and, ultimately, shaping the reception – and possibly the production – of both the TV show and the Schumacher films. As the critic George Melly noted in 1970, 'we all knew Robin and Batman were pouves.'[63]

But just as earlier attempts to control homoerotic readings of Batman and Robin's relationship not only failed to repress them entirely, but paradoxically made them visible and set them into circulation,[64] so the discourse that constructs Nolan's project as gritty, masculine and 'realistic' has to establish itself in opposition to an alternate version, and again, paradoxically, bring to light the very meanings it is trying to wipe out.

Jonathan Gray suggests that 'the tale of *Batman Begins* is one of how to escape a dark shadow ... audience and critical reception of *Batman and Robin* had been so near-universally caustic that it had set up a strong paratextual perimeter and a flaming hoop through which any subsequent Batman text would need to pass.'[65] However, while Gray's image of a flaming hoop has appropriately campy, circus connotations, *Batman Begins* is, in fact, more a tale of how to cast a shadow or draw a veil over the garishly bright colours of Schumacher's interpretation. The paradox is, of course, that darkness can only be defined in contrast to its opposite.

Therefore, though Nolan and his crew apparently take pains not to mention Schumacher by name – Nolan sources the 'I like your tailor' remark vaguely to 'one of the Batman films' – the sense of an alternative approach consistently shapes their sense of what they are doing, what this Batman is like, and even, because of their close identification with the main character, who they are.

So, Schumacher is 'ludicrous' and the TV show is 'ridiculous', while the more 'theatrical' and 'exotic' scenes of *Batman Begins* are justified by Nolan as 'rooted in science'. Bale's use of his own genuine anger and discomfort as fuel for the performance is contrasted to the whining of 'a guy in a suit', a 'little acting ninny': this is 'Batman without frills'. The journalists make explicit what Nolan and his team only suggest: Schumacher's films were 'bloated, camp disasters', 'Day-Glo nightmares' and 'mindless camp'. As noted in Chapter One, 19 out of the 27 reviews in this sample compared Nolan's film to Schumacher's previous instalments. Overwhelmingly, the comparisons favoured Nolan, but more notable is the fact that Schumacher was mentioned so frequently in reviews of a film that was meant to erase his efforts from popular memory.

Sight and Sound concludes that 'Nolan's spirited take on this franchise wipes the slate clean after the tired mess of *Batman & Robin;* it is a welcome new beginning.'[66] The image echoes the production discourse's claims of a straight and thorough reboot, but the reality is more complex. Rather than wiping the slate clean, *Batman Begins* wrote on a page already indelibly marked with the traces of previous Batman films. Rather than a clean blank, ready for Nolan's new project, the 'Batman' of 2005 was a palimpsest, already carrying the faint shapes of Burton's Batman, Schumacher's Batman, Miller's Batman, O'Neil's Batman and countless others, back to Kane's original of 1939.

Furthermore, despite the implications of 'rebooting' as a memory-wiping start from scratch – echoed by the title itself, *Batman Begins* – Nolan's film did not, in fact, even attempt to start with a completely blank page, for two fundamental reasons. Firstly, as we've already seen, rather than presenting itself as Nolan's independent authorial take on Batman, the film was promoted as a faithful adaptation of 'the comics', and those previous, carefully selected interpretations of Batman were foregrounded through paratexts like the production notes, which heavily reference Kane and Miller, and the DVD documentaries, with their direct comparison of film scenes and comic-book images. *Batman Begins* was presented as a fresh start to the film franchise, but it was also pitched in terms of fidelity and continuity to a long-standing mythos. It was successfully sold as both appealingly new and authentically traditional: it played cleverly on the double meaning of an 'origin' story as both a beginning and a return.

Secondly, as I've suggested, the production notes and official paratexts only partially attempt to wipe Schumacher's Batman from the slate, because this trace of an alternative, previous interpretation was also needed to give Nolan's film its definition. To demonstrate the novelty and value of a new approach, the producers had to retain some contrasting traces of the bad old one in the production discourses; and rather than erasing it, they in fact made the bad object visible again, as a point of comparison. Rather than repressing discussion of Schumacher's Batman, Nolan's film prompted it to be talked about far more than it had been since 1997. To understand this process more fully, we can refer to the work of Michel Foucault.

Foucault says of the containment and policing of sexuality in Victorian culture that rather than 'a censorship of sex ... there was installed rather an apparatus for producing an even greater quantity of discourse about sex.' As queer theorist Alan Sinfield wryly summarises, 'rather than the Victorians repressing sex ... they went on about it all the time.'[67] This explosion of discourse was particularly important in terms of categorising, controlling and policing deviancy and aberration, with significant implications for homosexuality. 'The nineteenth century homosexual,' writes Foucault,

> ... became a personage, a past, a case history, and a childhood ... nothing that went into his total composition was unaffected by his sexuality. It was everywhere present in him: at the root of all his actions because it was their insidious and indefinitely active principle; written immodestly on his face and body because it was a secret that always gave itself away. It was consubstantial with him, less as a habitual sin than as a singular nature. [...] The sodomite had been a temporary aberration; the homosexual was now a species.[68]

The distinction, Sinfield points out, is 'between taking things from a chain store, which many youngsters might do at some time, and being labelled "a thief": with the latter, thievishness is made to seem the core of your personality.'[69] However, just as the attempts to censor and control gay readings of Batman and Robin stories in the 1950s in fact increased their visibility, so Sinfield observes that

> nineteenth-century legal, medical and sexological discourses on homosexuality made possible new forms of control; but, at the same time, they also made possible what Foucault terms 'a "reverse" discourse,' whereby 'homosexuality began to speak in its own behalf, to demand that its legitimacy or "naturality" be acknowledged, often in the same vocabulary, using the same categories by which it was medically disqualified. Deviancy returns from abjection by deploying just those terms that relegated it there in the first place.'[70]

'Even a text that aspires to contain a subordinate perspective,' Sinfield states, 'must first bring it into visibility; even to misrepresent, one must present.'[71] This is precisely what we saw in the discourses around Nolan and Schumacher, with their attendant values of dark, gritty, masculine, stripped-down realism, and bright, glitzy, effeminate, bloated, campy theatrics. To confirm the qualities of Nolan's Batman, the discourse had first to remind its readers of Schumacher's.

> Any utterance is bounded by the other utterance that the language makes possible. Its shape is the correlative of theirs: as with the duck/rabbit drawing, when you see the duck the rabbit lurks around the edges, constituting an alternative that may spring into visibility. Any position supposes its intrinsic *op*-position. All stories comprise within themselves the ghosts of the alternative stories they are trying to exclude.[72]

Batman, by nature, is multiple. As I suggested in the Introduction, and is clear from this chapter, this multiplicity has been subject to repeated attempts at control, reduction and containment. But Batman, by nature, must remain multiple. He is a composite of many different Batmen; his richness and resonance is due to in large part to his diversity, his potential for change, all the things he has been, and all the things he can be. All Batman stories comprise within themselves the ghosts of the alternative Batman stories they are trying to exclude; and the discourse around *Batman Begins* shows that Nolan's reboot was no exception. Rather than starting with a clean slate, it sketched a new Batman over the traces of the previous authors' work; but the Batmen from before – the alternates, the ghosts, the other interpretations, even the aberrations – can never fully be erased, and keep coming back.

The Selective Tradition

We saw in Chapter Two that the production discourses worked hard to establish a sense of fidelity between *Batman Begins* and its 'source', suggesting a more traditional relationship of adaptation than was in fact the case. Several reviews picked up on this framework, as they did with the construction of 'realism', and discussed the film's source material within the terms established by the official paratexts, sometimes naming the exact titles that were foregrounded in the official paratexts – The *Long Halloween, Year One* and O'Neil's 1970s Ra's al Ghul stories – as the key inspirations.[73]

The reviews demonstrate some variation in terms of the comic-book texts identified as the 'original', but only within a narrow margin. As we saw in Chapter One, four of the 27 reviews mention Kane, while 11 refer to Miller. Manohla Dargis, for instance, praises *Batman Begins* in *The New York Times* as a 'tense, effective iteration of Bob Kane's original comic book,'[74] while Nev Pierce, writing for the BBC online, describes the film as 'influenced by Frank Miller's seminal comic *Batman: Year One'* and credits it as 'easily the most engrossing and faithful screen adaptation of his adventures', implying that the fidelity is specifically to Miller. Sandhu, in the Telegraph, suggests that Nolan's film 'recalls … Frank Miller's 1986 graphic novel.'[75] Kenneth Turan agrees that

> Nolan, who co-wrote with comic book specialist David S. Goyer, has in effect brought the franchise back to its modern origins. That would be the appearance in 1986, three years before the first Tim Burton film, of Frank Miller's somber and ominous graphic novel *Batman: The Dark Knight Returns*, which repositioned Bob Kane's 1939 Caped Crusader as a contemporary figure of almost existential torment.[76]

Total Film takes a similar view, allowing for both a 1939 origin and an equally important modern reworking, which now serves – as the title *Year One* suggests – as a new start point. Again, we have the sense of both a fresh beginning and a faithful return embodied in the same text.

> Frank Miller reinvented Bob Kane's iconic character in *Batman: Year One* and *The Dark Knight Returns*. And while *Sin City*'s comics genius isn't credited, Nolan and David S Goyer's script is indebted to Miller's exploration of Batman's bruised psyche and his noir-styled depiction of a Gotham wracked by organised crime more than costumed superfreaks.[77]

Steve Biodrowski, unusually among these reviews, recognises the complexity of the adaptation process with his comment in

Cinefantastique that 'elements of Frank Miller's *The Dark Knight Returns* and *Batman: Year One* are skilfully woven in with other bits and pieces from Batman's long comic book career', but again, Miller is the only creator mentioned by name.[78]

Whichever specific source is identified, though, the implication is the same: Nolan's film comes closer to an 'original', a 'true' version, than previous Batman films, while Schumacher's movies, by contrast, are described by Sandhu in the *Telegraph* as modelled on the 'fly-weight, jokey 1960s television series' and by *CNN* as 'big screen versions of the over-the-top, campy 1960 TV series';[79] adaptations of an aberrant or at best flimsy text. As the *Cinema Crazed* blog enthuses of *Batman Begins*, 'they finally got it right. Finally. Batman is finally the character I've read on the page since I was a child,'[80] and Roger Ebert, admitting that he has loved Batman since his own childhood, agrees. 'This is at last the Batman movie I've been waiting for.'[81] *Empire,* as we saw, promises that Nolan will restore Batman to his 'rightful place', and speculates that 'that this could very well be the film that Batman fans have spent their lives waiting for'.[82] In faithfully following the comic book (rather than the TV show) Nolan has, it's implied, finally captured the essence of the character. As such, we encounter a further, and final meaning of 'realism' carried by Nolan's reboot: the implication that his film depicts Batman 'accurately', as he was meant to be, in a faithful rendition of the 'originals' (whether Kane's 1939 incarnation, or Miller's modern reinterpretation). Nolan's film, it is suggested, gives us the true Batman.

The comic-book source is narrowed down in these reviews to a handful of texts, exactly as the production discourses suggested: a faithful adaptation of 'Batman' becomes, through a successful sleight of hand, a film that follows the template of Batman set out in a small group of stories from within a relatively slim chronological window. The 'originals' are, as discussed in Chapter Two, all drawn from between 1971 (O'Neil's 'Daughter of the Demon') and 1997 (*The Long Halloween*). As such, they all share a rough understanding of how Batman and his milieu work, in terms of character and tone, and often overlap or pay homage to each other on the level of specific details. O'Neil's 'The Man Who Falls', for instance, quotes directly from Miller's *Dark Knight Returns*, and Loeb and Sale's *Long Halloween* continues chronologically from Miller's *Year One*, remaining within the continuity established by, and developing characters from, the previous series. Loeb and Sale's *Long Halloween* and Miller and Mazzucchelli's *Year One* were both released during O'Neil's reign as Group Editor of Batman titles, and so were subject to the guidelines of his Bat-Bible, which ensured a level of continuity and consistency.[83] Most of these reviews, however, narrow this source material down even further, recognising only Miller's *Year One* and *The Dark Knight Returns* as key influences on *Batman Begins*.

We can identify here what Raymond Williams, one of the pioneers of modern cultural studies, called a 'selective tradition'. Williams observes, in his book *The Long Revolution*, that

> Even most specialists in a period know only a part of even its records. One can say with confidence, for example, that nobody really knows the nineteenth-century novel; nobody has read, or could have read, all its examples over the whole range from printed volumes to penny serials. The real specialist may know some hundreds; the ordinary specialist somewhat less; educated readers a decreasing number: though all will have clear views on the subject. A selective process, of a quite drastic kind, is at once evident, and this is true of every field of activity.[84]

As Williams notes, the drastic narrowing-down process of the selective tradition expresses certain values and emphasises certain traits, through the works that are chosen. A list of novels from the 1950s, or indeed graphic novels of the 1980s, will be based around a consensus of 'what seem to be the best and most relevant works,'[85] and this selection will, of course, in turn be informed and governed by contemporary notions of quality and relevance. We must remember, says Williams, that 'the cultural tradition is not only a selection but also an interpretation.'[86] He further proposes that these traditions can change over time, in a process of 'continual selection and re-selection ... particular lines will be drawn, often for as long as a century, and then suddenly with some new stage in growth these will be cancelled or weakened, and new lines drawn.'[87] However, as the discussion above suggests, the consensus around the 'seminal' and most influential Batman comic books and graphic novels of recent decades remains stable, with no signs as yet of reevaluation or revisionism.

What values, then, does this tradition carry; and what type of Batman does it propose as the 'real' version of the character? As we saw, Miller's *Year One* and *Dark Knight Returns* were singled out in particular by reviewers as the most influential Batman texts of the 'modern' era. *The Dark Knight Returns* has been discussed exhaustively elsewhere, from online fan debates to published scholarly analysis: readers wanting a more detailed analysis of this specific text are directed to the relevant chapters of Geoff Klock's *How to Read Superhero Comics and Why*, Roz Kaveney's *Superheroes! Capes and Crusaders in Comics and Films*, Richard Reynolds' *Superheroes: A Modern Mythology* and my own 'The Best Batman Story: *The Dark Knight Returns*' in Alan McKee's edited collection *Beautiful Things in Popular Culture*.[88]

However, we can draw out a set of key values and associations from the tradition as a whole. Firstly, as suggested in Chapter One, these works helped to create and perpetuate a discourse of authorship within comics: the sense that an individual artist and writer – or an artist/writer, in Miller's case – was not just allowed but encouraged to offer their own distinctive 'take' on the character. This discourse, whereby Miller's Batman can coexist alongside Loeb and Sale's from *The Long Halloween*, Morrison and McKean's from *Arkham Asylum*, and Moore and Bolland's from *The Killing Joke*, enabled the promotion and reception of Nolan's Batman as distinct from, but equally valid as, these other interpretations.

That said, while the culture of authorship allows for heterogeneity – the *Batman Begins* documentary DVD alone shows a variety of different Batmen in various styles – these interpretations all fall within certain parameters. Each carries a sense of 'quality' and 'maturity', closely connected to the culture of the graphic novel that emerged in the mid-1980s, with *The Dark Knight Returns* as one of the key examples of this new format. The graphic novel brought with it improved production values – better quality paper, printing and colour – an elevated cultural status, as comics briefly entered the mainstream and earned broader recognition, and a slightly older, more sophisticated (though still largely male) readership. These factors in turn influenced the medium, encouraging greater experiment in comic-book artwork, more ambitious literary aspirations in the writing – some of which, inevitably, resulted in pretension and purple prose – and a greater engagement with 'mature' themes, which led to bold and valuable work like Peter Milligan's gender explorations in *Shade: The Changing Man* (1990–1996) and *Enigma* (1993), but also to an increased reliance on scenes of sex, violence and sexual violence that ranged from the hackneyed to the misogynistic: Mike Grell's *The Longbow Hunters* (1987) provides a notorious example. While O'Neil and Adams' Ra's al Ghul stories were initially published prior to the graphic novel boom, they have since been retroactively incorporated into the tradition through trade paperbacks that reprint the original stories on high quality paper and re-colour the artwork using modern digital techniques.

It would be a stretch to describe these Batman stories as visually 'realistic'. The culture of individual interpretations during this period enabled more artistic freedom than in previous decades, when artists remained anonymous and styles more standardised. Alex Ross and Dave McKean's painted artwork in *Kingdom Come* and *Arkham Asylum* approaches photorealism, but Miller's stylised figures and Klaus Janson's scratchy pen-work in *The Dark Knight Returns* invite us into a consistent visual universe rather than attempting to reproduce the world as we see it, while Tim Sale's *The Long Halloween* and David Mazzucchelli's art for Miller's *Year One*, in turn, both offer an entirely distinct, and equally stylised, representation of the environment, cast and main character. Despite their differences, though, these texts all share a *noir*-influenced aesthetic: a dramatic and extensive use of shadow – inked in deep black and often reducing figures to silhouettes – coupled with a subtle, muted use of colour. This last trend was, again, enabled by the improvement in printing quality and digital techniques, and helps to distinguish the 'modern' Batman of this period, cloaked in sombre, understated shades, from the brighter, brasher comics of the 1950s and 1960s.

A further distinction – and a further sense of darkness at a thematic level – can be found in the relationship between this selective tradition and broader Batman history. Miller's *Dark Knight Returns* coincided with DC Comics' twelve-part 'Crisis on Infinite Earths' storyline,[89] which rebooted continuity and erased the sillier, science fiction Batman adventures of the 1950s and 1960s – along with a host of the more frivolous supporting characters – not just out of existence, but out of official memory. As I have summarised elsewhere:

> Its principal aim was to clean up the mess of narrative parallel universes which DC's writers had established over the past forty-five years, in order to start afresh with a single, easy-to-follow continuity. It achieved this aim by combining all the possible earths into one, and killing off all the characters who didn't fit. The stories which had occurred 'pre-Crisis' were therefore made unofficial, outside continuity, and would never be referred to again.

> In practice the Crisis did make DC's narrative universe more accessible to new readers. However, it also served the purpose of wiping out almost five decades of superhero history, and re-writing its main characters according to the more 'serious', 'adult' ethos of the mid-1980s … Post-Crisis, the embarrassing moments of the 1950s and 1960s could simply be wiped out of history.[90]

As we saw with the branding initiatives in Chapter Two, the fictional and non-fictional worlds overlapped at this moment; just as the introduction of a new sidekick and enterprise within the story-world justified the new monthly titles *Red Robin* and *Batman Incorporated*, so the containment of Batman's diverse meanings in 1986, when the camp whimsy of previous decades was wiped from history, was enacted within the fiction through the destruction of multiple alternate worlds.[91]

While *Dark Knight Returns*, paradoxically, stood outside mainstream continuity itself, as an alternate-future story, it also represented a new sense of seriousness and gravity; 'it set the tone to grim, grainy, rainy and gritty, and convinced a host of subsequent writers and artists that the key to an "adult" comic was hard-hitting vigilant-ism with an edge of political commentary and an S&M twist to the superhero costumes.' Again, in my own words:

> It was the prime text of the 'post-Crisis' period: the *Crisis on Infinite Earths* maxi-series had forced DC's universe into a slimmed-down, supposedly more manageable form, razing off worlds that didn't fit and mercy-killing swathes of characters. It was a holocaust not just of geography but history, as origins were rebooted and the past wiped out. From this point onwards, whole pockets of history were buried: and invariably, it was the more embarrassing, campy episodes that were repressed, never included when the origin was retold. Batman's early days now officially involved pilgrimages to train with Asian martial artists and mystics, and trials by combat in Gotham's red-light district: there was no Ace the Bat-Hound, no science fiction alien adven-tures, no Rainbow Batman costumes in this history, and anyone clinging to that kind of nostalgia was suffering false memory syndrome. It wasn't a dream, it wasn't an imaginary story. It never happened anymore.[92]

Bat-Girl was gone, Bat-Mite and Ace the Bat-Hound were gone; and so were various alternate Batmen from those lighter, more play-ful science fiction stories, such as the Negative Batman, the Zebra Batman and, most notoriously of all, the Rainbow Batman, depicted on the cover of *Detective Comics* #241 (January 1957) in a bright pink costume.

Although it was *Year One*, released in 1987, that literally took the character back to square one and defined a new, hardboiled begin-ning, *Dark Knight* epitomises the armoured, military toughness and no-nonsense rationality that underpinned the Crisis, helped to shape Burton's 1989 movie, and in turn influenced Nolan's Batman. It was a reboot kicking the Rainbow Batman in the crotch and stamping on silliness; a tank crushing decades of colourful characters and light-hearted adventures. It engaged with contemporary politics and media, pushed Batman to new extremes of vigilantism and violence and eschewed bright fantasy in favour of painstakingly described street-level combat. In the tradition of O'Neil's Ra's al Ghul, a villain inspired more by the secret agent genre than by the superhero tradition, Miller kept both his heroes and villains down to earth. Demigods like Green Lantern and Wonder Woman are out of the picture, while Superman, the most science fiction element in this urban narrative, is depicted initially through his effects – a streak of cool blue and the sizzle of heat vision – and Joker, similarly, appears first as a sober, blank-faced mental patient, rather than a manic clown. While, as noted, *The Dark Knight Returns* takes place in a possible future, *Year One* continues the hardboiled urban tone through its focus on Batman's early career, at which point – rather than having died or departed – the more abnormal and superhuman members of Batman's supporting cast have not yet shown their faces. *The Long Halloween* follows its lead with an emphasis on Gotham's mafia families.

Despite their authorial variations, all the texts in this tradition work within the established post-Crisis continuity, to the extent, as noted, of quoting from and overlapping directly with each other's narratives. Although O'Neil's 1970s work predates the Crisis, his Ra's al Ghul stories were among the few aspects of Batman's history that escaped the reboot, and were officially approved as having 'really happened'. O'Neil and Adams' comics of this period are effectively precursors to *Dark Knight Returns* and *Year One* in their attempt to present a grittier, more serious and plausible Batman, and were also intended as a reboot; an antidote to the camp of the 1960s TV show and the comics that surrounded it. O'Neil remembers that his first Batman story with Neal Adams was

> a conscious desire to break out of the *Batman* TV show; to throw in everything and announce to the world 'Hey, we're not doing camp.' We wanted to re-establish Batman not only as the best detective in the world, and the best athlete, but also as a dark and frightening creature – if not supernatural, then close to it, by virtue of his prowess.[93]

Sam Hamm describes O'Neil's version as 'unlike anything that had appeared in the Batman titles for years'; the creators, ignoring the 1960s television and comics, 'had remembered – and been true to – an altogether different Batman.'[94] Again, note the appeal to an original, a valid essence of Batman that can be abandoned and lost, but also rediscovered and revived: the same combination of novelty and fidelity to an ur-text lies behind the idea of Miller's *Dark Knight* as a reinvention of Kane's 1939 vision, and in turn, of course, it circulated widely again in the promotion of Nolan's film. This selective tradition therefore appeals to an earlier tradition and a conventional sense of authorship – whether Kane's 'original', or Miller's 'modern origin' – as a guarantee of its own authenticity, and by contrast implies that the camp of the TV show and Schumacher's films were deviations from the fundamental 'truth' of Batman, as imagined by the character's first author and then re-imagined by the influential graphic novelists of the 1980s.

Therefore, just as *Batman Begins* was faithful not so much to a source text, or even a set of source texts, as to an underlying mode of comics authorship through its creative reuse and revision of existing motifs and narrative strands, so it also fundamentally adapted, and adopted from the modern tradition, this powerful sense of rebooting. *Batman Begins* was to Schumacher's *Batman & Robin* what O'Neil's 1970s Batman and Miller's *Dark Knight Returns* had been to the 1960s TV show and the associated comics: it drew from its source material not so much specific plotlines or dialogue as their underlying impulse to wipe a camp slate clean, to paint black over Day-Glo colours for a new start. By establishing a connection with O'Neil's Ra's al Ghul stories and Miller's *Dark Knight Returns/Year One*, the *Batman Begins* publicity discourses tapped into this already existing theme of a fresh – although, ironically, darker and grimmer – beginning. On one level, what the film adapts is the very concept of the comic-book Crisis as a rebooting device.

In his introduction to *Dark Knight Returns*, Alan Moore celebrates Miller's achievement in the same terms that Nolan used to praise Burton's 1989 movie; for helping to erase the memory of the TV show from public consciousness, and restore Batman's plausibility. Again, the implication is of reinventing, not inventing: like *Batman Begins*, the very title *The Dark Knight Returns* carries a double-barrelled resonance. The novelty of Miller's approach, it is suggested, lies partly in taking the character back to his roots.

> Whatever changes may have been wrought in the comics them-
> selves, the image of Batman most permanently fixed in the mind
> of the general populace is that of Adam West delivering outra-
> geously straight-faced camp dialogue while walking up a wall
> thanks to the benefit of stupendous special effects and a camera
> turned on its side. To lend such a subject credibility in the eyes of
> an audience not necessarily enamored of super-heroes and their
> trappings is no inconsiderable feat ... [95]

'Everything is exactly the same, except for the fact that it's all totally different.' Again, we can recognise the relationship between unchanging mythic template and narrative progression that Eco identified as essential to Superman stories, and the dynamic of familiarity and novelty that shapes comic-book authorship, and in turn informed Nolan's approach: a regular process of rebooting, revision and creative collage, whereby existing pieces are rearranged in a new formation, underpins Batman's success and survival as a cultural icon. Acclaimed auteurist interpretations of Batman are never entirely new, but rather inventive reworkings of the old; a new origin is always a selective retelling of the existing myth. 'The continuity', as Richard Reynolds suggests, 'is a *langue* in which each particular story is an utterance.'[96] Every new expression, or Batman story, relies on and calls upon the existing archive, the mythic structure and framework, just as every sentence relies on and refers back to the system of language.[97] A beginning, for Batman, is always also a return.[98]

Miller makes a similar boast about his own work in the introduction to *Year One*, with a further claim that his interpretation returns to an earlier, more authentic version; its power lies not in starting from scratch, but in its reactivation of older meanings. *Year One* is not just a clean page for 1987, but also a return to another 'year one', the original story of 1939; or for Frank Miller, a return to 1965, when he was eight years old.[99]

> If your only memory of Batman is that of Adam West and Burt
> Ward exchanging camped out quips while clobbering slumming
> guest stars Vincent Price and Cesar Romero, I hope this book
> will come as a surprise. For me, Batman was never funny. I was

eight years old when I picked up an 80-page annual from the shelf of a local supermarket. The artwork on one story looked good and scary ...[100]

Miller then digresses into a hardboiled narration about cold moonlight, shafts of concrete, 'a burglar alarm, the old kind' – of course, the old kind – and the appearance of Batman as 'glistening wet, black against the blackened sky, a monster, a giant, winged gargoyle.' This evokes the essence of the character for Miller as a child, and of course it equally describes the Batman he restores to the public consciousness through *Year One*.

Once more, the resonance and power of this Batman is highlighted through its continuity with an earlier 'original' ('Batman was never funny') and its opposition to an alternative, inferior approach: and again, this oppositional term is identified specifically as 'camp'. The 'dark' Batman of the modern tradition, with noir visuals, muted colour, rugged masculinity and rationalised continuity, is defined against the bright, silly – in Hamm's words, 'outlandish ... garish'[101] – caped crusader of the television show, and the Rainbow Batman who epitomises the campier pre-Crisis comics. The specific texts in question may be different, but the opposition is exactly the same as that which defined Nolan's Batman against Schumacher's. The camp Batman is associated with 'slumming', a debauched, grubby lapse in quality from the hard, rigid essence of the character; this false memory needs to be wiped out, as it was in the Crisis on Infinite Earths, and replaced with the true, dark origin intended by Kane in 1939. By drawing a straight line from the 'original' source through Miller's 'modern origin' – itself hailed as a 'return' to the essence of the character – to Nolan's faithful, back-to-basics, grittily masculine approach, any camp incarnations can be constructed, by contrast, as a detour, deviation or dead end.

As Andy Medhurst points out in his important essay 'Batman, Deviance and Camp', this binary structure, which associates the 'good' Batman objects with darkness, violence, machismo, rationality and authenticity, and the 'bad' with brightness, camp, homoeroticism, silliness and aberration, carries blatantly weighted value judgements about masculinity and sexuality.

The one constant factor through all of the transformations of Batman has been the devotion of his admirers. They will defend him against what they see as negative interpretations, and they carry around in their heads a kind of essence of batness, a Bat-Platonic Ideal of how Batman should really be. The Titan Books reissue of key comics from the 1970s each carry a preface from a noted fan, and most of them contain claims such as 'This, I feel, is Batman as he was meant to be.'

Where a negative construction is specifically targeted, no prizes for guessing which one it is: 'you ... are probably also fond of the TV show he appeared in. But then maybe you prefer Elvis Presley's Vegas years or the later Jerry Lewis movies over their early stuff ... for me, the definitive Batman was then and always will be the one portrayed in these pages.'[102]

Again, this hierarchy is based around notions of 'truth' ('essence of batness') and 'realism' ('how Batman should really be'): 'definitive' versions are associated vaguely with authorial intention ('Batman as he was meant to be'), and linked to an equally vague sense of origin and roots ('their early stuff').

'Why do they insist so vehemently that Adam West was a faggy aberration, a blot on the otherwise impeccably butch Bat-landscape?' asks Medhurst, suggesting that the 1989 film advances the cause of the 'rival Bat-archetype, the grim, vengeful Dark Knight whose heterosexuality is rarely called into question (his humourlessness, fondness for violence and obsessive monomania seem to me exemplary qualities for a heterosexual man).'[103] Rather than just an aesthetic distinction between Day-Glo and dark, the opposition between rival Batmen is, as Medhurst points out, loaded with implications about traditional heterosexual masculinity – of a muscular and moody variety – as the truthful, authentic essence of the male heroic archetype, which camp and homoerotic variants deviate from, degrade and corrupt. The camp Batman is resisted so vehemently because, despite his apparent frippery and theatrical frivolity, and the complaints that he fails to be dark, serious and grim enough, he nevertheless poses a threat. Mixing the bright, silly Batman into the myth is seen to undermine the character's pure essence, as if swirling bright pink into pure black.

Underlying this denial and resistance, as Medhurst suggests, is homophobia in a quite literal sense: an intense discomfort with any readings of Batman as potentially gay. Unsurprisingly, professional journalists avoid any explicit criticism of the Adam West or Joel Schumacher Batman as homoerotic; the distaste is concealed and carried by code-words like theatrical, ludicrous, outlandish, garish, Day-Glo and camp. Internet commentators tend to be less cagey. While many Batman fans, worried about the associations of Schumacher's films, used the same terms in their opposition – 'Burton's Batman was dark, mysterious, shadowy and gothic. Schumacher's Batman was campy and cartoonish' – some were also prepared to make the explicit link to homosexuality. 'Batman is not gay but I do wonder about Schumacher. All his butt shots and crotch shots tell me that he is a little camp himself. And he keeps raving about how Val and George looked great in rubber ...'[104] As noted, this discomfort, and the attendant impulse to 'protect' Batman and Robin from gay readings, dates back to the 1950s and the attempts to, in Medhurst's phrase, 'heterosexualise' the characters as a response to Wertham's discussion of their homosexual overtones.[105] 'Bat-fans have always responded angrily to Wertham's accusation,' Medhurst points out.

> One calls it 'one of the most incredible charges ... unfounded rumours ... sly sneers' and the general response has been to reassert the masculinity of the two heroes, mixed with a little indignation: 'If they had been actual men they could have won a libel suit.'[106]

In editorial terms, this heterosexualisation took the form of introducing various female love interests and attempting to remove any potential for male bonding – killing off Alfred and replacing him with Aunt Harriet; creating a new Batgirl and killing off Robin[107] – while, as Medhurst notes, fans continue to defend what they perceive as Batman's heterosexual honour.[108]

Again, though, note that in reinforcing the distinction between the 'original' and the deviant, and attempting to separate 'authentic' darkness from camp colour, these reactions, whether professional or amateur, continually bring the bad object back into the light. The slate can never be fully wiped clean, either of the celebrated original Batman or the despised aberrant one; the myth of Kane's 'dark' source material is needed to authenticate each new gritty version as an accurate return to the character's intended essence ('Everything is exactly the same') but the memory of the Rainbow Batman is equally necessary to define the dark outlines and subtle shades by contrasting them to Day-Glo, garish colour. Much as these discourses claim that they, and the works they celebrate, want to erase the camp Batman from memory, they need first to bring him back and keep him in mind, in order to reinforce a sense of their own difference and opposition. If, as I've suggested, the camp meanings of Batman are never fully repressed, the advocates of the 'dark' Batman are partly responsible; it is the creators and critics who try to push it down that keep bringing it up, and those who claim they want us to forget Schumacher's movies, the pre-Crisis comic books and the 1960s TV show that constantly remind us of all three. As an example, consider again Sam Hamm's introduction to the 1970s stories, celebrating O'Neil and Adams' reinvention of the Batman as 'a dark and frightening creature':

> Then came the infamous television series ... the sight of live actors in gaudy costumes behaving like their comic-book prototypes ruthlessly exposed the fundamental silliness of the source-material. It could have been worse; just imagine if Bat-Mite, or Ace the Bat-Hound, had made it to the small screen.[109]

In praising O'Neil's first Ra's al Ghul story as 'the point at which the "dark side" of the Dark Knight began to show through the cracks,' Hamm unwittingly lets the fun side, the silly side of the Caped Crusader show through the darkness. In his attempt to make readers thankful for the grown-up 1970s saga – 'some dimly perceived game of intrigue and conspiracy, played out across continents, the participants shadowy factions ...' – he has to invoke the memory of Bat-Mite, and so, inevitably, conjures up the fifth-dimensional elf in a Batman outfit for readers who might have forgotten the character or never known of his existence.

'Any utterance is bounded by the other utterance that the language makes possible,' Sinfield argued. 'All stories comprise within themselves the ghosts of the alternative stories they are trying to exclude.' Medhurst, in turn, suggests that 'it's impossible to be sombre or pompous about Batman because if you try the ghost of West will come Bat-climbing into your mind, fortune cookie wisdom on his lips and keen young Dick by his side.'[110] The ghosts of those killed in the Crisis also refused to go gently into that good night; rather than disappearing forever, they were marginalised, relocated to another dimension that, in another case of the fictional universe echoing and enacting the industry practice of the real world, was simply called 'limbo'. The multiple worlds were closed down, but not permanently; they hovered at the outskirts, like half-forgotten dreams. Batman, in his darkest, most rigid and repressed incarnation, is constantly haunted by spectres of himself – by variants and alternatives, possibilities and past lives – and as the next chapter will show more clearly, the ghosts can come back.

'If one wants to take Batman as a Real Man,' Medhurst proposes, 'the biggest stumbling block has always been Robin.'

> The Wertham lobby and the acolytes of camp alike have ensured that any Batman/Robin relationship is guaranteed to bring on the sniggers. Besides which, in the late 1960s, Robin was getting to be a big boy, too big for any shreds of credibility to attach themselves to all that father-son smokescreen. So in 1969 Dick Grayson was packed off to college and the Bat was solitary once more. This was a shrewd move. It's impossible to conceive of the recent, obsessive, sturmund-drang Batman with a chirpy little Robin getting in the way.[111]

The process was not quite as clean-cut as Medhurst suggests: O'Neil's 'Daughter of the Demon' from June 1971, which introduced Ra's al Ghul and falls firmly within the gritty, post-camp phase, opens with Batman looking aghast at a Polaroid of Robin with his hands tied behind his back and green fish-scale pants riding up his bare thighs. 'Young master Dick!' exclaims Alfred. 'Yes, Alfred,' Bruce grimaces, 'as I feared! He's a captive ... or WORSE!' Clearly, the new era of darker stories had not entirely ruled out either camp melodrama or the potential for homoerotic tension; Dick was now grown up and studying at Hudson University, but that didn't prevent scenes, all in the same action-packed episode, of Batman dramatically wrestling a leopard and rescuing his partner from captivity (or WORSE). 'Batman! Good to see YOU, friend!' 'Same here, ROBIN!'

However, Medhurst is of course correct that the 1970s Robin and Batman no longer share a domestic space, and also that this, with obvious exceptions like the story above, tends to work against gay interpretations: fewer readers, to borrow Wertham's phrase, are likely to enjoy a homoerotic 'wish dream' of one man living on his own, while another lives miles away in student accommodation. In the subsequent decades, *Year One* and *The Long Halloween* avoided any mention of Robin simply by setting their stories before his arrival in Batman's life, a precedent followed by the monthly title *Legends of the Dark Knight*, which kept its chronology firmly in 'year one' for 99 issues. *The Dark Knight Returns* arguably neutralised the potential for gay meanings by introducing a female Robin, Carrie Kelley. *Arkham Asylum* referred to Robin only briefly in passing, *The Killing Joke* acted almost as if he'd never existed,[112] and the 1988–1989 story *A Death in the Family* had Jason Todd, Dick Grayson's successor as Boy Wonder, killed by the Joker as the result of a reader phone-in. As ever, it was impossible to keep the bright, chirpy little kid out of the darkness for long – Dick Grayson made a special guest appearance in *Legends of the Dark Knight* #100 (November 1997) and entered the Loeb/Sale narrative in the sequel to *Long Halloween*, *Dark Victory* (1999–2000), while in mainstream continuity Jason Todd was quickly replaced by a new Robin, Tim Drake. However, it can safely be argued that the selective tradition of key texts which *Batman Begins* constructs as its source material marginalised Robin to the point of disappearance.

As Medhurst observes, the strategies that seek to 'protect' Batman from accusations of homosexuality – from the editorial decisions to get rid of another Robin and bring in another Batgirl to the online fan declarations ('NO HE'S NOT GAY! Everytime you see him, he has a new trophy on his arm!!! He's a cool geezer'[113]) are informed by a culture 'where homosexuality is deemed categorically inferior to heterosexuality'.[114] We can see in this process the concept of hegemony, which Raymond Williams describes – drawing on the work of Antonio Gramsci – as 'the relations of domination and subordination.' While hegemony works to make ideas that serve the status quo seem like naturalised, common sense – 'HE'S NOT GAY! He's a cool geezer' is a particularly crude example – Williams points out that, except in extreme circumstances, hegemony is not a rigid, uniform system or a directly imposed set of rules. Rather, it saturates our everyday lives, not only in political and economic activity, but also in culture; not only at the abstract level of ideology, but also in the way we live, in our 'practices and expectations', our 'perceptions of ourselves and our world'.

> It thus constitutes a sense of reality for most people in the society, a sense of absolute because experienced reality beyond which it is very difficult for most members of the society to move, in most areas of their lives. It is, that is to say, in the strongest sense a 'culture', but a culture which also has to be seen as the lived dominance and subordination of particular classes.[115]

However, because it exists through practice, in everyday life, 'a lived hegemony is always a process'.

> It is a realized complex of experiences, relationships, and activities, with specific and changing pressures and limits. In practice, that is, hegemony can never be singular. ... Moreover (and this is crucial, reminding us of the necessary thrust of the concept), it does not just passively exist as a form of dominance. It has continually to be renewed, recreated, defended, and modified. It is also continually resisted, limited, altered, challenged by pressures not at all its own. We have then to add to the concept of hegemony the concepts of counter-hegemony and alternative hegemony, which are real and persistent elements of practice. [...]

> The reality of any hegemony, in the extended political and cultural sense, is that, while definition it is always dominant, it is never either total or exclusive. At any time, forms of alternative or directly oppositional politics and culture exist as significant elements in the society.[116]

Sinfield agrees: 'Despite their power, dominant ideological formations are always, in practice, under pressure, striving to substantiate their claim to superior plausibility in the face of diverse disturbances. ... ideology has always to be *produced*.'[117] It is this process, this constant 'inter-involvement of resistance and control',[118] that shadows every assertion of Batman's 'essence' ('This ... is Batman as he was meant to be') with the ghost of what he could also be and has been, that haunts the grittiest moments of *Batman Begins* with the memory of Adam West climbing the side of a wall. Every dark, serious Batman, so to speak, has the mischievous Bat-Mite at his shoulder; every black-armoured Dark Knight has a rainbow costume in his closet.

We have seen that each bold claim for the 'truthful', 'essential', 'original' Batman has to engage with a sense of the inauthentic and aberrant, and so, deliberately or unwittingly, brings it back to light. However fiercely a producer, author or fan scribbles darkness on the slate in an attempt to start a new page for Batman, the Day-Glo colours of the past always peek through. It happened in the 1950s, when the censorship of gay readings only circulated them more widely. It happened after Burton's gothic Batman, when Schumacher took the franchise back to the camp aesthetic of the TV show; it happened in the 1980s and 1990s comics, when Robin reentered the 'year one' continuity, and restored the solitary Batman to a Dynamic Duo. We will see in the next chapter that it also happened when the Crisis tried to wipe out the carnival from Batman's universe, and the worlds in limbo refused to disappear; it took years, but they came back.

'It can be persuasively argued,' Williams goes on, 'that all or nearly all initiatives and contributions, even when they take on manifestly alternative or oppositional forms, are in practice tied to the hegemonic: that the dominant culture, so to say, at once produces and limits its own forms of counterculture.'[119] We saw this process, also, in the way that promotional discourses stressing the realism, rationality, gravity and masculinity of Nolan's reboot inevitably brought Schumacher's films to mind, prompting discussion of the very objects they were trying to wipe from the public memory. As Sinfield put it, 'Even a text that aspires to contain a subordinate perspective must first bring it into visibility; even to misrepresent, one must present.'[120] But the counterculture – the camp, in this case – can also be seen in another form, within those Batman texts that strive the hardest to stamp it out. 'If the word "camp" is applied at all to the eighties' Batman,' says Medhurst, 'it is a label for the Joker.'

> This sly displacement is the cleverest method yet devised for preserving Bat-heterosexuality. The play that the texts regularly make with the concept of Batman and the Joker as mirror images now takes a new twist. The Joker is Batman's 'bad twin', and part of that badness is, increasingly, an implied homosexuality. This is certainly present in the 1989 film, a generally glum and portentous affair except for Jack Nicholson's Joker, a characterization enacted with venomous camp.[121]

Medhurst finds a further example in *Arkham Asylum*, 'the darkest image of the Bat-world yet.'

> Here the Joker has become a parody of a screaming queen, calling Batman 'honey pie', given to exclamations like 'oooh!'... and pinching Batman's behind with the advice 'loosen up, tight ass.' [...] The Bat-response is unequivocal: 'Take your filthy hands off me ... Filthy degenerate!'[122]

Medhurst notes that the 'degenerate' gay Joker, in an age of AIDS awareness, has an unpleasant connection with the 'dominant cultural construction of gay men at the end of the 1980s ... as plague carriers'.[123] The Batman who dominates *Arkham Asylum* – dark, uptight, repressed, troubled, heterosexual to the point of homophobia – may create his own counter-hegemonic force in the Joker; and the Joker as resistant, dissident figure may well in turn, carry a charismatic, creative energy as an avatar of camp – Nicholson's performance was seen by many, including Medhurst, as the highlight of Burton's film – but he nevertheless remains on the margins, marked as a deviant. He scrawls his playful speeches in red ink across the rigid frames of *Arkham Asylum* and sprays graffiti across the art gallery of Burton's movie, but inevitably faces containment and defeat at the end of the narrative. While these glimpses of camp suggest the possibility of alternative readings that could privilege the counter-hegemonic figure of the Joker in the 'dark', aggressively heterosexual Batman texts, we must remember that the stories are loaded against him. Granted, these narratives could be read against the grain, as celebrations of Joker as queer hero, but this is not their intended meaning, and their structures are weighted against such an interpretation: we would, for instance, have to ignore the Joker's death or incarceration, his inevitable, ultimate punishment for deviance and the triumph of the Dark Knight, as he walks free from Arkham and leaves the 'filthy degenerate' inside. No text is closed against alternative readings; but some readings can present more of a struggle than others.

It would be an oversimplification to claim that the 'dark', grim and violent phase launched by O'Neil and Adams in the early 1970s, and accelerated by Miller in the mid-1980s, ruled out and repressed all possibilities of either camp or homoeroticism in Batman himself. The example of Robin's kidnap above shows that it would be entirely possible to draw gay readings from one of O'Neil's classic 1970s stories, and Geoff Klock has perceptively argued that *The Dark Knight Returns* reveals 'a complex dynamic' between Batman and his antagonists which does not simply, as Medhurst suggests, displace deviant sexuality onto the Joker.[124] For instance, Batman narrates, as he and Two-Face crash through a window together, 'we tumble like lovers':

> And the Joker's intriguing combination of feminine and masculine signifiers – the delicate application of makeup, a 'tough-guy' build, speech affectations, aggressive physical violence – must be seen in light of the fact that the issue devoted to him opens with Batman dressed as a woman.[125]

However, once more, this is not the dominant reading of Miller's work, or more broadly, of the selective tradition on which *Batman Begins* draws. We have seen from the celebrity introductions quoted above that the graphic novels and trade paperbacks of the 1980s stress the 'darkness' of this era as a return to the character's pure, original, authentic essence, and the 2008 anthology of critical essays, *Batman Unauthorised*, helps to confirm this interpretation. Robert Brian Taylor's 'Keeping It Real in Gotham' starts the book with the firm statement that 'of all the mega-popular superheroes, it is Batman and his universe that are the most grittily realistic.'

> The world Batman inhabits isn't the same fanciful, brightly coloured comic book macrocosm of Superman and Spider-Man, at least it shouldn't be, despite several attempts to turn it into one. I'm looking at you, Adam West and Joel Schumacher. Batman thrives in a pulp-noir universe, where his acts of heroism are more mundane and yet more titillating – the brutal disarming of a knife-wielding thug, with the snap of broken bone, deep in the shadows of some Gotham back alley. The characters who occupy Batman's universe can get hurt, even paralyzed – just ask Barbara Gordon. Sometimes they die.[126]

A more absolute and confident confirmation of Batman's 'essential' darkness could hardly be imagined; and as the opening salvo in a volume which, however 'unauthorised', is guest-edited by Dennis O'Neil, it carries cultural authority. More importantly, it joins the dominant perspective epitomised by almost all the commentators in this chapter: Taylor's is not a lone voice advocating the gritty, 'realist' Batman, but part of a powerful chorus.

Taylor is uncompromising in his ruling about what Batman and his milieu 'are', or at least should be like. The 60s TV show and the Schumacher films are scolded as attempts to degrade and falsify the character's essence. Violence is described with a grim enjoyment and a hardboiled delivery: 'just ask Barbara Gordon', Taylor tells us grimly, referring to her shooting in *The Killing Joke*. As we saw in the production notes, with their conflation of character, cast and crew, in Martyn Palmer's newspaper piece ('Nolan told him to bulk up fast'), and the Empire review ('Nolan isn't messing about'), in their enthusiasm to embrace the Dark Knight, male fans often seem to adopt a tough-guy manner, as if wrapping themselves in the mantle of their chosen Batman.

The films, Taylor goes on, 'are extremely condensed peeks into Batman's world that should be built on the most basic and powerful of the Dark Knight's major thematic elements.'

> The tone of the comic has wavered over the years – there was a sci-fi infusion in the late '50s, and the campiness of '60s live-action television series carried over into comics for a while as well – but the character has always worked best when writers return him to his pulp roots: Batman's a regular guy with a scarred psyche who uses his skills as a fighter and as a detective to protect the people of Gotham ...[127]

Taylor frowns at Burton's films for remaking 'Batman's world as more of a fantasy construct'; elements such as 'deadly circus performers ... further removed Bruce Wayne from a more tangible reality. Then Joel Schumacher took over the franchise ... and things got worse.' Taylor declines to even discuss *Batman Forever* in detail, except for a scathing examination of its storyline that 'further drives the series into an illogical fantasy world ... a blast of '50s sci-fi hokum.' Nolan, on the other hand, offers a 'return to the more starkly grounded Gotham popularized in comics such as *Batman: Year One*, Frank Miller's down and dirty prequel.' Nolan is praised for scaling down the 'more fanciful comic book background' of Ra's al Ghul, rationalising the character's immortality and integrating him 'into his no-supernatural-crap version of the Batman universe that is far superior to Burton's and Schumacher's takes on the character'.

> And it's not just Ra's that Nolan gets right. From the Batmobile – extrapolated from real-world tank design – to the other villains in the film – brutish mobster Carmine Falcone and sociopathic psychologist Jonathan Crane, a.k.a the Scarecrow – Nolan properly reins in the outlandish elements to a point where Batman's

universe is only one or two steps removed from our own. ... boy, it makes for great drama when things are that simple. It's a lesson that all caretakers of the Batman mythos would do well to follow ... Frank Miller knows this.'[128]

To Taylor, Miller and *The Dark Knight Returns* capture the fundamental truth of Batman, taking him back to his roots. The opposing terms in this binary structure – the deviations and wrong turns, the waverings from the truth path – were already clear from Taylor's first tirade ('I'm looking at you, Adam West and Joel Schumacher') but he repeats them for good measure. In the dark corner is the 'realistic' Batman, represented by Frank Miller and Christopher Nolan: a world of authentic tanks, brutish gangsters, snapping bone, psychological torment and regular guys. It's a simple world, but – oh boy – it makes for great drama. In the rainbow corner is the Batman of Adam West and Joel Schumacher, trailing a world of fanciful bright colours, sci-fi hokum, circus stunts, illogical plots and supernatural crap.

We can note that in order to condemn it, Taylor has first to describe this alternative tradition in some detail; to demonstrate the 'reality' of his own preferred Batman, he has to outline the 'fantasy' version he despises. As Williams argued, the enforcing of dominant values is a push-and-pull dynamic rather than a simple imposition – hegemony 'has continually to be renewed, recreated, defended, and modified' – and though Taylor picks an easy battle, arguing in favour of the Batman epitomised by popular graphic novels and the most recent blockbuster films, he still sweats and struggles as he wrestles the Rainbow Batman to the floor.

But things change; moods shift, and trends turn. Taylor is clearly ramming his point home because he feels his brutal Batman needs protecting. 'It's too bad the folks at DC don't always listen to Frank. In the last few years, the people in charge have made a couple of truly boneheaded decisions ... enough to drive a serious-minded Batman enthusiast crazy.'[129] Recent developments in mainstream continuity – 'incredibly dopey' characters and 'larger-than-life' villains – prompt Taylor to warn his reader (assumed to be another 'serious-minded

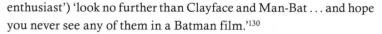

enthusiast') 'look no further than Clayface and Man-Bat . . . and hope you never see any of them in a Batman film.'[130]

Taylor clearly realises, on some level, that hegemony is a process, and that the dominant has to be defended: why else would he show such fury as his chapter builds to a climax, with increasingly aggressive outbursts against 'mind-blowingly ridiculous fantasy/sci-fi drivel' and 'fantasy hogwash' and 'supernatural bullshit'? 'Paradise dimension?' he sneers of a recent, multiple-world plot twist. 'God, I hate this stuff . . . Sleazy? Sure. Also monumentally stupid.'[131]

The selective tradition, Williams notes, 'a version of the past which is intended to connect with and ratify the present. What it offers in practice is a sense of *predisposed continuity*.' The term, particularly suited to comic-book heroes, aptly summarises the argument put forward by critics like Taylor, that Nolan's Batman goes back (through Miller) to Kane's original, and therefore to the character's essence, or roots. It is a powerful tradition, but it is also vulnerable.

> Powerful because it is so skilled in making active selective connections, dismissing those it does not want as 'out of date' or 'nostalgic', attacking those it cannot incorporate as 'unprecedented' or 'alien'. Vulnerable because the real record is effectively recoverable, any many of the alternative or opposing practical continuities are still available.[132]

As Sinfield observes, dominance and dissidence are not absolute, and no meanings can be rigidly contained; although he agrees that, at each specific historical moment, one side can push harder than another for its chosen interpretation.

> There can be no security in textuality: no scriptor can control the reading of his or her text. And when, in any instance, either incorporation or resistance turns out to be the more successful, that is not in the nature of things. It is because of *their relative strengths in that situation*.[133]

In the discourses around Nolan's Batman – from the key texts in the selective tradition that informed it, to the production notes stressing the masculine qualities of cast, character and crew – the side that pushed for a 'dark', grim, gritty Batman was by far the strongest. But dominance and dissidence are not absolute. The weight can shift, and the dynamic can change. The selective tradition is strong, but temporary; the Crisis may reorder the worlds for 20 years, but alternative stories are still available, waiting in limbo.

In 2006, when Grant Morrison began writing the monthly *Batman* comic and therefore took effective control of mainstream Batman continuity, things did change; and because Nolan's second Batman film, *The Dark Knight*, entered an intertextual network of Batman texts, where it intersected with, shaped, was shaped by and read through a matrix of other stories, *The Dark Knight* became part of this shifting territory, and should be seen in this context. The final two chapters look in detail at this recent transformation to mainstream Batman continuity, and then at the perspective it presents, in turn, on *The Dark Knight*.

CARNIVAL ON INFINITE EARTHS: CONTINUITY AND CRISIS

4

Carnival of sorts

We saw in the last chapter that the Joker of the 1980s and 1990s can be identified as the exiled, abject figure of camp and homosexuality in the Batman mythos after its once-diverse, carefree complexity was progressively closed down and, in Medhurst's term, 'hetero-sexualised' through various containment strategies: the removal of Robin as a potential partner and the introduction of various, short-lived female love interests, the return to a 'darker', grittier portrayal with O'Neil and Adams' 1970s stories, the culling proc-ess of the Crisis, and the dominance, from the mid-1980s onwards, of the Frank Miller-style representation, which shaped mainstream audiences' understanding and expectations of Batman through both the graphic novel boom and through its influence on Burton and Nolan's films. As Medhurst persuasively argues, Joker is often loaded with stereotypical signs of deviance and homosexuality – over-the-top exaggeration, outrageous flirtation, theatrical make-up, arch performance, screeching and posturing – while Batman remains the upright, solid, unmoved and humourless straight man to the villainous pantomime queen, his own heterosexuality enforced by the contrast ('filthy degenerate!').

We can expand productively on this understanding of Joker through Mikhail Bakhtin's theories of carnival. These theories intersect with the concepts of intertextuality and the model of Batman texts as a matrix, which I outlined in Chapter Two, and will lead us towards a new, richer and more complex interpretation of Batman himself.

In earlier stages of human society, as Bakhtin explains in *Rabelais and his World*, serious ceremonies and rituals coexisted with parodic, comic versions. Primitive folklore paired its earnest religious organisations with 'comic cults which laughed and scoffed at the deity ... coupled with serious myths were comic and abusive ones; coupled with heroes were their parodies and doublets.'[1] In early Rome, 'the ceremonial of the triumphal procession included on almost equal terms the glorifying and the deriding of the victor. The funeral ritual was also composed of lamenting (glorifying) and deriding the deceased.' Yet as societal structures shifted, 'such an equality of the two aspects became impossible', and the serious and the comic formed into a new hierarchy. 'All the comic forms were transferred, some earlier and others later, to a nonofficial level. There they acquired a new meaning, were deepened and rendered more complex, until they became the expression of folk consciousness, of folk culture.'[2]

'Carnival festivals,' Bakhtin tells us, 'and the comic spectacles and ritual connected with them, had an important place in the life of medieval man.'

> Besides carnivals proper, with their long and complex pageants and processions, there was the 'feast of fools'... nearly every Church feast had its comic folk aspect, which was also traditionally recognised. [...] Civil and social ceremonies and rituals took on a comic aspect as clowns and fools, constant participants in these festivals, mimicked serious rituals such as the tribute rendered to the victors at tournaments, the transfer of feudal rights, or the initiation of a knight. Minor occasions were also marked by comic protocol, as for instance the election of a king or queen to preside at a banquet 'for laughter's sake' (*roi pour rire*).[3]

This folk activity – a genuinely popular culture of the marketplace and the streets, fuelled by laughter and belonging to the ordinary people – was unexamined by studies of 'the popular' and omitted from the epics and myths of literature. Yet – perhaps precisely because it was left alone – it was central to the structures of everyday life during the Renaissance and the Middle Ages, shadowing and mocking each formal event.

> A boundless world of humorous forms and manifestations opposed the official and serious tone of medieval ecclesiastical and feudal culture. In spite of their variety, folk festivals of the carnival type, the comic rites and cults, the clowns and fools, giants, dwarfs and jugglers, the vast and manifold literature of parody – all these forms have one style in common: they belong to one culture of folk carnival humour.[4]

The rituals based on laughter

> were sharply distinct from the serious official, ecclesiastical, feudal, and political cult forms and ceremonials. They offered a completely different, nonofficial, extraecclesiastical and extra-political aspect of the world, of man, and of human relations; they built a second world and a second life outside officialdom, a world in which all medieval people participated more or less, in which they lived during a given time of the year.[5]

Bakhtin describes this dynamic between official ritual and its carnival inversion, the formal calendar and its parodic opposite, as a 'two-world condition'.[6]

The parallel to Batman's narrative universe and cast of characters is already suggestive. In his personal sense of order and duty, his broad alignment with the law and his steady alliance with the police department, his civilian role as a figurehead of bourgeois society and captain of capitalist industry, his obsessive planning and organisation both in public and private, even his tendency towards solemn ritual – from the original vow to avenge his parents to the candlelit induction of Robin, from his annual visits to the site of his parents' death to his regular graveside vigils – the modern, 'dark' incarnation of Batman/Bruce Wayne can clearly and firmly be located on the site of official structures and routines.[7]

'Parodying doubles have become a rather common phenomenon in carnivalized literature', Bakhtin observes. In Dostoevsky, 'almost every one of the leading heroes of his novels has several doubles who parody him in various ways.'[8] Batman's regular opponents, similarly, invert and caricature aspects of his persona in diverse and inventive ways, reflecting them in distorting mirrors and showing them as grotesque or ridiculous. The waddling, squawking Oswald 'Penguin' Cobblepot, in tuxedo and top hat, satirises Wayne's role as an old-money society gentleman; the former District Attorney, Harvey 'Two-Face' Dent – handsome lawyer or scarred gangster, depending on the angle – makes visible the ugly tensions between Wayne's double lives as philanthropist and vigilante. Riddler subverts Batman's detective skills by wasting his time with elaborate, essentially pointless puzzles; Scarecrow uses Batman's own methods – fear as a weapon – but reveals them as monstrous.[9]

The second tier of villains, filling out the bill, is a sideshow of novelty attractions rather than complex inversions of the protagonist. The dumb giant Solomon Grundy and sewer creature Killer Croc are freak show monsters; Harley Quinn, Joker's moll, is the acrobatic jester her name suggests. The roster of Batman villains is essentially a circus, and of course, Joker is the ringmaster, the 'Clown Prince of Crime', the master of ceremonies whose declaration at the start of *Arkham Asylum* – 'let the Feast of Fools begin!' – serves as a parodic fanfare to Batman's entrance, a mocking initiation of a Dark Knight. That Joker has no secret identity is significant: Bakhtin points out that the fools of medieval culture 'were not actors playing their parts on a stage, as did the comic actors of a later period, impersonating Harlequin. ... but remained fools and clowns always and wherever they made their appearance.'[10] It is worth noting that while Harley Quinn does have a civilian past, her given name was Harleen Quinzel; she was, in a sense, always the clown, even before she knew it.[11]

Each of the main villains is Batman's circus counterpart, imitating and exposing the absurdity in his solemn obsessions. Batman's self-made symbolism – his construction of identity around a totemic creature – looks less resonant when we see how similar it is to a little man who models himself on a penguin. His tormented duality and the struggle between man and mask looks less like tragic heroism when taken to ridiculous extremes by Two-Face, who sews two suits together in an over-literal representation of split personality. Even his on-off lover Catwoman gently mocks Batman's ritualised focus through her own playful appropriation of feline mannerisms, and inability to resist any crime with a cat in the name. And Wayne's painstaking, pedantic branding – Batmobile, Batplane, Batboat, Batarang – looks less like corporate power and more like the games of a spoilt, lonely rich boy when his clownish adversary wheels out bright green Joker-copters and fashions his own silly utility belt.[12] In a further, perfect parallel with Bakhtin's concept of a 'two-world condition', the multiple-dimension model of the DC Universe included a reverse, dark-mirror equivalent on Earth-3, where an evil Owlman, member of the Crime Syndicate of America, enjoyed a successful criminal career.

As counterpoints and contrast, the villains are locked into a ritualised dance with Batman; on one level, he justifies their existence, and they justify his, just as each medieval carnival was linked to a sacred feast. Without Batman, the villains would have no challenge, no real *raison d'être*, and the reverse is also true; the two sides, particularly the love-hate pairing of Batman and Joker, define and, in a sense, create each other. We saw a hint of this dynamic in *Arkham Asylum*, where Joker's provocative 'deviance' was used to demonstrate the Dark Knight's rigid heterosexuality: they are a gothic variation on Sinfield's model of opposites. 'As with the duck/rabbit drawing, when you see the duck, the rabbit lurks around the edges, constituting an alternative that may spring into visibility. Any position supposes its intrinsic *op*-position.' The ambivalent and complex relationship between Batman and Joker is a focus of my discussion later in this chapter and the next, but it is worth noting here that the idea of their mutually dependent existence was flagged up long before the 'dark', modern period. Joker refuses to kill Batman in a 1973 story ('No! Without the *game* that *the Batman* and I have played for so many years, winning is *nothing*'[13]), and even their first encounter in 1940 sees Batman declaring 'You may be the *Joker* but I'm the

King of Clubs', identifying them both as playing cards from the same deck.[14]

When the villain is temporarily triumphant, law is overturned and rules are suspended; carnival comes to Gotham. Joker's underlying mission, in common with carnival, is to make the city into a circus.[15] Not content with embodying clownishness in his own person, his crimes are based around spreading laughter, infecting the world with his own spirit.[16] Just as Batman's vow is to enforce order and structure, to impose rules not just on himself but on society, so Joker's project is to overturn them, to make his own comic essence universal. To borrow again from Bakhtin, his laughter is 'not an individual reaction to some isolated "comic" event. Carnival laughter is the laughter of all the people ... it is universal in scope; it is directed at all and everyone, including the carnival's participants. The entire world is seen in its droll aspect, in its gay relativity.'[17]

> The main arena for carnival acts was the square and the streets adjoining it ... the central arena could only be the square, for by its very idea carnival *belongs to the whole people,* it is *universal, everyone* must participate in its familiar contact.[18]

The square, Bakhtin writes, becomes in carnivalized literature 'a setting for the action of the plot.'[19] In the brighter, lighter Batman stories, all of Gotham is this public square, serving as a playground for the costumed characters and clowns: the giant typewriters, golf clubs and coffee cups that decorate the city's architecture add to the sense of urban circus.[20]

Carnival, however, is always a 'temporary suspension'; a 'temporary liberation from the prevailing truth and from the established order'.[21] Carnival's parodic culture is, in Bakhtin's phrase, a 'world inside out'[22]; but the world cannot remain inside out, or it becomes something quite different; a society without norms to resist or rules to subvert, where villains, by default, enforce rather than disrupt the status quo. This is the mirror-world of Earth-3, where the Joker-analogue falls into the uneasy role of hero; but in such a permanently inverted universe, Batman cannot exist either, and is reworked into Owlman, a quite different character. The dynamic between Batman and his villains, the serious knight and the troupe of fools, depends on the regular restoration of order and its equally-regular subversion. '... The official feast asserted all that was stable, unchanging, perennial: the existing hierarchy, the existing religious, political, and moral values, norms and prohibitions.' However, at the same time, the 'festive character was indestructible: it had to be tolerated'.[23]

Yet this easy-going, predictable dance, where each player knows his place and takes it gladly, is already reminiscent of an earlier era of comic books. We can apply Bakhtin's model readily to the routines of classic Batman stories – a villain does his or her totem-based thing, the hero responds with a Bat-themed smackdown; subversion enjoys its brief moment, but is put safely away in jail until next time – but this ritualised playtime belongs to the pre-Crisis period, to the TV show and, at a push, to the gaudy pantomime of Schumacher's films, not to the dark, 'down-and-dirty' tradition of *Year One* and its successors, or the back-to-basics, gritty realism of *Batman Begins*. Even Bakhtin's description of folk carnival as a 'gay parody' – though he intends it simply to mean brightly merry – inevitably recalls the camp adventures of the 1950s and 1960s, and the playful spirit that the 'dark', 'realist' tradition of the 1970s and 1980s attempted to close down. In 1986, the parallel world of Earth-3 – and all the other alternate worlds, with their alternate Batmen – were destroyed or combined into a single continuity, and their inhabitants wiped from official memory.

A comparable process of closure and containment was imposed on carnival. 'During the domination of the classical canon in all the areas of art and literature of the seventeenth and early eighteenth centuries,' writes Bakhtin, 'the grotesque related to the culture of folk humor was excluded from great literature ...'

> During this period (actually starting in the seventeenth century) we observe a process of gradual narrowing down of the ritual, spectacle and carnival forms of folk culture, which became small and trivial. On the one hand the state encroached upon festive life and turned it into a parade: on the other hand these festivities were brought into the home and became part of the family's private life. The privileges which were formerly allowed

the marketplace were more and more restricted. The carnival spirit with its freedom, its utopian character oriented toward the future, was gradually transformed into a mere holiday mood. The feast ceased almost entirely to be the people's second life, their temporary renascence and renewal.[24]

Yet – as we learned from the previous chapter – subversive, dissident energies are difficult, if not impossible, to destroy completely. As Bakhtin says of the people's feast: 'We have stressed the word almost because the popular festive carnival principle is indestructible. Though narrowed and weakened, it still continues ... having lost its living tie with folk culture ... the grotesque underwent certain changes.'[25]

Those energies are difficult to destroy, but they can be pushed into a corner. The carnival-grotesque was preserved in traditions such as the *commedia dell'arte*, but even following this formalisation the figure of Harlequin was excluded from 'the serious and respectable stage' in the late eighteenth century.[26] 'Unlike the medieval and Renaissance grotesque, which was directly related to folk culture and thus belonged to all the people', this new, reduced figure, an exiled fool stripped of his celebration, was a 'private, "chamber" character. It became, as it were, an individual carnival, marked by a vivid sense of isolation.' Its laughter remained, 'but laughter was cut down to cold humour, irony, sarcasm. It ceased to be a joyful and triumphant hilarity. Its positive regenerating power was reduced to a minimum.'[27]

With the removal of this regenerating laughter, the clown became a sinister, uncanny figure. 'The world of Romantic grotesque is to a certain extent a terrifying world, alien to man. ... something frightening is revealed in that which was habitual and secure.'[28] The fool of folk carnival was a 'gay parody' – 'in the diableries of the medieval mysteries ... the devil is the gay ambivalent figure expressing the unofficial point of view ... there is nothing terrifying or alien in him.'[29] – while in Rabelais, 'the devils are excellent and jovial fellows ... the devils and hell itself appear as comic monsters.' By contrast, 'the Romanticists present the devil as terrifying, melancholy, and tragic, and infernal laughter as somber and sarcastic.'[30] 'The result', Bakhtin concludes, 'is a broken grotesque figure'.[31]

Again, the description lends itself immediately to the Joker of the 'dark' modern tradition: the horrific, pale figure of *Dark Knight Returns* who twists his own neck, 'with a devil's strength ... what's left of his spine goes ...' and dies with a manic laugh and a chilling crack of vertebrae. This is the Joker who brings his own ghastly private carnival to Jim Gordon's house in *The Killing Joke*, dressed in a Hawaiian holiday outfit: Barbara Gordon opens the door and stares at the palm tree pattern on his shirt, then at the pistol in his hand. 'She thinks she's a coffee table edition,' Joker muses as Barbara writhes on the floor, clutching a gunshot wound, '... there's a hole in the jacket and the spine seems to be damaged.' Nobody laughs: not even him. This is the Joker of *Arkham Asylum*, king of the madhouse, his face long and white as a bone, his 'gayness' – in every sense – turned into a threat, and his riddles tailing off aimlessly, pointless exercises in sadness and shock. 'Listen: how many brittle bone babies does it take to ...' 'Shut up,' Batman snarls, but the joke wasn't going anywhere.

Needless to say, the other villains are equally reduced. The Two-Face of *Arkham Asylum* is introduced as a naked, savage figure who can't make it to the bathroom on his own. Catwoman, in *Year One*, is a disillusioned dominatrix; the Penguin of *Long Halloween* is as grotesque as the Joker, all oversized monocle, bushy eyebrows and tiny, sharp fish-teeth. Again, the jokes are rarely funny, and struggle for the bleakest humour: Catwoman, in *Dark Victory,* asks Riddler 'what's green and brown and red all over?' Crouched on a toilet, the little man offers 'A ... frog in a blender?' 'No,' snarls Catwoman, leaning into the dank, dirty cubicle. 'A Riddler with his eyes scratched out.' This is a sorry carnival, a sordid circus.

It is particularly telling that the formal calendar dominates these grim, seedy stories, with a reduced, stilted sense of celebration, and the fun drained out of every festival. *Year One*, from its title onwards, closes down possibilities and imposes a new, definitive post-Crisis origin for the character: this is the new official history, and its events are even tied down to specific dates, each day documented twice-over by its two solid, reliable male narrators. Bakhtin argues that the 'brimming over-abundance' of folk carnival, 'the all-people's element', stands in direct contrast to the 'private, egotistic "economic man"... the drabness of everyday existence.'[32] The captions in *Year One*, offering a report on each day in Jim Gordon's careful penmanship and Wayne's more fluid cursive, are a perfect example of the controlling structures that contain carnival. We now know exactly what Batman was doing on January 4th, the first day of the story; and on February 12th, and 21st, and 26th, the next scenes. His first year is documented in precise detail, in gritty, downplayed 'realism' – the muted colour and deep shadow of Mazzucchelli's Gotham City – and literally in the black and white of Wayne's diary, backed up by Gordon's report on, appropriately, a yellow legal pad. There are gaps in the diary, of course, but there is very little room for any radical imagining: between January 4, when Wayne arrives in a blue-and-grey Gotham, and February 21, when he smashes bricks and karate-chops trees in the washed-out, snowbound grounds of his manor, it is unlikely that he dressed up in a rainbow costume.

We saw in the previous chapter that this newly imposed continuity and stricter chronology helped to define the Batman of the 1980s and 1990s. *Legends of the Dark Knight* was generally confined to 'Year One', meaning it followed the tone and rules Miller had established in *Year One* itself: an inexperienced, stripped-down Batman, no boy sidekick, and a low-key roster of villains, rather than the colourful city-as-circus (and extended universe as playground) that characterised the 1950s and 1960s. New origins like 'The Man Who Falls' built on *Year One*'s template, faithfully copying its key events – to the extent of copying individual panels – and filling in backstory in the same gritty, realistic vein, completing the gaps in Bruce Wayne's official biography with scenes of FBI training, Korean martial arts and shamanic trances. *The Long Halloween* and *Dark Victory* also follow on from Miller's early-career reboot, developing the gangster families from *Year One*, redefining the costumed villains as bleak grotesques and providing a new, more *noir* introduction for Robin; but, even more significantly, they subtly echo its calendar structure. Both *Long Halloween* and *Dark Victory* are based around United States holidays – Mother's Day, Valentine's, St Patrick's Day, the Fourth of July – their rhythm reinforced by the fact that each series ran just over a year, with new episodes appearing monthly. Again, a strict, structured chronology regulates the narrative. Batman's captions, again in journal format, frequently remind us of the date, even the time and location ('The morning of February the 15th. Selina Kyle's brownstone'), while the details and specifics of the narration leave little room for imaginative interpretation, or gaps for alternative versions of Wayne's early career. Most notably of all, the villain of *Long Halloween* is 'Holiday', revealed as a pathetic, bespectacled figure with a shrivelled arm, terrified by memories of his gangster father; even his chosen weapon, a .22 with a baby's bottle teat as silencer, is infantilised. At the end of *Dark Victory*, he is beaten by Julian Day, a little-known villain with the months of the year tattooed around his bald skull. 'The Calendar Man is being forgotten,' Day scowls at Holiday, pointing a gun at him. 'And that is unacceptable.' A more perfect example of the shrunken, enfeebled modern festival described by Bakhtin – joyless, pitiful, individualised and ruled by the calendar – could hardly be imagined.

Wayne, in these realist retellings, can be read as the solid, normative contrast to the terrifying and yet tragic clownishness of Joker and the other villains. Bakhtin writes that

> the grotesque images preserve their peculiar nature, entirely different from ready-made, completed being. They remain ambivalent and contradictory; they are ugly, monstrous, hideous from the point of view of 'classic' aesthetics, that is, the aesthetics of the ready-made and the completed.[33]

So Joker and his freaks, stunted remnants of folk culture – 'fragments of half-dead forms' – come into conflict with Wayne, 'the bourgeois conception of the completed atomized being ... the petty, inert 'material principle' of class society'.[34] Of course, even within the 'dark' modern stories, Wayne is a split personality himself; his complete, bourgeois persona is just a front. Yet Bakhtin contrasts this rigid duality with the more fluid sense of growth and renewal that characterised folk carnival.

> Even in the seventeenth century some forms of the grotesque began to degenerate into static 'character' presentation ... this

degeneration was linked with the specific limitations of the bourgeois world outlook. The last thing one can say of the real grotesque is that it is static; on the contrary it seeks to grasp in its imagery the very act of becoming and growth, the eternal incomplete unfinished nature of being. [...] The fact is that the new concept of realism has a different way of drawing the boundaries ... it cuts the double body in two.[35]

Despite his divided self, then, Wayne/Batman remains a static and contained figure – two neat halves, cleanly separated – compared to the protean force of carnival, the 'phenomenon in transformation, an as yet unfinished metamorphosis, of death and birth, growth and becoming.'[36] The modern Joker retains some traces of this energy: in his *Killing Joke* origin, for instance, he is born again as a hysterical living corpse, half-laughing, half-weeping as he crawls out of a transforming river of chemical sewage, baptised in the rain. 'Birth-death, death-birth', writes Bakhtin, 'such are the components of life itself ... death is included in life, and together with birth determines its eternal movement.'[37]

The dark, grim Batman, on the other hand, wears one of the 'masks offered by degenerate, petty realism':[38] itself a reduction of a carnival motif, a once-magical device emptied of its positive, celebratory charge and loaded with more sinister connotations.

In its Romantic form the mask is torn away from the oneness of the folk carnival concept. It is stripped of its original richness and acquires other meanings alien to its primitive nature; now the mask hides something, keeps a secret, deceives ... the Romantic mask loses almost entirely its regenerating and renewing element and acquires a somber hue. A terrible vacuum, a nothingness lurks behind it.[39]

We can draw a further valuable parallel between Bakhtin's theories of carnival and his concept of dialogism, discussed in Chapter Two. Bakhtin, we recall, saw meaning as defined by the relationships surrounding every utterance, formed in a dynamic between the speaker, the addressee and the context; meaning is therefore a process, shaped through conflict and conversation. He sees this 'dialogization' as fundamental to the novel, which 'permits a multiplicity of social voices and a wide variety of their links and interrelationships': various styles such as 'authorial speech, the speeches of narrators, inserted genres, the speech of characters' intermingle and react with each other as the novel shifts between forms and voices.[40] Bakhtin refers to this internal dialogue using a Russian word connoting 'different-speech-ness'; it is usually translated into English as *heteroglossia*. We might consider, as examples, Bram Stoker's *Dracula* (1897) with its letters, transcriptions and documents, or Irvine Welsh's *Trainspotting* (1993) a babel of dialects and idiolects: comics, arguably, are an even more diverse collection of competing signs and forms, as words in different fonts, sizes and colours carry sound effects, tone of voice and volume, in addition to multiple narration and dialogue.

Yet this many-voiced diversity, says Bakhtin, is threatened by traditional criticism that has no way of dealing with 'the distinctive social dialogue among languages that is present in the novel.'[41] Conventional analysis and approaches, he claims – 'philosophy of language, linguistics and stylistics' – assume and impose a reduced, simplified model of the individual, monologic utterance: one person with one voice. 'These forces', Bakhtin stresses, 'are *the forces that serve to unify and centralize the verbal-ideological world*. A unitary language

> ... makes its real presence felt as a force for overcoming this heteroglossia, imposing specific limits to it, guaranteeing a certain maximum of mutual understanding and crystallizing into a real, although still relative unity – the unity of ... literary language, 'correct language.' A common unitary language is a system of linguistic norms. ... forces that struggle to overcome the heteroglossia of language.[42]

Bakhtin identifies various schools of thought – 'the poetics of the medieval church, of "the one language of truth"... the idea of a "universal grammar"' – as expressions of a project to unify, centralise and control. 'The victory of one reigning language (dialect) over the others, the supplanting of languages, their enslavement, the process of illuminating them with the True Word'; the incorporation of exceptions and deviations into a 'unitary language of culture', and the academic treatment of plural, individually complete linguistic systems as a 'single proto-language'; all these approaches are examples of the 'centripetal' forces on the life of language, pulling it inward, shrinking it and trying to reduce it to a single, unified entity. Working against those energies are the 'centrifugal' forces of heteroglossia, throwing language outwards like a spinning firework. Every utterance, or text, is 'a point where centrifugal as well as centripetal forces are brought to bear'; every utterance is 'a contradiction-ridden, tension-filled unity of two embattled tendencies in the life of language.'[43]

Already, we can recognise a fascinating, intertextual dialogue of echoes, links and parallels between Bakhtin's argument and the ideas that circulated through the last chapters. The relationship between centrifugal and centripetal forces reminds us of the constant tension between repressive and resistant discourses, for instance, and the dynamic push-and-pull that characterises the struggle for interpretation, meaning and power in the accounts of Foucault, Sinfield, and indeed Medhurst; twinned energies locked in a never-ending battle of mutual opposition and dependence, each needing each other for definition. Traditional authorship theory, which prefers to treat each piece of work as the coherent, self-contained expression of a single individual, rather than an assemblage of styles and voices which in turn enters into in a larger cultural conversation and joins an intertextual network, can be seen as part of the reductive critical project that Bakhtin describes. 'Stylistics has been ... deaf to dialogue', he writes. 'A literary work has been conceived by stylistics as if it were a hermetic and self-sufficient whole, one whose elements constitute a closed system presuming nothing beyond themselves, no other utterances.'[44]

We saw in Chapter One that Barthes proposed the figure of the scriptor as a more accurate representation of authorship's mediating and editing process than the towering Author-God of conventional criticism: Nolan's role in selecting and stitching together elements from existing Batman texts into a new tapestry, I suggested, embodies this role, where the art and act of creation lies in assemblage, an awareness of intertextual contexts, and a contribution to a broader, cultural conversation, rather than a claim to pure invention. Bakhtin preempts that model with his description of the prose writer confronting 'a multitude of routes, roads and paths that have been laid down in the object by social consciousness ...'

> the prose writer witnesses as well the unfolding of social heteroglossia *surrounding* the object, the Tower-of-Babel mixing of language that goes on around any object; the dialectics of the object are interwoven with the social dialogue surrounding it. For the prose writer, the object is a focal point for the heteroglot voices among which his own voice must also sound; these voices create the background necessary for his own voice ... [45]

This scriptor-figure 'welcomes the heteroglossia and language diversity of the literary and extraliterary language into his own work ... it is in fact out of this stratification of language, its speech diversity and even language diversity, that he constructs his own style ... he can make use of language without wholly giving himself up to it.'[46] Bakhtin contrasts this to a more conservative model of authorship, whereby the writer 'strips the word of others' intentions', cutting their links with other utterances and losing 'their connection with specific contexts', attempting to claim the word as a uniquely individual utterance. *'Everything that enters the work must immerse itself in Lethe, and forget its previous life in any other contexts.'*[47] The parallel with DC Comics' editorial revisions of the mid-1980s, which imposed a similar sense of amnesia on all the events and characters who were excluded from the single-world, single-continuity post-Crisis narratives, is irresistible.

Yet the most suggestive connection comes in Bakhtin's description of heteroglossia as born from low-level, street and market culture, in relation to poetry's lofty, narrowing project of 'cultural, national and political centralization of the verbal-ideological world':

> ... on the stages of local fairs and at buffoon spectacles, the heteroglossia of the clown sounded forth, ridiculing all 'languages' and dialects; there developed the literature of the *fabliaux* and *Schwänke* of street songs, folksayings, anecdotes, where there was

no language-center at all, where there was to be found a lively play with the 'languages' of poets, scholars, monks, knights, and others, where all 'languages' were masks and where no language could claim to be an authentic, incontestable face.[48]

Heteroglossia was 'consciously opposed to this literary language. It was parodic, and aimed sharply and polemically against the official languages of its given time. It was heteroglossia that had been dialogised.'

We can take the extra step and add: it was heteroglossia that had been carnivalised. Like carnival, heteroglossia existed in tension with the official, formal structures that sought to control and contain it. As such, we can read the various strategies that attempt to narrow and secure Batman's meanings, reducing him to one world, one note, one continuity, one level of 'truth' and accuracy – an official ruling that Batman is a dark, gritty, tortured vigilante, and that any other interpretations are aberrant or plain incorrect – in the same vein as both the formal structures that incorporated and contained carnival, and the academic approaches Bakhtin describes that attempt to fit the diversity of many voices into a reductive interpretive system, and strip the dialogue of prose writing into a single-authored unity. From various angles, in various forms, we are witnessing the same fundamental process: the compression of many into one, the narrowing of potential into singularities, the repression and suppression of alternates into a simple, unified whole. The underlying motif of the Crisis on Infinite Earths – a complex network of intertextual possibilities shrinking to a reduced, linear explanation – chimes throughout this discussion. *E pluribus unum.*[49]

By locking down the intertextual matrix of Batman narratives that shapes and surrounds Nolan's reboot to a simple, straightforward dyad of 'fidelity' between source and adaptation, and shrinking the potential pool of Batman stories that could have informed the film to a handful of distinctly authored narratives from a specific and strictly ordered tradition, the discourses around *Batman Begins* perform the same process of narrowing down a diverse network of texts to a straight line of influence, reducing many worlds to one, and closing the carnival, replacing it – as we saw in *Year One* and its successors – with the formal calendar of official continuity and canon.

Yet as we have also seen, forces of repression are never fully successful; they invariably exist in tension, defined by and to an extent depending on an opposing energy. ('Any position supposes its intrinsic *op*-position. All stories comprise within themselves the ghosts of the alternative stories they are trying to exclude.') Bakhtin points out that any text and discourse 'cannot fail to be oriented toward the "already uttered", the "already known":

> ... the dialogic orientation of discourse is a phenomenon that is, of course, a property of *any* discourse. It is the natural orientation of any discourse. On all its various routes toward the object, in all its directions, the word encounters an alien word and cannot help encountering it in a living, tension-filled interaction.[50]

Despite the focus of traditional criticism on the singular voice of each utterance – as the unique expression of an individual author, rather than a contribution to a matrix of cultural dialogue – Bakhtin sees dialogic interplay as a fundamental element of every text. Even the most stripped-down, contained, individual utterance only achieves a 'tension-filled unity of language',[51] haunted by the repressed voices of the others from which it inevitably borrows and with which it inevitably interacts. Each utterance exists in a relationship with the other texts that define it through their difference: just as the gritty, realist Batman required the contrast of the camp Batman to delineate its own dark edges, and as the repressive, straight Batman of the graphic novels needed the deviant Joker as contrast to his own rigid heterosexuality, a text cannot rid itself of all influence and surrounding context. Every text, says Bakhtin – even in the most repressive interpretive system – always coexists with what it is not. Even when the dialogue between multiple earths is denied and the universe reduced to a singularity – one world, one official continuity – each story carries the shadow of its opposite, the ghost of its alternate, the possibility of what it could have been, the potential other that it represses or reacts against. 'The word is shaped in dialogic inter-action with an alien word that is already in the object,'[52] Bakhtin writes. Through speech and through practice, language creates 'a multitude of concrete worlds.'[53]

As noted, those ghosts of other worlds and possibilities can never be fully contained, and never go away. And as promised, they come back. The next section explores the changes to continuity that opened up Batman's narrative universe in the second half of the 2000s, under the authorship – more appropriately, the scriptor-ship – of Grant Morrison. Morrison's run on the flagship *Batman* title and its spin-offs, from 2006 until 2011, drew on the entire history of the character, reopening the closed archive of the 1950s and 1960s, and reanimating characters and stories that had been ruled out of conti-nuity by the Crisis.

Tellingly, Morrison showed his hand and hinted at his inten-tions years before he took over the monthly *Batman*, not least in his graphic novel *JLA: Earth 2*, published in 2000. For the first time since the Crisis, *Earth 2* brought back the parallel, opposite universe, and Batman's alternate, Owlman. Diversity and multiplicity were creep-ing back into the Dark Knight's controlled story-space.[54]

Continuity

I have emphasised above that Batman is inherently multiple, and suggested that the character is an amalgam of all his different forms, stories and histories. I have also discussed the official continuity that periodically attempts to close down, repress, reboot and wipe from memory individual iterations of Batman that no longer suit the inter-ests of the character's producers, or (and the two are closely related) are no longer popular with audiences. Furthermore, I have suggested that Batman texts exist within a matrix, and interact in a complex network across media platforms.

These three statements may seem contradictory. However, they propose three distinct, coexisting models of continuity; effectively, three different frameworks within which the history and identity of Batman and his milieu operate. That these three distinct paradigms can all apply to and shape the character is a result of Batman's rich and diverse history across various media: the same does not apply, for instance, to a more recent figure like Harry Potter, or an equally long-lived but less popular character like Tarzan. I will return to the relationship between these models, and their implication for Batman as a cultural icon, in the conclusion; but it is worth developing and expanding on them more fully here.

We could call the first sense of Batman the *myth*. 'Metatext' would also serve – in Reynolds' words, 'a summation of all existing texts plus all the gaps that those texts have left unspecified'[55] – but 'myth' captures better the sense that this Batman belongs to everyone; to the public, to popular memory, to a modern folk culture. It is in this sense that I propose that Batman could survive as a cultural icon if DC Comics closed down every monthly title now, and Warner Bros. cancelled all its superhero films.[56] Batman is sufficiently embedded in popular culture – the essential template of his character, iconography, cast and setting familiar to millions, and his history dating back to before World War Two – to retain his public recognition and broader popularity as a cultural reference without the backing of regular comics and blockbuster films. The majority of film viewers, of course, have little or no interest in the comic books – recall the comparative box office and sales figures in Chapter Two – and their sense of Batman is already shaped more by unofficial or nostalgic texts than by the official, ongoing comic book narratives. Batman is kept in the public eye by political newspaper cartoons such as Patrick Chappatte's 'Savior of the Economy', showing a Bat-signal calling for Obamaman,[57] and Ben Jennings' 'DIY Police', with British Prime Minister David Cameron in an amateur Batman suit and Nick Clegg as his boy sidekick,[58] far more than he is by the regular comic book that actually bears his name. However, many of the dedicated fans who follow Batman closely are also talented enough to create and distribute new, unofficial adventures to a global audience, and could readily provide a continuing stream of Batman narratives if DC were to release the character from copyright. Sandy Collora's fan-film *Batman: Dead End* (2003) and John Fiorella's *Grayson* (2004) are only the most celebrated examples of this small-scale but high-quality creativity.[59]

It is this sense of Batman as myth that comprises all his contradictory variants, but is loose and flexible enough for the contradictions not to matter. Batman fights crime in Gotham City, aided
by his trained mind and physique, and supported by his wealth
and ingenuity rather than any superpowers. That essential framework can hold Frank Miller's Batman, Joel Schumacher's Batman,
Patrick Chappatte and Ben Jennings' Batman, Bob Kane's Batman,
and even – with only a little generosity in the interpretation – Adam
West's Batman. This Batman encompasses everything he has ever
been: he is ridiculous and fearsome, a fatherly protector, a big boy
scout, a grim vigilante and a gothic guardian. Each individual story
and iteration is an expression of the archetype, a part of the whole;
the myth is the *langue* from which each story is the *parole*, and each
new narrative also contributes to the whole, building our many-
faceted sense – partly a shared sense, partly entirely individual – of
what Batman is. The figure at the heart of this process is a mosaic
icon: a collage of images and graffiti, portraits and texts, some serious and dark, some light and silly. It is never finished, it catches the
light differently depending on your angle, and it belongs, in its crazy,
glorious complexity, to all those who help construct it; that is, all of
us who can imagine Batman.

The second framework is what I described earlier as a matrix: we
could also call this the *brand*. This is a smaller, more contained and
more controlled network of texts, defined by their current status as
Warner Bros. Batman products: expressions of the contemporary corporate template, rather than a broader, folk identity. However, as we
saw in previous chapters, there are distinctions and variations within
this more official conception of Batman. The main character of the
1990s animated show is quite different from the protagonist of the
two other recent cartoon series, *The Batman* and *The Brave and the Bold*.
The Batman of the *Arkham Asylum* video game is quite different from
the Batman of the *Arkham Asylum* graphic novel. The Batman of *Dark
Victory* has a first meeting with his sidekick that is quite different from
their meeting in *All Star Batman and Robin the Boy Wonder*. Yet as we
also saw, the stories within this matrix can overlap, intersect and borrow from each other. The animated series lent its new characters to the

regular comic books, and shares its voice actors with the video games; the blockbuster films both poached from and in turn, shaped the comics. This sense of Batman is more rigid than the first: it attempts to exclude previous readings now seen as aberrant, and replace them with a current range of approved Batman texts, which – from the video games with their elaborate, brutal combat routines, through the 'realist' Nolan reboot and the re-released 1970s stories to the 'Dark Whopper' burgers – currently conform to a far narrower reading of the character than the diverse, messy and all-encompassing 'mythic' icon.

The third framework is the most rigid. This is the rulebook of continuity *canon*; the strict sense of what counts and what happened, what is 'true' and what isn't, in the mainstream Batman comic book universe.[60] It is within this system that the Crisis wiped out an archive of stories from the past. It is this system that Harley Quinn only entered when she was introduced to the regular comic book title from the animated series. It is within this system that *The Dark Knight Returns* is only a possible future, until such time as its key details are incorporated, and thus approved, within the monthly comics such as *Batman* and *Detective*. Those two titles represent the highest level of the canon; in Batman terms, they are the Bible, and of course they were governed, under O'Neil, by a Bat-Bible. As Pearson and Uricchio note, the increase of Batman texts across various platforms in the late 1980s necessitated 'explicit editorial statements about the canonical and non-canonical.'[61] The DC Comics site currently offers the official origin as a two-page comic that echoes, and further condenses, the story of 'The Man Who Falls';[62] each new retelling of the origin sequence becomes the approved version.

Contemporary continuity is policed in more detail by fans, who document each official event in Batman's fictional career on both Wikipedia and the more specialist DC Database, and explain it on forums like *Comic Book Resources*, where more experienced members attempt to offer definitive answers based on their knowledge of the Batman archives.[63] The canonical narrative of the DC Database covers Bruce Wayne's training and overseas sojourn in detail, and orders key works into a clear chronology, with the events of *Year One* followed by *The Long Halloween*, *The Killing Joke*, *A Death in the Family* and *Knightfall*, leading through to the most recent episodes of *Batman Incorporated*.

This obsessive encyclopaedic record of Batman's fictional life may seem a long way from Umberto Eco's account of Superman continuity, first published in 1972, as an 'uncontrollable flux' that retains the illusion of a 'continuous present'.[64]

> The stories develop in a kind of oneiric climate – of which the reader is not aware at all – where what has happened before and what has happened after appear extremely hazy. The narrator picks up the strand of the event again and again, as if he had forgotten to say something and wanted to add details to what had already been said.[65]

The dreamlike realm Eco describes, where Batman's history can be picked up like a fireside yarn, is far more immediately reminiscent of the 'folk', mythic hero I described above; a figure more like Robin Hood or Anansi, a character with many faces and adventures who belongs to the storyteller, the *griot*, rather than the global corporation, the multi-platform product and the rigid publishing and distribution cycle. As Batman moves across those three forms, from the myth through the brand to the rules of canon, the framework becomes less dreamlike and more focused on 'realism'; governed not by the loose continuity of sleep, where a figure can change shape (from West's Batman to Miller's Batman) while still, somehow, remaining the same person, and where stories can cut and jump while still, somehow, encouraging us to follow, but by more rigid frameworks like the editorial Bat-Bible and the mantras of verisimilitude that guided Nolan's project. The process of narrowing from 'myth' to 'canon' clearly enacts and echoes the relationship we explored above, between Bakhtin's concept of carnival as a metaphor for heteroglossia and dialogism, and the controlling, containing forces of dominant culture, whether at the level of social ritual or disciplinary 'stylistics'.

And yet already we can identify a continuum between these categories, rather than the strict distinction that the discourse of the gritty, realist, modern Batman attempts to construct. Rather than a clear hierarchy of binary oppositions (dark versus rainbow) we can identify a spectrum, shifting from dreamlike freedom – Batman can fly to other planets and meet space policemen – to grounded rationality – Batman is 'probably the best martial artist alive, and one of the best gymnasts.'[66] Tellingly, the looser and more liberated continuity has always allowed some space to play, even in the darkest days of the modern, gritty Batman. Shortly after the publication of *Year One* and 'The Man Who Falls', with their defining, street-level template for Batman's early years, DC launched its 'Elseworlds' series of imaginary tales, which explored diverse possibilities for Batman and other characters, outside strict continuity. While *The Long Halloween* was carefully filling in the calendar blanks of Batman's official history, *Gotham by Gaslight* (1989) placed Batman in the Ripper's Victorian London, *Red Rain* (1991) faced him with Dracula, and *The Blue, The Grey and The Bat* (1992) relocated him in the American Civil War.

These more experimental stories – appearing post-Crisis, but in many ways embodying the globetrotting, time-hopping spirit of earlier decades – are not featured in the version of Batman's 1980s and 1990s identity presented by the *Batman Begins* documentaries and production material; they are retroactively edited out, presumably to preserve a more coherent and straightforward portrayal of Batman's gritty, urban realism. However, the very fact that *The Dark Knight Returns*, central to the dark, modern tradition, is itself only a possible future, works to undermine any simple opposition between the 'realist' 1980s stories and their more fantastical pre-Crisis counterparts. The spirit of 'what if' and dreamlike speculation were never entirely purged from Batman's adventures, and while many of the resulting stories were kept apart from the rigorously policed mainstream canon through the separate imprint of the 'Elseworlds' sub-brand, others, like *Dark Knight Returns* and the future stories that appeared in *Legends of the Dark Knight*, retain an ambiguous standing.

More revealing yet is the strand of stories that explicitly constructs Batman as a folk hero of many faces, playing with his multiple forms and shifts, and specifically evokes a group storytelling tradition. During the gritty, social-realist 1970s tradition, the comic book episode titled 'The Batman Nobody Knows', from 1973, had a trio of 'ghetto-hardened kids' relating their personal experiences of Batman to Bruce Wayne. Mickey saw the crimefighter as a half-bat demon, Ronnie as 'Muhammed Ali – Jim Brown – Shaft – an' Superfly all rolled into one', while Ziggy recalls a ten-foot tall shadow with 'big bat-ears.'[67] A 1997 issue of *Legends of the Dark Knight*, called 'Stories', performs a similar exercise: a group of Gothamites trapped in an elevator remember their own version of Batman, including a vampire-fighting creature of the 1930s, a gimmicky hero of the 1950s and the more recent armour-clad vigilante.[68] In a neat intertextual borrowing, an episode of *The New Batman Adventures* animated series from October 1998 reprised the 1970s set-up, with kids sharing their stories: but now the title was 'Legends of the Dark Knight', and one of the kids – herself based on Frank Miller's female Robin – related an episode from *The Dark Knight Returns*. Finally, the DVD compilation *Gotham Knight* (2008), intended as a tie-in to bridge *Batman Begins* and *The Dark Knight*, opens with 'Have I Got a Story for You': three kids, in a now-familiar scene, tell tall tales of the Batman they encountered, from a vampire to a combat robot. Writer Josh Olson admitted he was paying tribute both to the 'Legends of the Dark Knight' episode of the 1990s and the 1973 comic book: 'The first time it's stealing, the second time it's borrowing, the third time you're creating a genre.'[69]

Already, then, we can recognise distinct nods to a folk cultural, mythic figure – the multifaceted, fluid Batman who belongs to the storyteller and to his listeners' imagination – even within the 'realist' range of branded products attached to Nolan's films, and the rigid structures of modern comic book canon. However, even canon itself behaves more like Eco's 'oneiric climate' than we might expect, whatever its claims to realism and rationality. Its boundaries are elastic – snapping back tightly into place, but able to stretch – rather than brittle. As drastic events like the Crisis show, even in its acts of control and censorship, its approach is editorial: it is about revising, writing over, deleting and replacing. The very fact that continuity can erase swathes of comic book history demonstrates that its ethos is based in change and fluidity, rather than permanency.

Despite its associations with continuity bibles, canon is not absolute gospel but a database that allows for constant tweaks, reboots and revisions. Metaphorically, its ideal medium is not stone tablets, but Wikipedia.

But the beauty of word processing and online editing is its apparent lack of traces. The deleted text can be recovered from electronic limbo, and the debates behind each Wikipedia entry are visible behind a tab, but they remain comparatively hidden. Each change is smooth; each replacement can seem seamless. Continuity can incorporate additions and delete details that no longer fit, and cover up the join. As such, it retains the dreamlike potential for sudden shifts and second thoughts that Eco identified in earlier, pre-Crisis continuity; the difference is that it conscientiously hushes them up, denies their previous existence and pretends, for the most part, that things were always this way. Like Orwell's 'doublethink' politics from *Nineteen Eighty-Four*, it represses a previous truth, and rewrites not just the present but the historical past. As I have suggested, continuity is always a palimpsest bearing the signs of previous texts; even if canon insists the 1960s television Batman never officially happened, it still exists in the broader cultural memory of Batman as myth, and it keeps peeking back through the gaps. The one-issue story *Planetary/Batman: Night on Earth* (2003), for instance, had Batman phasing through different versions of himself, from the 1939 gothic vigilante through the brick outhouse of *Dark Knight Returns* to the gallant, ridiculous Adam West caped crusader.[70]

But, that said, canon can attempt a thorough – never complete, but thorough – job of cleaning the slate and revising the past. As such, it is similar to but distinct from the vague continuity described by Eco, whereby 'at a certain point, Supergirl appears on the scene. She is Superman's cousin, and she, too, escaped from the destruction of Krypton.'

All of the events concerning Superman are retold in one way or another in order to account for the presence of this new character (who has hitherto not been mentioned, because, it is explained, she has lived in disguise in a girls' school, awaiting puberty, at

which time she could come out into the world; the narrator goes
back in time to tell in how many and in which cases she, of whom
nothing was said, participated during those many adventures
where we saw Superman alone involved).[71]

This kind of rewriting still regularly takes place; it is simply less
crudely – or less charmingly – performed, and commonly known as
the *retcon*, from 'retroactive continuity'. Over the past twenty years,
for example, the key detail as to whether Bruce Wayne's parents were
murdered by a specific gangster named Joe Chill – thus enabling
Batman's revenge on an individual – or by an unnamed and uni-
dentified villain, making Batman's war on crime more general, has
changed twice, in events of a similar scale and nature to the Crisis
on Infinite Earths. *Zero Hour*, in 1994, erased Joe Chill from history;
Infinite Crisis, of 2005–6, brought him back. No grand announcement is customarily made to herald these changes, though; the shift
in official history is signalled in a panel or a line of dialogue, and
with that small revision, a character's fundamental motivation can
change and a series of stories go in or out of continuity – in this case,
Mike W. Barr's *Batman: Year Two*. This four-part series, first published in *Detective Comics* and therefore occupying the highest level
of canon, was originally, as the title suggests, intended to continue
from Miller's *Year One*, and mapped out Batman's next 12 months
with authority. As suggested above, however, the Batman entry at
the *DC Database* now omits it, moving straight from *Year One* to *Long
Halloween* in its chronological account; there is no crossing-out, no
sign of erasure, just a clean-cut and invisible join. On the other hand,
the fan-written Wikipedia entry for *Year Two* gives a clear sense
of continuity's flexibility and ambiguity, and the fact that, in the
absence of clear editorial announcements, it can be open to speculation and debate. 'Canonical status' here earns a section to itself:

> This story has since been deemed non-canonical due to conti-
> nuity revisions in the Batman universe as a result of the *Zero
> Hour* storyline, by story editor Dennis O'Neil. This is the sec-
> ond time a Mike Barr story has been retconned out of existence;
> the first was the one-shot *Batman: Son of the Demon* (although

elements of *Batman: Son of the Demon* seem to have recently been put back into continuity by current Batman writer Grant Morrison). After the events of *Infinite Crisis*, Joe Chill's arrest has been restored into continuity, meaning the story could very well be canonical.[72]

We see here the two sides of canonical history, viewed from inside and outside. From a position within the official account of Batman's fictional life, *Year Two* has simply, for the moment, dropped out of sight without a trace. If it remains non-canonical, then the current Batman will never remember or refer to the events of Mike W. Barr's story; though he does now know Joe Chill, who was reintroduced and reinterpreted in *Batman* #673 (2008). Taking a broader view, though, the collective fan memory has obviously not forgotten *Year Two*, and it remains within the bigger, less restrictive, public myth of Batman as a cultural icon, ready to reenter the official canon if editorial decisions approve it; this approval may well manifest itself as an explicit reference to *Year Two* in a current storyline, rather than a literal announcement.

Julian Darius' *Improving the Foundations*, Geoff Klock's *How To Read Superhero Comics and Why* and Richard Reynolds' *Superheroes: A Modern Mythology* collectively provide, through their individual case studies, an unsurpassable account of the way continuity has operated since Batman's inception. Darius explains, in fascinating detail, the evolution of the origin story from 1939 onwards, and shows how elements were, over the years, added, dropped, incorporated into the canon or suggested but then forgotten. Inventive but daft tales about Batman's history as 'the original Robin', in *Detective Comics* #226 (December 1955) were simply allowed to drift, then picked up again, reworked and retold more successfully a year later (as 'The First Batman', from *Detective Comics* #235 in September 1956), with the new story replacing the old. Elaborate additions to Bruce's childhood narrative – the child is put into the care of his Uncle Phillip and housekeeper Mrs. Chilton, who turns out to be the mother of Joe Chill – were introduced in 1969, and again, dropped when they failed to serve any significant future narrative use, or capture the imagination of either other writers, or the comic's fans.[73] Before the wholesale, deliberate and sweeping housecleaning process of the Crisis, Darius shows, there existed a messier, less formalised but similar system whereby, every so often, a new origin story would re-edit the previous narratives, trying to make sense of the diverse additions and elaborations of the past years.

Just as a new origin sequence can write earlier details out of the official story – if Joe Chill didn't kill Bruce's parents in the latest version, he never did – so Geoff Klock demonstrates that when a new story becomes popular with fans, gains resonance, earns authority through repetition in other stories, and is editorially approved as the current 'truth', it writes details retrospectively into history.[74]

> When Batman takes a rifle shot to the chest, which any reader assumes would kill him instantly, it reveals metal shielding. Batman says, 'Why do you think I wear a target on my chest – can't armor my head,' and with that one line, a thirty-year mystery dissolves as every reader runs mentally through previous stories, understanding that plate as having always been there. […] *his* Batman is almost always wounded, sometimes badly, and the Batarang is reconceived as a kind of bat-shaped throwing star that disarms by slicing into the fore-arm, rather than its former, sillier portrayal as a boomerang that disarms criminals by knocking weapons out of their hands. The strength of Miller's portrayal leaves readers with the impression that all of Batman's fights must have been of this kind, but that they have been reading a watered-down version of the way things 'really happened.'

The strongest version, Klock concludes, 'is retroactively constituted as always already true.'[75] Again, that Klock's example is *Dark Knight Returns* confirms the ambiguous relationship between Miller's speculative future and present-day canon: while the graphic novel, strictly speaking, remains outside mainstream continuity, the Bat-shuriken and bulletproof chest-plate have become an established part of the regular Batman's armoury.

Reynolds confirms this process of addition, revision and rearrangement through reference to T.S. Eliot's 'Tradition and the Individual Talent':

> what happens when a new work of art is created is something that happens simultaneously to all the works of art which preceded it. The existing monuments form an ideal order among themselves, which is modified by the introduction of the new (the really new) work of art among them. The existing order is complete before the new work arrives; for order to persist after the supervention of novelty, the whole existing order must be, if ever so slightly, altered ... [76]

This account of continuity's operation – the way in which an approved change to the top level of the Batman canon alters not just the present day, but the character's history – is necessary in order to understand the importance of Grant Morrison's recent work on the flagship Batman titles.

Taste the Rainbow

As already suggested, there was precedent for Morrison's approach to Batman. His *Earth 2* had reintroduced Owlman's alternate earth for the first time since its elimination in the Crisis. His reworking of *Animal Man*, a little-known, second-string character (1988–1990), became an exploration of the characters left in limbo by DC's housecleaning event; his British superhero story in *2000AD*, 'Zenith' (1987–2000), expanded into an epic battle across parallel earths. His four-issue *Flex Mentallo* (1996), itself spinning off from *Doom Patrol* (1989–1993) was a further celebration of diverse, multiple dimensions, Silver Age fantasy and queer subversion.[77]

Morrison played a part in returning previously lost worlds and histories to the DC Comics universe as a co-writer of the year-long narrative *52* (2005–6), which concluded with the revelation that, rather than a single earth, 52 different alternate continuities were once again officially in play.[78] The Elseworld milieu of *Gotham by Gaslight* now occupies Earth-19, for instance, while the future of *The*

Dark Knight Returns is currently located on Earth-31, and Owlman is Batman's dimensional neighbour on Earth-3. On a far smaller scale, but perhaps most significantly, Morrison's *JLA Classified* #1 (January 2005) found Batman declaring 'I'm opening the Sci-Fi closet, Alfred. Don't tell my friends in the GCPD about this,' and revealing a flying saucer in a previously hidden storeroom. Already, the author's intentions were clear; even his choice of the word 'closet' signalled that he understood the connection between the repression of pre-Crisis diversity and the containment of gay readings. While Morrison had previously perpetuated the representation of Batman as dark, grim and gritty through *Arkham Asylum*, *Gothic* (1990) and *JLA* (1997–2000), his work on *Batman* from 2006–2008 saw him bringing more playful, Silver Age sensibilities to the character.

Morrison sums up his approach in the introduction to *The Black Casebook*, a reprinting of stories from the 1950s and 1960s that inspired his *Batman* run. His account is so lucid in its awareness of the character's history, and the rules governing that history, that it is worth quoting at length:

I decided to treat the entire publishing history of Batman as the events in one man's extraordinarily vivid life. This for me was the story that hadn't been told yet; the story of how his life might include the complete trajectory of Batman as a character from the 1930s to the 2000s. [...]

I imagined a rough timeline that allowed me to compress 70 years' worth of Batman's adventures into a frantic 15 years in the life of an extraordinary man (I'm not suggesting this is canon and other writers may disagree with my scheme, but it helped me to develop a story capable of incorporating Batman's history itself as the driving force of the plot). This approach, however, required me to deal with and recuperate some of the more problematic areas of that long history, in particularly the despised 'sci-fi' Batman of the 1950s when the Dark Knight Detective was thrust awkwardly into stories involving other dimensions, time machines, space travel and colourful alien worlds.

Most Batman fans prefer to ignore the often surreal and outlandish stories of the 1950s, and for good reason, as they tend to
violate some of the basic 'real world' rules which help to make
Batman's adventures convincing to an older and more sophisticated audience. [...] This long-repressed material, most of
it erased from Batman's official history, became for me a rich
source of inspiration and allowed me to see the character from a
very different angle.

So I decided to introduce the revelation that Batman keeps a
'Black Casebook', his own version of the *X-Files*, where all the
bizarre, supernatural or logic-defying encounters of his career
can be recorded.[79]

Morrison concludes that these are the adventures Batman would 'probably much rather forget', but which are nevertheless 'carefully recorded'.
The contradiction captures the relationship between Batman as myth
and canon – the repressed stories remain in the archive, however
unofficial their standing in terms of the approved Batman narrative,
and can be brought back, in this case as odd memories, drug-induced
experiences and aspects of the unconscious. Morrison's reincorpora-
tion of these pre-Crisis tales into current continuity is a radical move:
according to the rules, by appearing in the mainstream *Batman* title,
at a stroke – through one reference in a single panel – they happened.
They always happened. They were never gone.

So, albeit as hallucinations, the results of sensory deprivation
or unexplained phenomena, the events of 'Robin Dies at Dawn'
(*Batman* #156, June 1963) in which the Dynamic Duo fight a huge
pink alien, Robin shouts 'Come on, Big Boy! I'm still waiting for
you!', Batman sobs over his partner's body ('Oh, Robin ... Robin')
and Dick Grayson runs into Bruce's bedroom in his pyjamas to wake
his friend from a dream about a 'tentacle-plant', are now back within
continuity. The events of 'A Partner for Batman' (*Batman* #65, June-
July 1951), in which Bruce shouts 'Robin, go limp! Go limp, Robin
...' and Robin weeps at the idea of being replaced by Wingman
('Just as I feared (sob!) They're planning to drop me!') are now back
within continuity. The events of 'Batman Meets Bat-Mite' (*Detective*

Comics #267, May 1959) whose title is surely self-explanatory ('It's an elf . . . an ELF DRESSED IN A CRAZY-LOOKING BATMAN COSTUME!') are now back within continuity.

Arguably the most revealing moment in the *Casebook*, though, is one that Morrison does not explicitly incorporate in his contemporary *Batman* stories, and claims he has never read ('I've only ever seen the cover images . . . I hope I'm in for a treat.') The scene is from 'The Rainbow Creature' (*Batman* #134, September 1960) and it takes place after Batman and Robin have battled the eponymous science fiction monster. Batman searches for a way to end a skirmish between the peaceful townsfolk and a band of rebel soldiers: 'Hmmm – there's a TOY SHOP on the street . . . it gives me an idea!'

Minutes later, according to the caption, Batman leaps from the door of the toy shop, his arms up in what is presumably meant to convey fear, but looks from his grin more like celebration, even worship. 'THE RAINBOW BEAST . . .' he exults, 'IT'S COME BACK!' Around him, rays of coloured light explode like stained glass, as the criminals run for their lives. But Batman quickly reveals his ruse: 'That's what made the rainbow colors – a TOY PRISM I placed on that table!' We see the shard of refractive glass, still radiating rainbows; now Batman's face is serious as he offers this science lesson, but Robin beams.

In an influential online article from August 2008, Duncan Falconer proposed that recent trends in superhero comics should be distinguished from the 'Dark Age' of the 1980s and early 90s – the grim-and-gritty tradition on which *Batman Begins* most obviously draws – and suggested 'The Prismatic Age' as a title to evoke their recurrent themes and motifs. He used Morrison's work as key examples of those contemporary trends, and drew his central term from a page of Morrison's *The Flash*, where a giant prism splits the hero into seven variants, each a different colour of the visible light spectrum: that is, a rainbow Flash. Falconer's image evokes the lighter approach that characterised many superhero narratives of the later 1990s and 2000s, as a reaction against the 'darkness'; but it also captures the sense of alternates, analogues and parallel iterations of characters that frequently recurred in these stories.

> The ideology of the Prismatic Age, what it insistently moves toward, is that *all* parts are active, all of the time. While not necessarily visible monthly, nor are they hidden or overwritten ... Summary of all incarnations, a distillate.[80]

This is not the place to summarise Falconer's extensive argument, except to note that it echoes, both in its imagery and its implications, the sense of Batman as myth that I described above. This is the hero as mosaic, made up of refracting tiles that throw back light in different colours and shapes depending on the angle;[81] this is the cultural icon who is everything he has ever been (though those aspects may not all be visible, they are never truly lost), who is multiple and infinite. This is also, though Falconer's focus is elsewhere, the return not just of light but of rainbows, not just of shiny neo–Silver Age reflexivity but of camp, even queerness. Batman, in the original story from 1960, uses a child's toy – kid's stuff, like a comic book itself – as a tool to create something at once glorious, ridiculous, hilarious and revelatory: no wonder his hands are up in both epiphany and horror. 'THE RAINBOW BEAST ... IT'S COME BACK!'

Marc Singer's extensive analysis of Morrison's oeuvre, which further traces prismatic imagery throughout the writer's recent work, suggests that 'Morrison seems well aware of the language and conventions of the "Prismatic Age"; if he has not read Falconer's piece, he is certainly operating on the same wavelength.'[82] Equally, if Morrison had genuinely not read 'The Rainbow Creature', he was entirely on the same page.[83]

It would be over-simplistic to claim that Morrison's approach, which retroactively integrated various pre-Crisis events and characters – associated with Silver Age silliness, camp, science fiction and play – into mainstream continuity, restored a sense of carnival to the modern-day Batman. Indeed, it could even be argued that, while Morrison brought these campy stories back into visibility, his quotation of them in the *Batman* title actually had the conservative effect of incorporating radical, repressed material back into the mainstream, bringing it to light but making it safe by adapting it to the dominant aesthetic and approach. The jolly image of Bruce Wayne's father in a bat-like masquerade costume, from 1956's 'The First Batman', is transmuted into villainous Dr. Simon Hurt in the same outfit, standing over a brutally beaten Alfred. The Batman of Zur-En-Arrh, a smiling alien policeman from 'Batman – The Superman of Planet X' (1958) becomes a full-page image of Bruce Wayne in the same ripped, ragged costume, snarling in the rain. The simple, flat drawings of the 1950s are adapted into the grim-and-gritty style of the modern age, retaining their strangeness but, arguably, losing all their innocence.

The major change that Morrison makes, then, is not so much to the present-day tone and aesthetic of Batman – his *Batman RIP* storyline is an intense, even disturbing exploration of Bruce Wayne suffering a mental breakdown – but to the history. By introducing Bat-Mite, the First Batman, the Batman of Zur-En-Arrh, even the pink 'Big Boy' Alien from 'Robin Dies at Dawn' as the current Batman's vivid memories, however inexplicable and hallucinatory, Morrison reinserts them firmly into Batman's past, and insists that, in one form or another, this period took place and must be reckoned with.

Morrison's two-part story 'The Butler Did It' and 'What the Butler Saw' (*Batman* #682–3, December 2008/January 2009) for instance, replays and retells Batman's entire career, opening with a familiar moment from *Year One* where Bruce first sees his battotem, then moving swiftly through visual quotations from 1939's 'The Batman Meets Doctor Death' and 'The Dirigible of Doom', and another glimpse of Robin's origin. So far, so familiar, as the contemporary comic revises Bob Kane, Jerry Robinson and Bill Finger's earliest stories into a more 'realistic' mode: a panel from Batman's first ever appearance in May 1939 is quoted verbatim, but translated into the sophisticated art style and computer colouring of the late 2000s.[84] This return to the character's origins, which are validated and expanded through a 'realistic' retelling, is exactly the approach we saw in the gritty tradition of *Year One*, 'The Man Who Falls' and *Batman Begins*.

However, having established the pattern, Morrison then uses it to perform the same act of validation on less stable material. Joker announces 'I just blew five million dollars on a helicopter that looks just like me!' while Batman and Robin smilingly punch out a pair of clowns. Batman kisses Kathy Kane, the 1950s Batwoman who was ruled out of continuity by the Crisis, and wonders '... when did it become like some endless game show?'[85]

'Whatever it is, they've certainly turned the place into Toytown, sir,' Alfred replies. 'Pop Criminals, I believe they've started to call them.'

The next panel, while drawn in the same 'realistic' style as the scenes borrowed from late '30s continuity, is a pastiche of the 1960s TV show. 'The Joker left a card,' Batman muses. 'An ace. Card begins with a "c." Remember it's a playing card.'

'Sea,' Robin exclaims, snapping his fingers. 'Playing "C"... "C" playing ... HOLY SEA PLANE DISPLAY IN GOTHAM HARBOR!' The dynamic duo leaps into action, socking a gallery of costumed villains.

History moves on, as Morrison has Batman reflecting on the changes in his own tradition. 'I'm tired of playing games with clowns and quizmasters and circus people. I trained to be a soldier. Crime. Madness. Horror. These are the things I understand.' Soon, we are reeling through a montage of O'Neil and Adams 1970s stories – a bare-chested Batman duelling Ra's al Ghul – and then Jason Todd is murdered (*A Death in the Family* 1988–1989), and Brian Bolland's Joker arrives at the door in his palm tree–patterned shirt to shoot Barbara Gordon, and Batman's back is broken (*Knightfall*, 1993–1994) and he is replaced by the armoured vigilante Azrael, and fights Hush (2002–2003), and Tim Drake's father is killed (*Identity Crisis,* 2004) ... and then Batman wakes up.

It was a dream, but those were genuine memories. We return to them in *Batman* #700 (August 2010), also authored by Morrison, and titled 'Time and the Batman'.[86] The opening story is set on the cusp of the change from camp to gritty; in real world terms, at the end of the 1960s, when O'Neil's stories reacted against the TV show. Again, Batman is pitted against a whole crowd of his arch-villains – a trope that recalls the Adam West *Batman* feature film of 1966 – and the tone starts out as relatively light entertainment, in 'Pop Crime' style. 'Who knows what this baffling box can do?' Riddler wonders, dressed in skin-tight, Day-Glo green. 'Lemme outta this, I'll clean your clock, Joker!' yells Robin. 'And all the rest of you, too!'

But times are changing. 'Jokerrrrrr,' Catwoman chides, as the Clown Prince of Crime becomes increasingly violent. 'You used to be fun!'

'I ... feel funny ... but funny's good,' Joker mutters, clutching his forehead. 'I brought you here to witness history. Maybe I'm not. Even. Me. But I promise to put a big cheeky smile on that baby face just as soon as the rush lets up!' He takes a toke of Scarecrow's fear toxin, and holds a knife to Robin's mouth. Batman kicks him brutally in the face: no cartoon 'Ka-Thwok', just blood. 'You can't handle all of us, Caped Crusader,' Riddler taunts. Batman's fist smashes out his teeth. 'Don't call me that again!' An era is over.

Morrison's first innovation, then, is not to return mainstream continuity to an earlier age, but to present Batman as, in Falconer's words, a 'summary of all incarnations,' rather than claiming Batman is only, and has only ever been, the current version. This Batman can be a grim soldier, a bright do-gooder, a father and a demon; and the totality of his life is – as the brief retelling above demonstrated – at once a rich archive, a crazy roller coaster, a joyride and a nightmare. The Joker's life is reconceived in a similar fashion.

> His remarkable coping mechanism, which saw him transform a personal nightmare of disfigurement into baleful comedy and criminal infamy all those years ago – happily chuckling to himself in the garage as he constructed outlandish Joker-Mobiles which gently mocked the young Batman's pretensions in the Satire Years before Camp, and New Homicidal, and all the other Jokers he's been – now struggles to process the raw, expressionistic art brutal of his latest surgical makeover.[87]

Joker reinvents himself in a new form as 'The Clown at Midnight', his mouth cut and stitched like Heath Ledger's in Nolan's *Dark Knight*, quoting Moore's *Killing Joke* ('And I'm looony, like a lightbulb-battered bug') and Morrison's own *Arkham Asylum* ('Aren't I just good enough to EAT!'). This is a Joker informed by the key texts of the 'dark' tradition;

but the difference is that the outlandish, the gentle mocking and the camp are reinstated as part of the character's history. This is still the figure of Bakhtin's modern carnival, twisted and uncanny, but it is a figure who remembers his past, when he brought something more life-affirming, genuinely comic, happy and, indeed, gay: a folk festival that transformed Gotham temporarily into Toytown. Morrison, as scriptor, in Bakhtin's words, 'welcomes the heteroglossia and language diversity … into his own work … it is in fact out of this stratification of language, its speech diversity and even language diversity, that he constructs his own style.' He returns Batman and Joker not to a single earlier era, but to something more complex: a matrix, a network, a conversation between past and present. Batman and Joker alike now become a Babel of voices, conflicting and contradicting. Batman's life is no longer structured by the calendar, but a confusion of illusions, memories and half-truths. 'It would be far easier to consider this a dream', he tells himself as he remembers, or thinks he remembers, his 1950s adventures. 'The boundaries between what's real and what's illusion have come to seem as threadbare as a moldering shroud.'[88] Rather than a clean duality between Wayne and Batman, with the mask hiding the nothingness of his civilian shell, Batman becomes, like Joker, a series of personae, in a cycle of renewal, birth, death and re-becoming.[89]

Stripped of his identity by subliminal messages, Bruce becomes a hobo, but then constructs a new costume from purple, yellow and red rags and rebrands himself as the Batman of Zur-En-Arrh. As his possibly imaginary friend Bat-Mite explains: 'Batman thinks of everything. Batman even prepared for psychological attack with a backup identity, remember?' Batman, building a new self based on a 1950s science fiction adventure, snarls 'I'm what you get when you take Bruce out of the equation.' At a later point, he declares 'Not Bruce. I'm Batman,' and confirms, even with his mask removed, 'I'm the Batman of Zur-En-Arrh.' Yet the text of his announcement is small, and his voice quiet, uncertain. The tone is still brutal, violent and grim – it even seems to rain all the time – but this is far from a one-note Batman, reduced to a single reading. It is not a return to the far-fetched adventures of the science fiction stories, or the knowing fun of camp; rather, it shifts uneasily between the dreamlike climate of earlier continuity and the rigid order of the modern period, between the oneiric and the realist. 'Are you really an alien hyper-imp from the 5th dimension,' Batman asks Bat-Mite, 'or just a figment of my imagination?' Bat-Mite hangs like a dark spider in the rain, silhouetted by the glow of incendiaries. 'Imagination IS the 5th dimension,' he scoffs. 'Some world's greatest detective you are.' I suggested above that the darkest, grittiest Batman has, metaphorically, a playful imp hovering at his shoulder, and a rainbow costume in his closet: Morrison literalises those repressed aspects, bringing them to the surface.

Morrison's second innovation is, through this increased fluidity and unsettling of borders, to interrogate the relationship between Batman and Joker. That the two are mutually dependent opposites, two sides of the same coin, has been a trope in both Batman comics and Batman criticism for many years.[90] Morrison's *RIP* storyline, while riffing off these readings, suggests a subtly different dynamic.

'Both of us trying to find meaning in a meaningless world!' Joker thinks to himself in 'The Clown at Midnight'. 'Why be a disfigured outcast when I can be a notorious Crime God? Why be an orphaned boy when you can be a superhero? You can't kill me without becoming like me. I can't kill you without losing the only human being who can keep up with me. Isn't it IRONIC?'

In *RIP*, they face off again. Joker's new incarnation, the 'Thin White Duke of Death', speaks entirely in lowercase, green ink, like a stalker's poison pen letters. 'ah heh,' he announces, 'love really *is* blind. It's only *me* again. remember *me*? you and i, we had a special arrangement. A yin/thang thing. holmes and moriarty, tweety and sylvester, hats and gloves ...'

> you think it all breaks down into symbolism and structures and hints and clues
>
> no, batman, that's just *wikipedia*

It's a damning insult, and it seems to capture the usual dynamic. Batman is order, structure and rationality: Joker is camp, pastiche, the breakdown of high and low culture (from literary antagonists to a cartoon cat) into an anything-goes cabaret.[91] Harley Quinn, in 'The

Clown at Midnight', calls Joker 'The Great Modernist in a postmodern tradition'.[92] Batman, in turn, self-consciously reiterates his own rules – 'Batman doesn't *use* a gun' – and derides Joker as a corrupted, abject figure, calling him a 'grinning freak'; not so far from a 'filthy degenerate'. Joker is heteroglossia – his every line a cross-referencing dialogue, stitched together from cultural scraps – and Batman is Wikipedia, the medium of canon and containment.

And yet this isn't the familiar Batman. This is Batman in the gaudy, purple, scarlet and yellow outfit of his Zur-En-Arrh persona. 'The colors demonstrate total *confidence*,' he tells Bat-Mite. '*Robin* dressed this way for years and survived.' His own speech is depicted in a scratchy white on blue, indicating a new, strange voice. Everything is exactly the same, except for the fact that it's all totally different. As Batman crouches on a roof, in an earlier scene – a reprise of a familiar motif, except for the costume and the fact that he's talking both to Bat-Mite and two gargoyles – he hallucinates grids around the city's buildings. 'A checkerboard, a blueprint, a machine designed to make Batman.' Once more, this positions Batman as the figure of imposed order, rationality and containment, an impression confirmed by the Joker's later complaint that 'every single time I try to think outside his toybox he builds a new box around me.' But the grids are illusory – an imaginary Emerald City surrounding the real Gotham – and the dynamic is more flexible than Joker implies. For Batman to keep building a new box around each deviation suggests constant improvisation and invention on his part. As already noted, the canonical history detailed on Wikipedia effectively tries to make sense of change, rearranging itself to construct a new history when stories are ruled out of or into continuity, but as such, its own borders have to be elastic. To incorporate and contain change, it must be open to change itself. 'A lived hegemony,' said Raymond Williams, 'is always a process. It has continually to be renewed, recreated, defended, and modified. It is also continually resisted, limited, altered, challenged by pressures not at all its own.' To keep up in its push-and-pull struggle, its dance with the counter-forces of dissidence and deviance, the dominant, Williams suggests, has to remain nimble and fluid itself.

But the radical result of this dancing duel between order and disorder, as depicted in *RIP*, is that, at times, the participant-opponents seem almost to change places. 'you really want to know how it *feels* to be the clown at midnight?' asks Joker. 'where there's only ever *one* joke and it's *always* on you?' Batman has entertained exactly that desire, earlier in the story: his captions here are a frantic scribble on lined pad, reminiscent of but quite different from the careful cursive journal of *Year One*. 'How do I learn to think like these monsters I've chosen to fight?? And not let my own mind be mangled out of all recognition in the process?'

'you got yourself *into* this whole horrible mess because *you* wanted to understand what it was like to *be me* ha ha,' Joker taunts, but he's not the only one who tried to get closer to his opponent: in 'The Clown at Midnight', Joker muses that 'he simply wants the goddamn Batman to finally get the goddamn joke', and in *RIP* he confesses 'I've been driven *literally in. sane*, trying to get him to loosen up.'

Of course, Batman wins. It takes him a while – *RIP* ended in 2008, but Batman only returns victorious in *Batman and Robin* #16, from January 2011, punching the Joker unconscious with a clean, old-school right hook. But the Joker's last speech before Batman's fist connects is revealing. 'I don't have to go back to the old gags. Starting today, I'm taking the act in a whole new direction. "The Joker Fights Crime!" The gravediggin' clown gets to be the good guy. "Tell me, I said . . . what could be funnier than that?"'

This comic signals a kind of closure, but also a kind of aperture, as it marks both the start of *Batman Incorporated,* and the end of Morrison's run on both *Batman* and his first spin-off title, *Batman and Robin*. Batman has fundamentally changed, announcing publicly that Bruce Wayne is his secret financier, and launching a campaign, as we saw in Chapter Two, to franchise the Batman brand across the world. He now invites multiples, many voices and many variants on his own identity: his new project, spreading his mission globally but allowing it to be inflected by different cultures, embraces a Japanese Batman, the Argentinean El Gaucho, a French Muslim called Nightrunner, the Hong Kong representative, Blackbat, and the African Batwing. Echoing both the 1955 'Batmen of All Nations' tale from *The Black Casebook* and Morrison's reprise of the characters in his more recent 'Black Glove' storyline, the initiative could be read as a worldwide Batman carnival, breaking down the rigid individualism that surrounds the lone vigilante of the 'gritty' tradition and inviting not just the immediate Batman family – Batgirl, Robin, Nightwing and Red Robin all guest star in Morrison's *Batman: The Return*, from January 2011 – but the broader public to participate in a more flexible, playful Batman myth.[93]

As noted in Chapter Two, *Batman: The Return* also depicts a heavy-duty, militarised Batman, modelled to a significant extent after Nolan's 'realist' representation. But this is no hardcore reboot of the character Morrison explored in *RIP*: the fundamental point, that everything happened and everything was true, remains intact. We have seen Batman as the gaudy, fantastical Zur-En-Arrh incarnation, talking to imps and gargoyles within a rainy urban setting and trying to think like the Joker, while the Joker tries to make Batman more like himself; that history is still within recent continuity. We have seen that Batman is only a few steps from carnival costumes and chaos himself, and that cannot be easily forgotten. More significantly yet, we can read back from Morrison's depiction of Batman to realise that, even in his darkest, most military, macho and rational incarnations, carnival was never far from the surface.

Frank Miller's *All Star Batman and Robin*, for instance, is a parade of cheesecake girl art and explosive action, with Batman as a brutal, bullying thug who tells the recently orphaned Dick Grayson 'you've just been DRAFTED. Into a WAR.' This is the comic that described its protagonist as 'the goddamn Batman'; the incarnation that Morrison's Joker despaired over, wishing he could see the joke. But in Episode 5 of Miller's story this stubbled, violent urban soldier announces 'I give with the LAUGH. That ALWAYS works', and falls from the sky with an insane cry of 'HA HA HA HA HA HA!' This, of course, is Joker's trademark, the words that fill the air around him during his baptism in Moore and Bolland's *Killing Joke*: yet at the end of that story, too, both Batman and Joker – caught in a struggle or an embrace, or both – seem ambiguously to be sharing the HA

HA HA that crowds and invades the frame, white text around their silhouettes. In *Arkham Asylum,* just before rejecting his archenemy's advances, Batman confesses 'I'm afraid that the Joker may be *right* about me. Sometimes I ... *question* the rationality of my actions.' 'Arkham is a *looking glass*', the Mad Hatter tells him, 'and we are you.' In *Dark Knight Returns,* it is Joker, fleeing from Batman in a fairground hall of mirrors, who protests that his adversary is 'out of your *mind* ... this is too weird ...'

Later in *Dark Knight Returns,* Batman's ally Oliver 'Green Arrow' Queen remarks 'You've always had it wrong, Bruce ... giving them such a big target. Sure, you play it mysterious – but it's a loud kind of mysterious, man.' This Batman, Geoff Klock observes, terrorizes people 'with cheap theatrics'.[94] But then hasn't he always? His earliest origin sequence has him deciding 'my disguise must be able to strike terror into their hearts. I must be a creature of the night, black, terrible ... I shall become a BAT!' *Dark Knight Returns* expands on that origin by showing the Waynes at the movie theatre, watching *The Mark of Zorro.* 'You loved it so much,' Bruce muses to his younger self. 'You jumped and danced like a FOOL.' Christopher Nolan switches the story to the opera, showing the young Bruce terrified, but in time inspired, by the masks and costumes of *Die Fledermaus.* At the film's end, Gordon shows Batman the Joker's calling card. 'Got a taste for theatrics, like you ...' Whoever tells and draws the story of Robin's origins, with whatever variations – from Bill Finger and Bob Kane in *Detective Comics* #38 to Jeph Loeb and Tim Sale in *Dark Victory* and Frank Miller with Jim Lee in *All Star Batman and Robin* – it always takes place in a circus. Batman's beginnings lie in the cinema or the opera, with him dancing like a fool and adopting a disguise; sure he's mysterious, but it's a loud kind of mysterious, with a taste for the theatrical. Robin, already dressed in the gaudy colours of the fantastical, Zur-En-Arrh Batman, was born in the Big Top. From his origin to his costume to his sidekick – from his first appearance through his camp spectacle to his darkest incarnation – Batman is, and has always been, also a figure of carnival.

So, just as we saw that the relationship between dreamlike continuity and rational canon was not so much a clear distinction as a continuum, so the relationship between Batman and Joker is not so much an opposition as a spectrum; they do not occupy opposite sides, but different points on the rainbow range of light thrown by a prism. They are not antagonists so much as alternates; Batman is defined against Joker as a part of himself, a possible other, rather than a rigid, binary reversal of all he stands for. Like Owlman, Zur-En-Arrh and indeed Bruce Wayne, Joker represents something that Batman could conceivably become, and to an extent always contains.

That measure – the extent to which the camp, the carnival and the chaos of the Joker-aspect within Batman is contained both within the fiction, by Batman himself, and outside, by the discourses of producers, authors, journalists and fans – should lead us to ask, as suggested at the start of Chapter Three, who benefits from those discourses: to examine, in Foucault's words, 'the will that sustains them and the strategic intention that supports them.' If we recognise that the relationship between dark, gritty Batman and rainbow, carnival Batman is not a natural opposition but a dynamic, a struggle between dominance and dissidence, a push-and-pull across a spectrum rather than a binary conflict, we can begin to explore what is at stake, and why one side pushes so hard, and whose interest it serves to insist that Batman is reduced to a one-note, rigid pillar of militarised heterosexuality.

Batman, I have suggested, is in one sense everything he has ever been: but the Batman of the modern, 'dark' tradition is a figure in denial, repressing aspects of himself, or, put another way, a character whose full rainbow spectrum has been repressed, and whose diverse totality has been denied. The value of Grant Morrison's Batman is that it brings those aspects openly back, making the sillier sides of Batman visible rather than pretending they never existed; but equally importantly, it suggests the conflict involved in Batman's character, and the containment he needs to constantly perform in order to keep his Joker-side in check.

It would be overly simplistic to celebrate the Joker wholeheartedly as an avatar of fun, carnival and playful camp; and equally crude to argue that Batman's constant denial is simply a policing of his inherent queerness, an uptight inability to embrace his own diversity. Just as Batman contains multitudes, so does Joker. 'My name is Legion', as the possessed man in the Bible declares, 'for we are many.'[95]

Joker can be seen as representing a positive, liberated folk culture; but in his modern form, as we have seen, he is also a terrifying grotesque. He is not simply a gay devil, an embodiment of becoming and transformation; he is also an avatar of death. In that light, Batman's patrolling of his own borders – his recognition of his potential to become like Joker, and his struggle to pull back from that boundary – can be read not as (or not only as) homophobic repression, but more generously, as an act of self-awareness, sacrifice and necessary control; a reining in of the terror he evokes and the fury that fuels him. If we acknowledge that Joker is a possible variant of Batman, and that Batman knows their characteristics overlap, we can see his refusal ever to fully succumb to that alternate self as a struggle that enriches, rather than diminishes his character, making it more complex; even a fan who objects to gay readings and clings to the idea of Batman as staunchly heterosexual could agree that a Dark Knight who struggles against his own Joker-like aspects is more interesting than a character without conflict.

Having established the dynamic between the two figures not as a clear-cut opposition, but a fluid, potentially interchangeable relationship, the next chapter brings this interpretation to bear on Christopher Nolan's *The Dark Knight*, and its symbolic treatment of contemporary political dilemmas, through the work of Jacques Derrida.

5

THE NEVER-ENDING WAR: DECONSTRUCTION AND THE DARK KNIGHT

Deconstruction

Deconstruction, the approach to texts and theory first pioneered by Jacques Derrida in the 1960s, has a reputation for being complex, challenging and 'difficult'. This reputation is not helped by Derrida's refusal to pin deconstruction down by labelling it as a theory or philosophy in itself,[1] or by the widespread general misuse of the term 'deconstructed' to mean anything from 'analysed' to 'playfully self-referential', or simply to describe a T-shirt with its seams on the outside.

However, the course we have been following in the previous chapters already overlaps with deconstruction: we have been practicing it without identifying it as such. This final chapter engages in a closer study of Derrida's ideas in relation to the processes that structure the texts of Batman, and draws explicitly on deconstruction both to clarify and sharpen our understanding of the dynamics discussed above, and to connect those ideas, in turn, to a reading of Nolan's *The Dark Knight* (2008) in the context of the post-9/11 'war on terror.'

We have explored above, for instance, the fact that any representation of Batman as 'dark', with all the connotations associated

with that term – straightness, realism, rationality, grittiness, toughness – inevitably depends, for its own definition, on an alternative
or 'Other'. This is the figure I have termed the 'rainbow' Batman,
with all its associations of camp, queerness, dream-logic, fantasy
and carnival. We saw that each new iteration of the 'dark' Batman –
O'Neil's in the early 70s, Miller's in 1986, Nolan's in 2005 – defines
itself against the Batman it is not, as a 'bad object'. The comics of the
1950s and 1960s, the Adam West TV show and Joel Schumacher's
two movies are used to represent the alternative.

And yet the previous chapter suggested that, rather than a clear
binary opposition, the dynamic at work here can more accurately be
seen as a shifting spectrum. The supposedly rational logic of post-
Crisis canon includes dreamlike rewriting and ret-con. The supposedly rigorous and fiercely controlled Batman is flexible and fluid
enough to contain multiple versions of himself: he has to be, in order
to keep the Joker – both the Joker as external figure, and his own
Joker-aspects – within ever-expanding, inevitably elastic boundaries.
('every single time I try to think outside his toybox he builds a new
box around me.') This unsettling of paired terms is fundamental to
deconstruction. Christopher Norris describes the approach as a dis-
mantling of seemingly binary terms 'to the point where opposition
itself ... gives way to a process where opposites merge in a constant
undecidable exchange of attributes.'[2] Rather than simply inverting the
received order of priorities, and returning Batman to an uncomplicated, 1960s camp, or adopting an alternate-earth reversed hierarchy where Batman is Joker and Joker becomes Batman, we saw that
Morrison suggests instead an uncertainty, a shifting pattern of chronology and identity where the sci-fi, camp and Pop years took place,
but possibly partly as hallucinations and dreams; where Bat-Mite
could be a fifth-dimensional imp or a product of the imagination,
and where Batman and Joker seem to temporarily change places in
their wary dance, countering and mirroring each other in an eternal
pas de deux.

We can draw on this reading of the Batman/Joker relationship –
which itself mirrors, echoes and symbolically represents the broader
Dark Batman/Rainbow Batman relationship – to understand one

of Derrida's key terms, *différance*. Derrida starts from the concept that language, within structuralist theory,[3] is 'a *differential* network of meaning.'

> There is no self-evident or one-to-one link between 'signifier' and 'signified', the word as (spoken or written) vehicle and the concept it serves to evoke. Both are caught up in a play of distinctive features where differences of sound and sense are the only markers of meaning. Thus, at the simplest phonetic level, *bat* and *cat* are distinguished (and meaning is generated) by the switching of initial consonants.[4]

'Bat' and 'cat' are 'dependent on a structured economy of differences', where one defines the other. Derrida's poststructuralist concept of *différance* combines this sense of 'difference' with the concept of 'deferral' to imply that meaning is always postponed, and in a continual process of being formed. If we look up the signifier 'bat' in a dictionary, for instance, we are given multiple possible signifieds, from various sporting uses as a noun through verb and verb phrases (to strike a ball; to take a turn as batsman) and a second use of the word (to blink or flutter eyelashes) before we reach the meaning that refers to the flying mammal of the order Chiroptera. But to understand what this kind of bat is, we would have to look up 'mammal' and 'Chiroptera', which then become signifiers leading us in turn to further signifieds (vertebrates, Eutherian), which we would have to follow through, as signifiers, to a next level of signification in turn. Rather than a definitive answer and origin, we find only a relentless intertextual deferment of meaning, where one reference leads us to another: what Derrida calls 'the indefinite referral of signifier to signifier ... which gives the signified meaning no respite ... so that it always signifies again.'[5] Within this model, language is 'always inscribed in a network of relays and differential "traces".'[6]

Again, the concept is familiar from previous chapters, which have already explored the poststructuralist approach to meaning as an endless dialogue across a multidimensional map, whereby the text, or utterance, intersects with and is formed through its relationship with other texts. But Derrida's specific coinage of *différance* helps us to understand more clearly that the distinction between 'dark' and 'rainbow' Batman incarnations is not a binary opposition but a process within which meaning is forever postponed.

This process is illustrated in Julian Darius' article 'Erasing Burton: *Batman Begins*, Realism, and the Anxiety of Influence'. Darius notes that James Mottram's introduction to the *Batman Begins* screenplay distinguishes Nolan's reboot not just from Schumacher's two movies, but from 'the high-camp theatrics particularly prevalent in the ABC 1960s TV series starring Adam West and the four preceding feature films – Tim Burton's *Batman* (1989) and *Batman Returns* (1992) . . .'[7] Yet Burton's *Batman* was, at the time, promoted in terms of its proximity to Miller's *Dark Knight Returns* and its distance from the TV show. Articles from the late 1980s assured fans that 'this movie will go back to Batman's roots: mysterious, brooding, dark, somber' and that 'it's a grim film . . . they have tried to do it seriously.'[8] When Schumacher's *Batman & Robin* was released in 1997, Burton's first movie was held up by fans and professional critics as a nostalgic, authentic object: 'the first film wasn't perfect but it was clearly the best one. And it was the one that captured the dark mood the best.'[9]

Darius concludes that 'What we're dealing with here isn't a simple dichotomy between campy material and realistic material.'

Rather, we're looking at a continuum between the two – a spectrum of options. On the one extreme is the 1960s television show. Indeed, certain 1950s and early 1960s Batman comics may be seen as even more unrealistic than the 1960s TV show . . . on the other extreme is *Batman Begins*. But while *Batman Begins* is more realistic than most of Batman's comic book appearances, even in today's more generally pro-realism comic book market, the film is not without its unrealistic elements: the microwave emitter used to partially vaporize Gotham's water supply comes immediately to mind.[10]

Darius identifies, through his own struggle to pin down points of comparison, the slippery, fluid patterns through which 'realism' (for which read darkness, grittiness) is both defined through difference and endlessly deferred – precisely the double meaning that Derrida captures in *différance*. While Darius attempts to fix endpoints – he begins by placing *Batman Begins* and the TV show at opposite extremes – they immediately slide away, as he admits that some 1950s comics are 'more unrealistic' than Adam West's Batman, and that *Batman Begins* also contains elements of fantasy. We might now try to position *The Dark Knight* as the definitive 'realist' Batman – as Darius points out, *Batman Begins*, despite its efforts to depict a convincing Gotham City, involves 'stylized' elevated trains, which are stripped from Nolan's sequel – yet *The Dark Knight* also includes fantastic elements such as Harvey Dent's elaborately scarred face. Each 'realist' Batman can only be defined as such in comparison to an alternative, yet there is no terminal point of 'truth' or absolute origin to be found. The earliest Bob Kane creations, often held up as a definitive ur-text and source of the 'authentic' Batman, are cartoonish and crude in their artwork, dialogue and storytelling. The 1970s O'Neil and Adams stories, as we saw in Chapter Three, can equally be read as campy, overblown melodrama. The 1960s TV series is arguably more 'realistic' than any comic book, simply through its use of filmed live action rather than drawn interpretations. Frank Miller's *All Star Batman and Robin* goes to such an extreme of dark, gritty machismo that it arguably becomes camp parody. To impose a binary distinction on this fluid intertextual relay is to fix it at a certain point and deliberately construct a contrast from a network that in itself offers no absolute sense of truth, origin or authenticity. As we have seen, such binary distinctions invariably have an agenda behind them, and serve a certain purpose: and when we see such a distinction imposed on the network of meanings, we should ask *cui bono* – who benefits?[11]

'Deconstruction,' Christopher Norris reminds us, 'is not simply a strategic reversal of categories which otherwise remain distinct and unaffected. It seeks to undo both a given order or priorities *and* the very system of conceptual opposition that makes that order possible.'[12] Simply put, deconstruction involves a close reading of a text, concept or theory, which seeks to unsettle its internal, structuring oppositions. Deconstruction suggests that every binary opposition is based around a 'violent hierarchy',[13] in which one is implicitly superior to the other. For instance, in the distinction between 'dark Batman' and 'rainbow Batman', the discourses around Nolan's films always privilege the former as good, authentic, truthful object. Rather than attack these structures from the outside, deconstruction, through its careful and in many ways sympathetic analysis,[14] inhabits the system, explores it from the inside, and identifies the weak point that destabilises its order from within. This weak point is an inherent contradiction, a paradox, often a specific word that can have two possible meanings and functions in two very different ways.[15] This ambiguous, problematic term at the heart of the system becomes the self-destruct button that Derrida pushes to unsettle the fixed binary, nudging it into collapse by triggering the bomb it always already contained within itself.

Yet deconstruction is not destruction. It does not destroy the system so much as dismantle its components and push it playfully into fluid, endless motion, revealing it as a shifting relay between terms rather than an absolute and unquestionable distinction. Derrida's interrogation shows that 'the privileged term is held in place by the force of a dominant *metaphor,* and not (as it might seem) by any conclusive logic.'[16] Structures, binaries, hierarchies and oppositions are simply strategies of containment, imposed on 'the unruly energies of meaning.'[17]

Already, the relevance of this approach to the discussions of the last few chapters should be obvious. The source/adaptation dyad, the original/aberration distinction, and most fundamentally, the core opposition between serious and camp, dark and rainbow, realistic and silly, straight and queer, are all attempts to lock down the complex interplay of meanings that flow around Batman and his multiple texts. As should also be clear, I have argued that these strategies reduce and significantly impoverish the character and his myth by presenting a narrow reading – the privileged term in the binary – as original, true and realistic, and repressing or subjugating the other aspects which are equally inherent to Batman, his rich history and his diversity. As such, these strategies deny the multiplicity, the variety and the capacity to adapt that make Batman what he is as a cultural icon, and that have, in a very real sense, enabled him to survive today, rather than leaving him as a one-dimensional, dated pulp hero whose adventures ended, as did those of so many other comic book characters, in the 1940s.

In Chapter Four, I suggested that 'carnival', with its double-faced function as signifier of both Joker's subversive folk festival and of Batman's equally inherent theatricality, was a key to unsettling the binary between the characters, to seeing their roles not as a simple oppositional conflict but as a fluid exchange and complex dance, and in turn to seeing each iteration of Batman in terms of his (and his writer/producers') relative rejection or embracing of the aspects embodied by Joker; his position on a spectrum of carnival, from the rigidly repressive 'dark' vigilante to the more open, playful 'camp' crusader. I proposed that Morrison's portrayal of Batman as the gaudy, fantastical Zur-En-Arrh, his reopening of Batman's Sci-Fi closet, and his exploration of the Joker/Batman relationship as a fluid game of control and resistance, with Batman's containing frameworks inevitably as flexible and elastic as the Joker's wild schemes, productively destabilises the oppositions that have governed the 'dark', modern Batman for decades.

Of course, we can draw this reading from Morrison's Batman without identifying his writing as intentionally and self-consciously Derridean; while Morrison is well-read, there is no reason to assume he is familiar with this specific theory. However, his work does suggest a deliberate play with and overturning of binary oppositions. In *Earth 2*, for instance, we quickly learn that, contrary to our expectations – and to the surprise of the main characters – Batman's home universe, rather than the Owlman alternative, is the one named 'Earth 2', the reversed-earth. The heroes' attempts to impose their own kind of truth and justice on the corrupt world of their counterparts is undermined by the inherent logic of the opposite universe, and it is Batman who realises they have to think outside the box: 'Failure is our only option if we want to win.' Bringing the two worlds into potential collision, Brainiac, the story's arch-villain, boasts that he is 'beyond "good" and "evil". Beyond the moral and conceptual framework which limits 3rd-level intellects such as your own. I am free to upgrade and evolve!' Following Batman's lead, the heroes thwart Brainiac by temporarily slipping out of their usual roles and softening the oppositions that govern their own morality. 'You didn't count on *us* deliberately doing something *bad*,' Superman points out, with Wonder Woman adding 'Like walking *away* in the middle of a crisis.'

Morrison's *Final Crisis* (2008–2009) sees Superman facing his selfish, cynical counterpart again. 'If we mix our matter and anti-matter particles,' he warns the evil Ultraman, 'we *annihilate* each other.' 'So let's commit the *ultimate crime*, you and me *together*, eh?' Ultraman sneers, ready to throw a killer, suicidal punch. Yet again, the solution lies in transcending these binaries; this time, it lies in Captain Adam, a third alternate Superman who sees beyond simple dichotomies. 'All I had to do was let go,' he announces, 'Let go of limits, expectations'. By relaxing his perception of good and evil, matter and antimatter, he brings Superman and Ultraman together into a composite that combines the former's stalwart dedication with the latter's necessary ruthlessness. '"Dualities?" he wonders. 'No. There *are* no dualities. Only symmetries. I am *beyond* conflict. Hate crime. Meet *selfless act*.'[18]

As these stories suggest, and as I noted at the end of Chapter Four, the opposition between darkness and camp is not the only pairing that structures Batman's role and representation. The fundamental concept of a man dressing as a bat and becoming a fearsome urban vigilante does inherently – from the first story of May 1939 onwards – contain the contradiction between ridiculous disguise and realist drama that in turn informs and shapes the twin discourses of Batman as ludicrous camp and Batman as serious crime-fighter. However, Batman also – again, from his first adventure onwards – expresses an ambivalent relationship to society and the legal system, between order and anarchy. The caption that introduced Batman's original appearance described him as 'a mysterious and adventurous figure fighting for righteousness and apprehending the wrong doer, in his lone battle against the evil forces of society … his identity remains unknown.'[19] Already, he stands alone, with a mission founded on essential principles of right and wrong, good and evil, rather than formalities of law-breaking and institutional correction: from the first story, his methods are contrasted to those of the police and Commissioner Gordon. The dynamic between control and chaos that plays out in the Joker/Batman relationship is not simply about order versus carnival, or repression versus libido; it also describes Batman's shifting position on a spectrum from cop to criminal, insider to outlaw. This fluid alignment, where Batman is again defined, and again, where any fixed meaning is deferred, through comparison with and contrast to a range of secondary figures – from *Dark Knight Returns'* uptight, upright Commissioner Yindel and the corrupt cops of *Year One*, through the pragmatic ethics of Commissioner Gordon and the two-faced morals of Harvey Dent, to the capricious selfishness of Catwoman and the epitome of anarchy, Joker – is central to a range of modern Batman texts. It also informs Nolan's films, and in *The Dark Knight* in particular, acquires a particular contemporary inflection: rather than questioning the distinction between cop and criminal, Nolan's sequel, engaging with 'post-9/11' social concerns, interrogates the relationship between terrorist and counterterrorist.

I suggest in this chapter, then, that *The Dark Knight* can also, like Morrison's authorship of the comic during the same period, be read through a deconstructive approach to Batman and the relationships that define him. However, while they have in common the fact that they can be interpreted as a destabilisation of oppositions, Nolan's focus is distinct from Morrison's, and explores (and explodes) a different set of paired terms. Just as Bakhtin's theory of carnival provided a way into reading Morrison's narrative, so we can find further tools for examining Nolan's second Batman film in one of Derrida's key case studies, 'Plato's Pharmacy'.

'Plato's Pharmacy' is a story about a story about a story. It discusses the *Phaedrus*, a Socratic dialogue that was recorded by Plato;[20] and within this dialogue, Socrates retells an Egyptian myth about the god Theuth[21] and the King of all Egypt, Thamus. At the heart of these nested narratives is the fable of Theuth coming to King Thamus and offering the gift of writing to the Egyptian people. Or at least, 'gift' is how the word is translated at this point: the original Greek is '*pharmakon*'. In Derrida's account, Theuth offers writing as 'a recipe for both memory and wisdom.'[22] The king declines it as 'a poisoned present.' Like the word *Gift* – innocent in English, but 'poison', in German – the *pharmakon* has been revealed as two-faced; it was offered by Theuth as a positive remedy, but rejected by King Thamus as an evil drug.

Thamus' distrust of this offer is based around a binary opposition that Derrida pursues through a series of language relays, following linguistic echoes to argue that the King's rejection is symptomatic of a deeper, underlying set of oppositions. Most obviously, Thamus makes his choice based on the claim that speech is superior to writing. Writing, he argues, is merely a set of lifeless inscriptions that substitute for the living presence of the speaker. 'Thanks to you and your invention, your pupils will widely be read without benefit of a teacher's instruction.'[23] This distinction is therefore bound up with patriarchal values that serve the monarch's dominant order – 'the king, the father of speech, has thus asserted his authority over the father of writing'[24] – and by extension justify the role of tutor-philosophers like Socrates and indeed Plato, which is why this particular fable was chosen. More broadly, though as Norris points out, 'in this respect, Egyptian mythology agrees with that other, Judeo-Christian account of God's creating word.'[25] This logocentric distinction, privileging the spoken word and presence of the symbolic Father (King, God, teacher, preacher and patriarch) over the external signs of written language, structures 'a quite extraordinary range of the world's religions and systems of thought.'[26] As Derrida explains:

> Plato had to make his tale conform to structural laws. The most general of these, those that govern and articulate the oppositions speech/writing, life/death, father/son, master/servant, first/second, legitimate son/orphan-bastard, soul/body, inside/outside, good/ evil, seriousness/play, day/night, sun/moon, etc., also govern, and according to the same configurations, Egyptian, Babylonian, and Assyrian mythology. And others, too, no doubt … [27]

Already, then, we can see that Thamus' act of rejection stands for a fundamental, wide-ranging hierarchical distinction, and furthermore, that it constitutes an act of control over ambiguity, reducing potential double-meaning to a singularity. The *pharmakon* was offered as a remedy and rejected as a poison; its meaning was revealed momentarily as fluid, but then quickly fixed in place. 'It is precisely this ambiguity,' says Derrida, 'that Plato, through the mouth of the King, attempts to master, to dominate by inserting its definition into simple, clear-cut oppositions: good and evil, inside and outside, true and false, essence and appearance.'[28]

Yet we can also see cracks appearing in this containment strategy. As we have already recognised in the previous chapters, any attempt to impose a clear-cut, binary opposition on a complex relay inevitably results in slippage and struggle. The relationship between cultural and textual energies is a process, not a neat division; black will always seep into white and colour will show through darkness. As Norris notes, Plato's text already invites deconstruction of its attempted opposites through the fact that, while Socrates speaks aloud as 'master of instruction' and bearer of the traditional patriarchal word, Plato 'obediently *writes it down.*'[29] Furthermore, Derrida observes that Socrates' attempt to validate speech over writing takes the form not of 'a rational discourse or *logos*', but 'a well-known rumor ... hearsay evidence ... a fable transmitted from ear to ear.' Socrates 'thus begins by repeating without knowing – through a myth – the definition of writing, which is to repeat without knowing.'[30] Thirdly, Derrida shows that Socrates describes, and derides, writing as an inferior version of legitimate discourse; yet in making this contrast he praises the 'good' discourse as that which 'goes together with knowledge and is written in the soul of the learner'.[31] Speaking is therefore, in a grand irony, celebrated as a form of writing: 'the good one,' Derrida points out, 'can be designated only through the metaphor of the bad one.'[32] As we have consistently seen, in defining one term as truthful, original, authentic and valid, its opposite is always made visible; and it is often shown, inconveniently, not to be such an opposite after all.

The key to the destabilisation of these oppositions, however, lies at the heart of the story. It was always already there, a bomb in the King's palace waiting to be detonated; and as is the nature of deconstruction, Derrida simply uses the tool that Plato provided himself to take the oppositions apart from the inside. In the story, as we have seen, Theuth presents writing as a 'remedy' that is rejected as a 'poison'. Derrida then shows that the two terms are not as distinct as Plato would like to claim, as the 'good' discourse (speech) is defined by and overlaps with the 'bad' (writing). Yet simply exposing the central term as a binary that can be reversed is not enough.

> ... this is not a question of simply *inverting* the received order of priorities, so that henceforth 'writing' will somehow take precedence over 'speech' and its various associated values. More than this, it involves the dismantling of all those binary distinctions that organize Plato's text, to the point where opposition itself ... gives way to a process where opposites merge in a constant *undecidable* exchange of attributes.[33]

Pharmakon, Derrida shows, has more than two connotations. It can be translated in various ways, with contradictory implications, as 'remedy', 'recipe', 'poison', 'drug' or 'philter'. Translation inevitably fixes its malleability and pins it down, depending on context, to a single signification, but the word is inherently multiple, constantly in motion between meanings.[34] Theuth, with a specific agenda, interrupts this motion and stops *pharmakon* at its positive aspect when he presents it as a gift:

> he *turns* the word on its strange and invisible pivot, presenting it from a single one, the most reassuring of its *poles*. This medicine is beneficial; it repairs and produces, accumulates and remedies, increases knowledge and reduces forgetfulness. Its translation by 'remedy' nonetheless erases, in going outside the Greek language, the other pole reserved in the word *pharmakon*. It cancels out the resources of ambiguity.[35]

So Theuth presents a positive side of the term (remedy, medicine) in making his pitch; but the King, Derrida suggests, sets the word in motion again, stopping it to reveal a second, more negative implication (suspect magic potion) and then a third (poison).[36] Thamus rejects writing on two fronts, for two reasons: it is both a dangerous

occult power and a harmful substance. The *pharmakon* is not, therefore, simply a two-faced opposition[37] but a dynamic, a set of relations
between different functions, a 'passage among opposing values'.[38]
Derrida's attempts to communicate the multiple meanings of *pharmakon* convey a sense of movement, fluidity and flow that does not
just overturn and reverse oppositions, but resists binary structures:
to translate it either as 'poison' or 'remedy' reduces the term to only
one of its many faces, but to render it as 'poison/remedy' would also
oversimplify its nature.

'The *pharmakon* is always caught in the mixture ... painful pleasure ... it partakes of both good and ill, of the agreeable and the disa-
greeable. Or rather, it is within its mass that these oppositions are
able to sketch themselves out.'[39] The *pharmakon* is not a binary opposition; it is a process, like energy travelling back and forth, rather
than a light switch whose only possibilities are off and on. It can be
stopped in its relay, to serve a particular purpose – as Theuth does
when he presents it as a positive, and when Thamus does, to reject it
on two counts – but these are interruptions of its to and fro, its flow.

These ideas already chime with our previous discussion of Batman
and Joker, darkness and camp, original and adaptation as a matrix,
network or relay rather than an imposed (and always hierarchical)
pairing, opposition or dyad. The parallels between Derrida's deconstructive approach and the Bakhtinian ideas explored in Chapter
Four should also be apparent, although the distinctions between the
two are also significant. While, as we saw, Bakhtin's concept of carnival overlaps with his theories of literary discourse and language,
his discussion of the grotesque is concerned primarily with the socio-
historical dynamic between festivals and rituals, whereas Derrida's
focus is more on the inner workings of textuality. Seen this way,
Bakhtin's object of study is broader, and concerned with patterns of
cultural repression and celebration, people and power, while Derrida
minutely unpicks the contradictions in writing and thought. In turn,
though, Derrida uses his close textual studies as the springboard for
a sweeping challenge to dominant belief systems: the detail of a single sentence or word becomes the explosive with which he unsettles
the hierarchies of Western ideology and philosophy.

As we saw above, for instance, he reveals '*pharmakon*' as the unstable keystone supporting not just a single narrative but a system of cultural binaries between writing and speech, father and son, legitimate and bastard, seriousness and play: when that key-word shifts, so do the structures on which it is built. As such, we could see Derrida as developing the implications of Bakhtin's work into a powerful and wide-ranging critical theory: a weapon that pinpoints and problematises a crucial, vulnerable contradiction, which then acts as a trigger to destabilise surrounding frameworks. In this respect, Derrida's focus is both more precise and more extensive than Bakhtin's; deconstruction interrogates the micro level of the word, scaling up its findings boldly, dizzyingly, to the macro level of philosophy and ideology, leaping the middle level of the novel's literary form and the city square's public forum that Bakhtin occupies.

I will go on to suggest that the depiction of poison and remedy as a fluid relationship rather than a binary itself offers a further insight into the Joker/Batman dynamic, enabling us to revisit the concept of the two figures on a spectrum rather than at opposite poles, and to see them also as occupying shifting, sometimes interchangeable positions on the range between good and evil, chaos and order, terror and counter-terror, as well as carnival and repression or containment and queerness.

Yet it is when Derrida extends the *pharmakon*'s destabilising power, and proposes that this always-ambiguous concept underlies, and undermines, a series of broader cultural oppositions, that 'Plato's Pharmacy' intersects more obviously with the details of the Batman myth, and specifically with Nolan's articulation of that myth in *The Dark Knight*.

Derrida has already suggested that the opposition between 'good' speech and 'bad' writing has implications far beyond this specific Egyptian fable, and the Greek retelling of it; it is a narrative that serves the logocentric, patriarchal authority that informed, and continues to inform, dominant systems of belief. The speech/writing binary echoes and reinforces the underlying hierarchical pairs – life/death, father/son, legitimate son/orphan-bastard, good/evil, seriousness/play – that structure Western tradition and philosophy.

But Derrida playfully pursues the linguistic trail of *pharmakon*, following a chain of 'pharmaceutical' metaphors[40] to suggest further oppositions. *Pharmakos*, for instance, carries the meaning of 'magician, wizard', but also 'poisoner' and 'scapegoat'; a figure in Greek culture who was sacrificed for the sake of the city in times of emergency.[41]

Yet like the *pharmakon*, the *pharmakos* carries not just doubled but multiple, unstable meanings. 'Wizard' and 'poisoner' already convey the two-sided aspect of the medicine that can kill or cure, and the further dimension of a dangerous, occult substance; but the 'scapegoat' figure is also a complex, contradictory role in itself. Derrida points out that while the sacrifice was a 'purification ... of the suffering city', designed to drive evil outside 'by violently excluding from its territory the representative of an external threat or aggression', the scapegoat was raised, fed and selected within the city boundaries, and so was 'at the very heart of the inside'.

> The ceremony of the *pharmakos* is thus played out on the boundary line between inside and outside, which it has as its function ceaselessly to trace and retrace. *Intra muros/extra muros.* The origin of difference and division, the *pharmakos* represents evil both introjected and projected. Beneficial insofar as he cures – and for that, venerated and cared for – harmful insofar as he incarnates the powers of evil – and for that, feared and treated with caution. Alarming and calming. Sacred and accursed.[42]

'The pharmacy is also, we begin to perceive, a theater,' Derrida proposes.[43] It is an arena for symbolic meaning, structured by oppositions that shift and lose their fixed positions once the key word, *pharmakon*, is revealed as unstable. The magician is suddenly indistinguishable from the poisoner and the medic; a dangerous gift becomes a remedy or cure. Just as Plato used figures from Egyptian myth to serve his argument, so we can place the archetypes from our modern myth on the same pharmaceutical stage. We can see in this setting, for instance, why Batman never kills Joker or even casts him successfully out of the city, but imprisons him instead, always uselessly and temporarily, in the limbo of Arkham, an asylum-city on the borders of Gotham;[44] because he is part of the city, part of Gotham's body, part of Batman, and his inevitable escape and return to the place and person that created him is part of the repeated ritual.

We can see Joker again in the further variations that Derrida draws from the *pharmakon*. He reminds us, for instance, that *pharmaka* means 'painter's colours', linked thematically and linguistically both to the magician, the writer and illusionist, and to the poison/cure of writing: 'the magic of writing and painting is like a cosmetic concealing the dead under the appearance of the living.'

> The *pharmakon* introduces and harbours death. It makes the corpse presentable, masks it, makes it up … deaths, masks, makeup, all are part of the festival that subverts the order of the city, its smooth regulation by the dialectician and the science of being. Plato, as we shall see, is not long in identifying writing with festivity. And play. A certain festival, a certain game.[45]

One aspect of the *pharmakon*, then, is make-up, the corpse covered in cosmetics. 'That chemical vapour,' Joker exclaims, recalling his own origin when he crawled back to life, baptised by drowning in toxic waste. 'It turned my hair *green*, my lips *rouge-red*, my skin *chalk-white*! I look like an *evil clown!*'[46] By extension, the *pharmakon* is linked to festival, carnival and play. Plato, Derrida tells us, celebrates play only when it is 'supervised and contained within the safeguards of ethics and politics', reduced and confined to safe, calendar-based formalities. We might think here of the Joker's taunting slogan in the advertising for *The Dark Knight*, 'why so serious?', and remember the fact that the viral campaign for the movie was based around 'Jokerised' versions of websites, posters and images, scribbled over with graffiti in wild red text. In a motif that recalls the almost-unreadable scarlet font of Joker's textual 'speech' in *Arkham Asylum*, the carnival Joker energy that infected the official publicity materials for *The Dark Knight* took the form of *writing*. Not even typing, but handwriting: scrawled, hasty, libidinal, mocking messages like lipstick on a mirror or spray paint on a wall, vandalising the steely blue seriousness of Batman's images with a slash of make-up.[47]

Writing is defined in Plato's account in contrast to the living immediacy of speech: as a set of external signs, rather than the authoritative presence of the King/Father/teacher, 'it is weakened speech, something not completely dead: a living-dead, a reprieved corpse, a deferred life, a semblance of breath.'[48] These images, again, recall Joker in his form as carnival grotesque. Yet Derrida pushes further. Writing is 'like someone who has lost his rights, an outlaw, a pervert, a bad seed, a vagrant, an adventurer, a bum. Wandering in the streets, he doesn't know who he is, what his identity – if he has one – might be, what his name is, what his father's name is. He repeats the same thing each time he is questioned on the street corner, but he can no longer repeat his origin.'[49] He is the lost son, 'wandering like a desire or like a signifier freed from *logos*, this individual who is not even perverse in a regular way, who is ready to do anything, to lend himself to anyone ...'[50] He is an 'adventurer' who 'simulates everything at random and is really nothing. Swept off by every stream, he belongs to the masses; he has no essence, no truth, no patronym ...'[51] He is the bad seed, the 'lost trace', 'everything in sperm that overflows wastefully, a force wandering outside the domain of life, incapable of engendering anything ... on the opposite side, living speech makes its capital bear fruit and does not divert its seminal potency towards indulgence in pleasures without paternity.'[52] Derrida links this prohibition against waste and lack of libidinal control to 'make-up, masks, simulacra ... games and festivals, which can never go without some sort of urgency or outpouring of sperm',[53] and with the Greek law around 'abstention from congress with our own sex, with its deliberate murder of the race and its wasting of the seed of life.'[54]

This is itself rich and potent material, and from it we can develop our understanding of the Joker-function within this oppositional structure. Joker can clearly be associated with one side of the binary: with writing, with poison, with masks and carnival, with rebirth and the living dead, with queerness and wasted seed, with a bad son and wandering vagrant, with a scapegoat raised within the city and sacrificed to save it, with a nameless, fatherless identity, with a free-flowing libidinal signifier that has no origin and belongs to anyone.

But so can Batman.

The *pharmakon* is, as we learned, never fixed in meaning; it flows from one term to another. Theuth, presenting this gift/poison to the King, himself embodies the ambiguous offering: 'in distinguishing himself from his opposite, Thoth also imitates it, becomes its sign and representative, obeys it and *conforms* to it ... he cannot be assigned a fixed spot in the play of differences. Sly, slippery and masked, an intriguer and a card, like Hermes, he is neither king nor jack, but rather a sort of *joker*, a floating signifier, a wild card, one who puts play into play.'[55]

But so is Batman. Every term cited above in relation to Joker could apply equally to his antagonist. Batman embodies masks, disguise and carnival. He is a cure for Gotham but also, as we'll see, a poison. He is the city's protector but is pursued by its police; he is an outlaw and adventurer, exiled from public society as a scapegoat. His life as 'Bruce Wayne' ended with his parents' death, and began again when he was reborn as Batman; his existence is governed by ritual repetition, endless and pointless symbolic attempts to avenge their murders through the cycle of a never-ending 'war on crime'.[56] As a myth, Batman risks being everything and therefore nothing; he is in danger of belonging to everyone, signifying so freely that his identity is lost.[57] As we saw in *Year One* and *RIP*, he even keeps a handwritten journal.

This reading of Batman helps us to understand, again, the processes of control that operate to keep him separate from Joker – both within the diegesis of the Batman fiction and extra-textually, through production, authorial and fan discourses. Batman's origin is, for instance, retold so many times, and so regularly, because of its importance to his identity: it reasserts the symbolic presence of his father, who appears surprisingly frequently in Batman narratives for a long-dead man.[58] Thomas Wayne's profession as doctor effectively turns the ambiguous *pharmakon* to its face as 'remedy' and 'cure', in an attempt to fix Batman's position on the 'good' side of this fluid structure; but more fundamentally, Bruce's memories of his father, and the assurance that he is following in his father's tradition, locate him as the 'good son', associated with patriarchy, presence and heterosexuality. This association also explains Batman's own drive to recruit first symbolic sons, then real ones – after years of having Robin as his ward, he formally adopted Tim Drake, then discovered a blood relationship in Damian Wayne. Although there is every practical reason for Batman not to have a brightly coloured sidekick, and his partnerships have almost invariably ended in tension and tragedy, Batman clearly feels a need to continue a symbolic patriarchy, to establish himself as a traditional and present father figure and therefore distinguish himself firmly from the queer, wasteful sexual energies of Joker. His corporate 'family', from the small group of allies such as Robin, Nightwing and Batgirl to his current global network in the *Batman Incorporated* series, is further evidence of this obsession with being not just a good son, but a good father: and each new recruit is brought into the fold through a solemn, quasi-religious ritual that casts Batman in the even more exalted light of spiritual father or priest.

The significance of this patriarchal order, of origins and identity, is demonstrated in Morrison's 'Zur-En-Arrh' storyline, discussed in the previous chapter. When Batman loses his sense of self and forgets the 'Wayne' name, abandoned by his father's symbolic presence, he becomes, quite literally, a vagrant and a wandering bum; he dresses in hand-sewn, gaudy rags and, as we saw, comes closer to overlapping, even crossing places with the Joker than he would ever allow in his usual, regimented and strictly controlled persona. Again, my point is not simply that Batman and Joker are interchangeable figures, but that they have the potential to be, and that various strategies are used both within and outside the fiction to separate them: the effort involved to keep Batman distinct from his trickster partner is as striking as the similarities between them.

The Dark Knight

The association of Joker with poison, both literal and metaphorical, dates back to his earliest appearances and echoes through his modern age incarnation. His first crime, in Spring 1940, was a poisoning ('The venom works well! Our little *game* is finished!').[59]

His first origin story, in February 1951, had him transformed by 'chemical wastes', a toxic immersion replayed in *The Killing Joke*. *Year One* ends with Joker threatening 'to poison the Gotham reservoir'; *The Dark Knight Returns* has Joker's followers, 'their skin ... painted chalk white, their hair dyed green', carrying out a copycat crime. However, the suggestion that Batman could also, despite his mission to 'cure' the city, have a corruptive influence, is a recurrent recent theme.

In *The Long Halloween*, Gordon muses of the costumed villains, 'So many are here. Nearly *double* from when you first appeared. Not that there is a direct correlation, but ... do you give it any thought?' 'No', replies Batman firmly, but adds, internally, 'I know what Gordon is implying. That my ... *presence* ... somehow *attracts* these men and women to my city ...'[60] In *Face to Face*, set in contemporary continuity, Gotham cop Bullock asks the same question: 'I've been thinking, *why* do villains *flock* here ... like birds? So many *clustered* ... they cling to Gotham and tell the *same* story over and over.'[61] In Azzarello's *Joker* from 2008, a petty crook watches the climactic hand-to-hand combat between Batman and the eponymous villain. 'I see *you*,' runs the narration. 'A disease. One that has been around longer than Gotham. The city infected. There will *always* be a Joker. Because there's *no cure* for him. No cure at all. Just a *Batman*.' Joker is presented as an eternal poisonous force, locked in a relay with his opponent: but Batman is no cure, either, and may be quite the opposite.[62] Michael Green and Denys Cowan's *Batman: Lovers and Madmen* destablises the relationship still further, with Joker styling himself as a doctor for Gotham's citizens in order to attract the Batman: 'Maybemaybe they need some medicine too. Poor sickies. I cut up the city ... I give the people their medicine ... but he still won't come. Doesn't he care?' Alfred, in turn, accuses Batman directly of creating the Joker. '*You* did this. You unleashed something foul and depraved. On those whose lives you swore to improve. A dead thing. Killed by you. That makes things more dead.' His imagery is vivid: *The Killing Joke* and Tim Burton's *Batman* also indirectly blame the Dark Knight for Joker's transformation, but Green evokes a sense of Batman as an evil magus reanimating a corpse.

This notion of Batman as *pharmakon* – poison and remedy, good doctor and dangerous magician – also informs *Batman Begins*, as Justine Toh discusses in her article 'The Tools and Toys of (the) War (on Terror)'.[63] Here, of course, Batman faces a form of proto-Joker in the Scarecrow, but the focus on toxin and cure, and the lack of clear distinction between them, remains central. More specifically, in *Batman Begins*, the key term is fear: Batman's childhood trauma becomes his tool, and he fights crime using, essentially, the same weapon as the Scarecrow. In one scene, their thematic overlap is literalised, as Batman intimidates Scarecrow using his own toxin – 'taste of your own medicine, doctor?' – and appears to him as a demon. The CGI hallucination sequences, though out of keeping with the film's claim for a certain form of 'realism', were, as we saw in Chapter Three, justified by Nolan as 'rooted in science'; while this may seem like a strained rationalisation, the blurring of boundaries between science, fantasy and magic is inherent to the Batman milieu. Key aspects of the Batman diegesis – such as Joker's transformation by chemicals into a corpse-like madman – are explained in terms of pseudo-science, but owe more to the folk- or fairy-tale. Batman's citywide sonar, and his ability to reconstruct a fingerprint from a shattered bullet in *The Dark Knight*, are similarly fantastical sequences with only a superficial basis in digital technology. Yet this mixing of science with magic is also entirely in keeping with the *pharmakon* and its multiple meanings: King Thamus rejected the gift not just as a poison, but as an occult artefact. Theuth, the masked trickster who embodies the *pharmakon*, is characterised 'by this unstable ambivalence. This god of calculation, arithmetic, and rational science also presides over the occult sciences, astrology and alchemy.'[64] Batman's conflation of ritual and rationality – his use of technology to conjure a spirit animal, his use of military strategy and deduction to create an urban legend – is entirely in keeping with a reading of him as the fluid *pharmakon*, the 'floating signifier' of Derrida's account.[65] More specifically yet, both Batman and Scarecrow in *Batman Begins* embody Derrida's argument that 'the fear of death is what gives all witchcraft, all occult medicine, a hold.' The *pharmakos*, in his fluid forms as doctor, magician and poisoner, 'is banking on that fear.'

It is the child in us that is afraid. The charlatans will all disappear when the 'little boy within us' no longer fears death as he fears a *mormolukeion*, a scarecrow set up to frighten children, a bogeyman.[66]

The final scene of *Batman Begins* signals that this theme of curative poison and poisonous cure will continue in the sequel. 'What about escalation?' asks Gordon. 'We start carrying semiautomatics, they buy automatics ... we start wearing Kevlar, they buy armor-piercing rounds ... and ... you're wearing a *mask* and jumping off rooftops ...' Here he wryly observes that the new guy in town has 'a taste for theatrics, like you ... leaves a calling card.' The card, of course, is a Joker, but it could equally apply to Batman, who has his own brand and symbol: indeed, one of the posters for *The Dark Knight* shows Joker holding up a Batman playing card, while Batman presents the Bat-shuriken that leaves his mark (and corporate marque). *The Dark Knight*, then, is built around the same central ambiguity between hero and villain, and much of its drama is based in this tension and potential overlap: Joker's agenda is to make Batman cross the boundary between them, and Batman struggles to resist. However, while the theme continues from the previous film, and develops the recurring idea of 'escalation' from the modern comic book tradition, as noted above, it also acquires a distinct socio-political inflection. Put simply, *The Dark Knight* is not about fear, but terror, with all the specific cultural associations that word evokes in the twenty-first century. The escalation from Scarecrow's small-scale frights to a broader, more serious threat is signalled in the first two minutes, when Joker's accomplices discuss his make-up. 'To scare people,' one of them explains. 'You know ... *war paint*.'

We saw in Chapter One that *Slate* writer Dana Stevens credited Nolan with turning 'the Manichean morality of comic books— pure good vs. pure evil—into a bleak post-9/11 allegory.' Of the 44 reviews of *The Dark Knight* I examined in this study, 22 referred to the film's political implications, ranging from direct identification and detailed discussion of imagery and themes relating to 11 September 2001 and the subsequent 'war on terror', to a passing recognition that the film describes Joker as a terrorist. More broadly, an online search for *The Dark Knight* including keywords such as 'Bush', 'Obama' and '9/11' turned up 62 further articles and news stories, including more extensive examination of the film's political themes and coverage of its unexpected, unofficial spin-offs, such as the 'Jokerised' images of Barack Obama.

Stevens' identification of *The Dark Knight* as a post-9/11 allegory was, then, far from unique. Sonny Bunch, as we saw, described it in *The Washington Times* as 'the first great post-Sept. 11 film.' Benjamin Kerstein, in *AzureOnline*, praised it as 'a surprisingly explicit allegory to our current age of terrorism, the challenge it presents to traditional ideas of heroism, and America's own ambivalence in confronting this challenge.'[67] Cosmo Landesman in the *Sunday Times* felt that 'the deathly pall of 9/11' hung over the film;[68] *The Philadelphia Inquirer*'s Carrie Rickey dubbed it 'a grim snapshot of America in the wake of 9/11'.[69] Yet while there was broad agreement that the film in some way articulated post-9/11 concerns, there remained surprising dissent over its political message. In fact, readings of the film's ideological agenda fell into several incompatible camps, with commentators drawing polarised interpretations from the same text.

Aside from the explicit description of Joker as a terrorist, and visual motifs such as the poster's image of a burning skyscraper and the slow camera glide into the side of a building, punctuated by an explosion, that opens the film, the journalistic discussion of *The Dark Knight* as an expression of post-9/11 concerns centred around a handful of key scenes, usefully summarised and contextualised by John Ip in his article 'The Dark Knight's War on Terrorism'. As Ip notes, several aspects of the film, such as 'the Joker's grainy homemade videos, cell-phone detonated human bombs, burnt out remains of buildings swarming with rescue workers', give the film 'a distinctly post-9/11 aesthetic', but its interpretation as a 'parable about the dilemmas that face society when confronting terrorism and terrorists' explores three specific policies.[70]

Firstly, Batman's snatch-and-grab of the money-launderer Lau from Hong Kong 'recalls the practice of rendition ... the capture and transfer, sometimes forcible, of a suspect for the purpose of allowing that person to face charges in the United States.'[71] Secondly, both Dent and Batman violently question and threaten suspects in 'scenes of torture and coercive interrogation',[72] which suggest the Bush Administration's authorisation of similar techniques on 'high value' Al Qaeda detainees. Thirdly, Batman develops a surveillance system that, Ip notes, 'is a clear allusion to the surveillance program run by the National Security Agency (NSA) after 9/11.'[73]

Spencer Ackerman, in *The Washington Independent*, argues that 'the concepts of security and danger presented in Christopher Nolan's new Batman epic, *The Dark Knight*, align ... perfectly with those of the Office of the Vice President ... *The Dark Knight* weighs in strongly on the side of the Bush administration.' Drawing on the three policies outlined by Ip, Ackerman proposes that Nolan's Batman must 'work, though, sort of the dark side, if you will. We've got to spend time in the shadows.'

> That quote, of course, is Dick Cheney's only explicit statement of purpose to the American people about where he thought U.S. foreign policy needed to go in the post-9/11 world, delivered on "Meet the Press" on Sept. 16, 2001.

> In the wake of that statement, Cheney and his allies created an unprecedented architecture of institutionalized abuse. The CIA would possess the power to kidnap suspected terrorists around the world, hold them indefinitely in undisclosed detention facilities — or hand them over to partner intelligence services that use torture — and torture them in the name of intelligence gathering. [...] The National Security Agency, in violation of the Foreign Intelligence Surveillance Act, would wiretap the communications of U.S. persons without warrants.[74]

'Attempting to understand Al Qaeda in order to confront it on its own terms was the stuff of the weak and the unsure,' Ackerman suggests. 'The Bush administration instead set out, in a morally Manichean way, to ensure that the U.S. became as fearsome as possible.' Matthew Yglesias, writing in *The Atlantic,* agrees that '*Dark Knight*'s Batman sees himself the way Dick Cheney sees himself ... heroes need to be backstopped by folks who are hard enough to walk on the dark side and to accept the public's scorn.'[75] Yet while the two authors agree that Batman's actions are analogous to Bush policy, Ackerman deplores the film's apparent endorsement of this approach – 'in the real world, this concept is ludicrous and anti-American'[76] – while Yglesias hesitates: 'does that mean that the movie is saying that Cheney is *right*? Well I think that's complicated.'[77]

Andrew Klavan's 'What Bush and Batman Have in Common', in the *Wall Street Journal*, offers a third reading. Klavan claims there is 'no question that the Batman film *The Dark Knight* ... is on some level a paean of praise to the fortitude and moral courage that has been shown by George W. Bush in this time of terror and war. Like W, Batman is vilified and despised for confronting terrorists in the only terms they understand. Like W, Batman sometimes has to push the boundaries of civil rights to deal with an emergency, certain that he will reestablish those boundaries when the emergency is past.' Yet Klavan applauds the film's conservatism and its portrayal of a hero who 'often must slink in the shadows, slump-shouldered and despised': only when more films adopt this 'real moral complexity', he claims, 'will we be able to pay President Bush his due and make good and true films about the war on terror.'[78] Similarly, conservative commentator Glenn Beck enthused that 'this is quite possibly the best movie on the war on terror I have ever seen.' Recognising the same key scenes as representative of rendition and surveillance, Beck is overwhelmed by the film's endorsement of his own beliefs: 'Batman is George W. Bush ... I mean ... eavesdropping, Batman starts eavesdropping and, you know, there's an outrage on it. He's, like, got to do what you got to do, brother.'[79]

By contrast, Steve Schneider cites the film's 'nods to terrorism, domestic surveillance and even sanctioned torture' as expressions of anxiety over 'the resurgent politics of hope', and sees Batman not as Cheney or Bush but Barack Obama, or a side of him.

> Shot largely on location in Chicago – the home, remember, of the 'new' Democratic party – the movie apportions progressive

activism between two mirror-image protagonists, Batman (Christian Bale) and crusading District Attorney Harvey Dent (Aaron Eckhart). The two of them, semiotically speaking, add up to one Obama: Batman is the (literally) black half, respected but feared by a citizenry that worries about his true allegiances and motivations. Meanwhile, Dent is lauded as the 'white knight' of Gotham, his bid to clean up organized crime a campaign swathed in respectability and charm.

'The film movingly illustrates,' Schneider concludes, 'that only Gotham can save Gotham – that, as Patti Smith once observed, "People Have the Power." (Or as somebody else has averred, "Yes, we can.")'[80]

Steve Biodrowski, in *Cinefantastique*, reads the surveillance and interrogation scenes as distinct from, and therefore critical of, Bush policy.

> Unlike the Bush administration, it is clear that Wayne does not anticipate an unending war that will permanently justify an expansion of his powers. In fact, in a subplot that riffs off of the domestic spying issue, Batman deliberately puts his surveillance power in the hands of the one man who objects to it morally, and Batman also provides him with the code that will self-destruct the device when its purpose has been served. This is precisely the opposite of the Bush-Cheney approach, in which crisis and emergency are not only embraced but deliberately prolonged as an excuse for maintaining a grip on power.[81]

Equally, although 'the film invites us to cheer when Gordon, a police officer, allows Batman, a vigilante, to interrogate the Joker ... the effort proves a total failure. The audience may enjoy a vicarious thrill at Batman's extra-legal measures, but taking off the velvet gloves is useless against the Joker's brand of villainy; getting down and dirty only plays into his scheme, such as it is.'[82] John Ip, finally, takes a similar stance, arguing that Lau's capture in *The Dark Knight* is not comparable to extraordinary rendition, that Batman's use of electronic tracking is quite different from the Bush administration's

'Terrorist Surveillance Programme', and that 'the use of torture and coercion in *The Dark Knight* is uniformly ineffective.'[83] The film, Ip proposes, 'is plainly not an endorsement of perhaps the most controversial aspect of the Bush Administration's war on terror. Indeed, it is better seen as a critique.'[84]

That the text can be read in such diverse ways, the interpretations coinciding on some points and conflicting in others, is testament to its complexity: specifically, it demonstrates the unstable, fluid terms and positions within *The Dark Knight*'s moral universe. As suggested above, these positions are occupied and embodied not just by Joker and Batman, but also by the other, secondary figures who shape them in a signifying chain of meanings, a shifting ethical network. Batman and Joker, like Dent, Gordon, Rachel Dawes and mob boss Sal Maroni, are not fixed in place but defined – and their definitions deferred – through dialogue, interaction, comparison and conflict with each other, like pieces on a game board or words in a dictionary.

Joker in particular, as we would expect, defies fixed meaning, and succeeds in frustrating Gordon, Dent and Batman's attempts to control him precisely through his unpredictability; yet key to his subversive power is the fact that he engages with their terms, seeming to make sense and, literally, speak their language as he echoes key phrases from their dialogue. For example, the slogan that became his catchphrase through the film's promotional campaign, 'Why so serious?' is contradicted by his early chiding to the mobsters, 'give me a call when you want to start taking things a little more *seriously*,' which in turn mocks Batman's grave solemnity and subtly preempts Dent's later line to Rachel as he offers her romantic commitment, 'let's be serious, then.'

Similarly, Joker's line during his handheld video, 'Starting tonight, people will die ... I'm a man of my word', enters into and subverts the other characters' ongoing discussions about trust. Batman asks Gordon, of Dent, 'Do you trust him?' and tells Alfred 'Need to know if he can be trusted', then, convinced of Dent's intentions, throws him a trust fund party. Dent and Gordon, at odds over the corruption in Gotham's police force, argue over where to keep Lau: 'You

trust them over at County?' 'I don't trust them here.' Between the
other characters, *trust* signals a bond, promise and (financial) pledge:
Joker twists the term, revealing that it can, in another context, be a
threat. His choice of a nurse outfit as he destroys a hospital can be
read as a similarly playful act of subversion; and his transformation
of a fire truck into a *truck on fire* is a particularly clever play on words,
literalising and deliberately misunderstanding the term.[85]

His origin story, notoriously, changes each time he tells it, effectively parodying the whole premise of *Batman Begins*, which painstakingly and 'realistically' rationalised Bruce Wayne's development
into a costumed crime-fighter: that he lies about his bullying father
makes his story a particularly dark and distorting mirror to Batman's
memory of Thomas Wayne. Even his 'calling card' is a range of different Jokers, a devil-may-care branding that mocks Wayne's obsessive consistency, while his vague plans for the 'aggressive expansion'
of his criminal operation parody Wayne's corporate vocabulary. His
own lack of truthful origin and fixed identity ('no name, no other
alias') contrasts with his demands that Batman 'take off your little
mask and show us all who you really are': again, he engages with the
terminology and tropes of the 'ordered' world Batman represents,
but refuses to be pinned down by them himself. Even his claim that
he has no plans, and is an 'agent of chaos' rather than a 'schemer', is
subtly undermined by the revelation that he intended to be arrested,
and must clearly have carefully prepared for each development –
sewing a bomb into a henchman's stomach, planting charges around
a hospital, paying off crooked cops – well in advance.[86]

Joker's very presence, then, is fundamentally subversive and
destabilising: even his own early vow to 'kill the Batman' is laugh-
ingly disavowed during the interrogation scene: 'I don't wanna
kill you! You complete me.' The line is partly camp provocation –
it quotes the romantic drama *Jerry Maguire* – but it also, of course,
recalls the idea of Batman and Joker as mutually-dependent, two
sides of the same coin. Yet the relationship between Batman and
Joker is, in fact, more complex than this image of simple duality suggests. Batman is constructed as uptight and bound by rules, yet when
he says of Joker's involvement 'this is different ... they've crossed a

line', Alfred points out 'you crossed the line first, sir.' A cop snaps at him when he tells the police to leave his crime scene alone: 'Us contaminate it? It's because of *you* these guys are dead.' Barbara Gordon yells at him 'You brought this craziness on us ... you did.' 'This is how crazy Batman's made Gotham,' Joker concludes in his video broadcast.

Joker transcends boundaries of life and death, posing as a corpse to trick Gambol and then returning from the dead; yet Batman also slips between categories. We first see him, or think we see him, as a copycat imposter; it is one of these wannabe Batmen who is captured by Joker, with the TV caption 'Batman Dead?' 'Will the real Batman please stand up?' reads Joker's taunting label, pinned to the lookalike's costume.[87] In the climactic showdown, Batman feigns death again, going down with a bullet in the chest then making a sudden recovery. Dent, in one of the film's most surprising twists, interrupts a press conference with the bold lie 'I am the Batman': after his disfiguring accident he also seems to return from the grave. 'I thought you was dead,' gasps corrupt cop Wuertz. 'Half,' Harvey retorts: ultimately, he has to die for his image as Gotham's 'white knight' to survive. Gordon, too, appears to be fatally shot, and is even mourned by his family before reappearing and saving Batman's life. Joker is far from the only character who shifts and switches, and rather than operating in a binary with Batman, he is part of a larger network, defined by and defining the other major and minor pieces including Gordon, Dent, Dawes, the cops and the mobsters. Nolan's camera, slowly circling Dent, Gordon and Batman during a rooftop conference, captures something of this fluid movement between players on Gotham's game board; tellingly, it is Batman who slips out of shot and vanishes.

Each character, from the central figure to the nameless extras, subverts and refuses easy binaries. Batman's surveillance system is an inherently ambiguous, problematic device, summarised neatly by Fox as 'beautiful, unethical, dangerous.' Ramirez, the cop who tells Batman he caused her colleagues' deaths, turns out to have been bought by the Joker's mob, and is herself responsible for Rachel's murder. The Joker's experiment with two boats is undermined by

both the 'scumbag selection' of prisoners and the 'sweet and innocent' civilians, but not before the citizens have voted to 'get their
hands dirty' and the convicts have shown compassion. Batman's
sonar initially fails to reveal that the Joker's thugs are disguised
as their opposite: the urgent correction reverses expectations. 'The
clowns are the hostages ... doctors are targets.'

While clear and unequivocal readings can obviously be drawn
from *The Dark Knight*'s shifting pattern, then, they involve stopping
the movement of its pieces at a certain point, in a specific arrangement, to fit a specific framework or agenda. A selective interpretation of the formation is certainly possible, but it is inevitably partial;
just as Theuth and Thamus both freeze the *pharmakon* at one of its
many angles when offering it as a gift or rejecting it as a poison, so
to read *The Dark Knight*'s Batman as Bush, Cheney or Obama is to
present only one of his faces. Klavan, Ip, Ackerman and Biodrowski
see clear constellations of meaning, but only by freezing the action in
one position, and therefore misrepresenting the dynamic as a static
pattern, rather than (in several senses) a *motion* picture.

If *The Dark Knight* has a political meaning, it concerns the blurring of boundaries, the instability of oppositions and the shades of
grey between black and white. The implications of its fluid, shifting moral universe can be read through Derrida's own discussion of
9/11 and its consequences. Interviewed by Giovanna Borradori mere
weeks after the events of 11 September 2001, Derrida immediately
questioned the binary oppositions established by Western media
coverage and the Bush administration's response.

> One can condemn unconditionally certain acts of terrorism ...
> without having to ignore the situation that might have brought
> them about or even legitimated them. [...] One can thus con-
> demn *unconditionally*, as I do here, the attack of September 11
> without having to ignore the real or alleged conditions that made
> it possible.[88]

Derrida sees the events of 9/11 as a symptom of an 'autoimmunitary
process ... that strange behavior where a living being, in quasi-*suicidal*

fashion, "itself" works to destroy its own protection, to immunize itself *against* its "own" immunity.'[89] In the case of the Bush administration and its 'with us or against us' war on terror, he suggests that the United States contributed to the attacks on its territory, both by welcoming, arming and training the hijackers who would then strike against it, and more broadly by creating the politico-military circumstances that would shape those hijackers' allegiances and harden their resolve.[90] The terrorist acts of 9/11 were, in turn, countered by a 'war on terror' that attempted to justify its own violations by instilling and perpetuating a culture of anxiety and impending threat. 'Terror' was countered not by its opposite, but by state-imposed fear. The perverse effect of the autoimmunitary is, Derrida explains, that it 'ends up producing, reproducing, and regenerating the very thing it seeks to disarm.'[91] Here he uses a familiar term: 'Once again the state is both self-protecting and self-destroying, at once remedy and poison. The *pharmakon* is another name, an old name, for this autoimmunitary logic.'[92]

'If the distinction between war and terrorism is problematic and we accept the notion of state terrorism,' Borradori asks, 'then the question still remains: who is the most terrorist?' 'The *most* terrorist?' Derrida repeats. 'This question is at once necessary and destined to remain without any answer.'

> Necessary because it takes into account an essential fact: all terrorism *presents itself* as a response in a situation that continues to escalate. It amounts to saying, 'I am resorting to terrorism as a last resort, because the other is more terrorist than I am; I am defending myself, counterattacking; the real terrorist, the worst, is the one who will have deprived me of every other means of responding before presenting himself, the first aggressor, as a victim.'[93]

As Derrida notes, the dominant power picks the terms, legitimizes the vocabulary and decides the official interpretation[94] – the 'other' terrorizes while the United States fights terror – but *The Dark Knight* questions these assumptions, as demonstrated by the range of contradictory political meanings drawn from different readings of its shifting signs. It suggests the fluidity of positions, bringing black into white territory and white into black until any fixed binary seems arbitrary; any labels are exposed as political convenience, any reading revealed as a matter of perspective. Moreover, through its exploration of morality not through twinned opposites but through a shifting constellation of points, it enables a 'characteristically deconstructive move', bringing in a third term through Harvey Dent – and mapping out a broader network through figures like Rachel, Gordon and Maroni – that undermines 'the classical opposition of friend and foe.'[95]

'The social order', writes Alan Sinfield, *cannot but produce* faultlines through which its own criteria of plausibility fall into contest and disarray.'[96] Hegemony, as a constant process and struggle, is not a smooth surface but an unstable terrain, and when a dominant framework is forced upon this complex, uneven structure, something sometimes has to crack, and spaces open. Popular stories, from Sinfield's Shakespearian examples to *The Dark Knight*, will engage with and explore those fissures. These are 'faultline stories ... the ones that require the most assiduous and continuous reworking; they address the awkward, unresolved issues, the ones in which the conditions of plausibility are in dispute.'[97]

> In these texts, through diverse genres and institutions, people were talking to each other about an aspect of their life that they found hard to handle. When a part of our worldview threatens disruption by manifestly failing to cohere with the rest, then we reorganise and retell its story, trying to get it into shape – back into the old shape if we are conservative-minded, or into a new shape if we are more adventurous.[98]

It is not necessary for Nolan to admit an explicit intention to address post-9/11 issues in *The Dark Knight*, and unsurprising that he does not;[99] part of the film's broad appeal, no doubt, is its openness to a range of political readings, and neither the director nor the studio would want to close down those possibilities. We can again see Nolan as scriptor, selecting, editing and arranging aspects of an ongoing cultural conversation in patterns that express his own interests and concerns. Just as he draws the Batman-Joker dynamic from the tradition of recent comics, and uses it to unsettle binary pairings, so his use of contemporary political motifs and themes such as the boundary between interrogation and torture, surveillance and intrusion, terror and counter-terror, can be seen similarly as a creative poaching and collage: neither a concerted political statement nor a superficial attempt at topicality.[100] Rather, Nolan could simply be seen as returning to his own evident interest in doubles who switch, opponents who overlap, and the shades of grey between black and white; issues he explores from *Following*, *Memento* and *Insomnia* to *The Prestige*. The pieces he arranges in *The Dark Knight* clearly have a cultural resonance more immediate and contemporary than the duelling magicians of *The Prestige* or the sleepless cop and killer of *Insomnia*, but it is in the symbolic pattern of pairs changing places, rather than in the specific references to surveillance, rendition and interrogation, that Nolan's characteristic themes are expressed.

Mapped across this particular cultural faultline, though, Nolan's authorial interests connect with and, consciously or not, explore the key contradictions of the 'war on terror', and, in Sinfield's words, enable people – from professional critics to casual viewers – to talk about an issue central to the first decade of the twenty-first century, working through its dilemmas and debating its terms. Nolan's fascination with reversals, conjuring tricks and switches intersects in this film[101] with both the contemporary tension between terror and counter-terror, and with the source material's already inherent tension around Batman as the city's problem and protector. His own authorial expression, the autoimmunitary logic of a terror created, sustained and encouraged by its targets, and the long-standing struggle between opposing terms that constitutes Batman as a broader myth converge in the film's closing moments, in Gordon's voice-over.

> ... he's the hero Gotham deserves, but not the one it needs right
> now. So, we'll hunt him, because he can take it. Because he's not
> our hero. He's a silent guardian. A watchful protector.

The title comes at the end, containing and restating the central paradox: scapegoat and saviour, poison and cure, dark and knight.

EPILOGUE: TIME AND THE BATMAN

Issue 6 of Grant Morrison's *Batman Incorporated*, with a cover date of June 2011, was titled 'Nyktomorph'. It developed the premise discussed in Chapter Two: Batman has become a global brand, financed by Bruce Wayne.

'What about the rumors that there have *always* been multiple Batmen and women?' a reporter asks him. 'Or that the *original* Batman is dead?'

'Or an avenging ghost, or an alien being,' grins Bruce. '... I can assure you, Batman has never been more alive.'

> But if the denizens of our *underworld* ever thought they knew what they were dealing with, those days are *over*. No one knows *who* Batman is anymore. Or how *many* there are. Criminals used to be afraid because they didn't know *where* Batman was. Things are *different* now. Thanks to *Batman Incorporated*, I can tell you *exactly* where Batman is.

A host of armoured figures gathers behind him: robotic Batmen, their chest-emblems and eyes glowing. 'Batman is *everywhere*,'

Bruce warns. 'And if he *didn't* exist, well…. I guess we'd just have to *invent* him.'

Later, with the same expression of slightly sinister enjoyment, Batman – in costume, without his mask – logs onto an internet discussion forum. 'You're in a *chat room*?' Robin asks incredulously, and reads aloud from the screen. 'Everyone in Gotham knows Bruce Wayne is Batman. It's obvious!'

'*I* didn't say it,' Batman points out. 'madhunter 303 did. And here comes "moneyrider's" response.' Batman has become an internet troll, an online trickster, spreading disinformation and conflicting reports. In disguise as Nero Nykto, 'the night-eye… the underworld's own private investigator', he offers criminals a rundown – again, partly true, partly fictional – of his own activities.

> *Wayne* arrived in *Paris*. *Batmen* sprung up. Batman is everything you fear. Wayne's in *Kuala Lumpur*, Batman's in *Hong Kong*. Batman's a *girl*. Then Batman's in *Melbourne*, Australia…Batman actually *tattooed* the words 'child molester' on the man's forehead. Stories that Batman was also in North Africa are unsubstantiated. So where do the rumors end? Where does reality *begin*? Some say Batman *died* and came back as a kind of *god*.

The episode ends with a double-page spread of eight panels, spanning the continents, scanning the global activities of Batman Incorporated – 'a ring around the world,' as Batman calls it. David Zavimbi, the Batman of North Africa, takes down a truck of bandits. Nightrunner, the Dark Athlete, subdues a French mob. Gaucho, in Argentina, punches out an army of monks; Blackbat, the Batgirl of Hong Kong, cracks heads together. Tim Drake, rebranded as Red Robin, defeats a voodoo gang. Dick Grayson disarms a crook with a well-aimed dart. A glimpse of the Dark Ranger, Melbourne's avenger, in a red-lit interior: the skyline behind him could be Australia, East Asia, it doesn't matter. And finally, Bruce Wayne as Batman shatters the frame with a single iconic punch. The title splashes across the two-page spread: NYKTOMORPH. Creature of the night.

This single issue summarises Grant Morrison's prior approach to Batman, but also escalates it to a higher level of intertextuality.

The title alone recalls Batman's origin sequence – 'criminals are a superstitious cowardly lot... I must be a creature of the night' – while evoking his fluid shape and shifting cultural form. The Gaucho and Ranger are veterans of the 1955 story 'Batman of All Nations'; Damian Wayne, the current Robin, is a product of the 1970s O'Neil and Adams' Ra's al Ghul epics. The African Batman is styled after the jet-powered black secret agent from 1973's 'The Batman Nobody Knows', while the motif of Batman as unknowable enigma – girl, ghost, alien – taps into the folk rumours and urban legends of more recent stories like 'Legends of the Dark Knight' and 'Have I Got a Story for You', discussed in Chapter Four. Red Robin and the Bat-robots originated in the 1996 Elseworlds title *Kingdom Come*, and have been brought firmly from a possible future into present-day continuity.

Morrison embraces and encourages the sense of Batman as a flexible fable – as everything you've ever heard or imagined about him – but explains it through the concept of corporate branding. Batman is everywhere, because he is a franchise. He can be a girl, or an African, a robot or a young man, because 'Batman' has become a global operation rather than a single person; although Bruce Wayne remains the patriarch and protagonist, the boss of the outfit, the guy in the costume.

What *Batman Incorporated* #6 does, in short, is allow the three levels of Batman's identity I sketched out in Chapter Four to converge at a single, textually rich point, in a super-compressed story. The broader myth, where Batman is all he has ever been, merges with Batman as brand, whereby the diverse shapes the character takes are rationalised through a framework of different formats for different purposes and markets. Finally, this broad sense of Batman as inherently multiple and flexible is authorised within mainstream continuity: everything in this issue, from the *Kingdom Come*-style bat-robots to the internet trolling and the Batmen of all Nations, actually and officially happened within the story-world. This is truly Batman *incorporated*, collecting everything and making sense of it, building the scraps and fragments into Morrison's creative collage.

For now, at least. Because just as *Batman Incorporated* #6 enters a dialogue with the ongoing and previous texts of Batman – the 1939 origin, the 1950s silliness, the 1970s globetrotting, 1990s Elseworlds and the 2000s Nolan aesthetic of military R&D – it also exists in dialogue with Batman's future, and with the potential changes yet to come. On the level of branding, the conclusion to Nolan's trilogy, the success of the *Arkham* video games and the possibility of a further movie reboot featuring Batman as a member of the Justice League have the potential to shape the comic book, while on the narrower scale of continuity, a future Crisis that closes down timelines and shuts down worlds could very easily negate all the events of Morrison's run. Even as I completed this paragraph, the DC Universe changed overnight, confirming that any assessment of a cultural icon like Batman can quickly become a record of a particular historical moment.

On 31 May 2011, DC issued a press release explaining that, in September of that year and following the cross-universe 'Flashpoint' storyline, 52 of its key titles would relaunch, renumbered from issue #1 and rebooted to make them more 'identifiable and accessible', reflecting 'today's real-world themes and events.'[1] The reading of Batman that Morrison articulated during his run on the key titles during 2006–2011 has been, since September 2011, entirely open to change, and the intersection he negotiated between the broad, diverse myth of Batman and the official continuity may, by the time this book is published, be wrenched apart.

The inclusive approach of Morrison's stories may be not just abandoned but rewritten, becoming a narrative dead end, a dream that Batman no longer remembers, a brief explosion of play and possibilities cherished only by diehard fans. *Batman Incorporated*, at the time of writing, seems headed for a quick conclusion in a one-shot titled *Leviathan Strikes*; the relaunched continuity of the 'New 52', or a subsequent Crisis, could collapse the universe back into one, wiping out Owlman and the Elseworlds and rebooting Batman without the Black Casebook, relegating the 1950s and 60s stories back into limbo. The Batman of official canon could be reduced, again, to a relatively flat figure, contained in a single dark dimension. This book may simply capture and record a brief period in Batman's cultural life: an explosion of possibilities, a rainbow flare, a flashpoint of colour before nightfall. If that were the case, what would be the consequence?

Morrison's authorship of Batman is, I have argued, a creative, inclusive collage of elements from every decade in Batman's career, offering a flexible model that depicts the character as a shifting figure, in tension with aspects of himself. This version of Batman, I have proposed, allows for his diversity and complexity, and presents the dynamic between Batman and Joker as a push-and-pull of conflicting, overlapping energies that both parallels the historical debates around the protagonist's meaning and offers a way of reading current stories, like Nolan's *Dark Knight*, in terms of a struggle with contradictions and an exploration of positions, rather than a simple, one-sided political message serving either left or right.

Throughout this book, I have argued that to insist on Batman as one thing only is to imprison and impoverish a rich, ridiculous, glorious mess of energies; not just a character, but a network of meanings, with a wildly diverse cultural existence. To see him simply as a silly camp crusader, in bright Pop colours, is to flatten him: but to see him only as a tortured, violent vigilante is also a narrow perspective that diminishes him, whatever the claims for realism and psychological complexity. Batman is more than carnival and camp, but he is also more than darkness. His evolution since 1939 has been a process, a dynamic, a struggle between those sides – or, more accurately, a shift between points on that spectrum, because I have argued that 'camp' and 'darkness' constitute a relay of deferred meanings, a range of different, mutually defining shades rather than clear binaries. Morrison's depiction captures that range and relay, the movement and flexibility. If his Batman stories were a brief, bright, prismatic flash, eclipsed by subsequent continuity and relegated to limbo, then reading Batman as a diverse and complex process, rather than a fixed character, would be made more difficult. But not impossible: it would simply take more work, and more imagination.

To insist that Batman is and only ever was a hard-ass, urban vigilante ignores not just a significant period of his history, but also the fact that, throughout the modern 'dark' tradition, the alternative, dissident version of Batman – the camp, Day-Glo, rainbow crusader – played consistently at the margins, hovering in limbo, reappearing through the gaps in his armour, or reshaping that armour in the case of the tightly body-sculpted costumes, complete with codpieces and nipples, of Schumacher's movies. This 'other' Batman, this 'bad object', was not just impossible to repress, but necessary for the very definition of the dark knight: every reworking of the character made its claim for authenticity and grittiness against the backdrop of Pop and camp. Darkness can only be seen as such as part of a spectrum of colours and contrasts: every 'realist' Batman needs the rainbow.

And the limbo into which camp was relegated is not a permanent purgatory. It only took one more Crisis to bring back the multiverse, after a 20 year absence; it only took one writer to bring the repressed stories of the 1950s and 60s back to the surface, and into official twenty-first century continuity. Doors close and worlds end, but they can just as easily be opened and begin again. Morrison's run on the title may be retconned and rewritten, with swathes of supporting characters massacred at a stroke, and the official Batman of continuity may become a lonely, uptight vigilante without friends or family; and then in 2039, a kid who grew up on *Batman Incorporated* might get his turn at the helm, and bring back the Gaucho, Nightrunner, Red Robin and Bat-Mite, calling them in like old friends to a reunion party. Every Batman exists in dialogue with what he has been, and what he can be; the moody, uptight Batman is always just a temporary phase, a teenager denying the childhood fun he may rediscover as an adult.

To recognise the constant presence of alternatives, and accept that other interpretations are always waiting in the wings, is vital to a full understanding of this cultural icon. Even during the height of the post-Crisis, post-Miller 'dark Batman' boom, compilations like *The Greatest Batman Stories Ever Told* (1988) reprinted 'Robin Dies at Dawn', with Dick shouting at a pink alien, 'Come on, Big Boy! I'm still waiting for you!', and 'The Jungle Cat-Queen', whose title ostensibly refers to Catwoman but could also describe Batman in a mask and fur leotard. The stories that Morrison brought back from limbo

were still available in the late 80s, alongside *Year One*, *Arkham Asylum*
and the spin-offs from Burton's movie: Andy Medhurst rightly notes
that the post-Crisis period attempted to make gay readings more difficult, but his article – written in the late 1980s, again – itself demonstrates that a casual fan could readily lay his hands on the campier
tales of the previous decades. Batman is a brand, but even as a cross-
platform product, his form is multiple, and subversive versions lurk
constantly at the margins. We have to seek them out, to remind
ourselves of the light that defines the shadow, and the shadow that
defines the light.

Without this fuller picture of struggle and process, Batman is
two-dimensional, and of limited interest to an audience outside the
dedicated comics market: just as the camp, Pop character's broader
appeal only lasted a few years in the 1960s, so the gritty graphic novel
boom had slumped by the early 1990s. Without a sense of Batman
as a dynamic between alternative positions, the character is just an
uptight, brutal bully or a daft scoutmaster; without an understanding
of Batman as a shifting stance across a range of possibilities, the protagonist of *The Dark Knight* presents only a simplified choice between
a Bush analogue or an Obama avatar, rather than an embodiment of
cultural dilemmas, a wrestling with contemporary contradictions, a
figure straddling a fault line.

To insist that Batman is one thing is, finally, to ignore the
fact that Batman is more than a character, more than a brand: he
is myth. As Alan Moore writes in his eulogy for the pre-Crisis
Superman, 'Whatever Happened to the Man of Tomorrow', 'this
is an IMAGINARY STORY... aren't they all?'[2] A whole archive of
adventures may be ruled out of official continuity, but they remain
in cultural memory. On one level, of course, all Batman stories
are imaginary, and therefore all equal. Even comics that are never
reprinted are still dissected and discussed – their pages scanned and
shared – by fans online. Decisions at company level fix the texts that
are readily available, and attempt to build structures around selective traditions – the notion that the 'dark' aesthetic of the 1980s dates
back to an authentic 1940s original, for instance, and that the camp
period in between was an aberration – but Batman always exists in

a dialogue, and dominant theories, as we have seen, always have to struggle against other voices to impose themselves. If we refuse to listen to all those voices – even those we disagree with – we again diminish the character to something less complex and less interesting. Batman, on one level, enacts a series of debates between authors, artists, journalists, campaigners and fans from 1939 to the present day, about issues that people felt a need to discuss: masculinity, childhood, violence, law, terror. To ignore the interpretations we dislike is to pretend that Batman is a monologue, rather than a conversation.

Batman is a myth: yet of course, Batman remains a property of DC and Time Warner, which is why this book, like most academic books about comics, has no pictures. DC can choose to enforce its interpretation with a heavy hand; in the last decade, the company has refused permission for and threatened legal action against representations and discussions of a gay Dynamic Duo. It would be misguided to suggest that corporate ownership has lost its relevance, even for a character with such widespread, long-term cultural circulation. But despite its ultimate ownership, DC is limited in its power to control Batman's meanings. It can decide what stories are true and false at the level of continuity, and construct a coherent brand identity. Yet even in the context of Nolan's rebooted franchise and its 'realist' aesthetic, popular journalism, reflecting and contributing to the everyday understanding of the character, continues to use 'Batman' as an umbrella term for a range of diverse incarnations: the evocation of Batman in British tabloids alone is a carnival of celebrity team-ups, from 'Joker David Cameron' and 'Jedward meet the Dynamic Duo' to Eddie Murphy's rumoured role as the Riddler, and Batman versus Al Qaeda.[3]

Batman Begins was meant to erase the memory of Val Kilmer's rubber-suited vigilante, but he was still referred to as Batman, or rather 'Fatman', in a story of 2010.[4] The 1960s TV show was supposed to be wiped out of the cultural consciousness by the O'Neil stories of the 1970s, but a story from 2008, the year of *Dark Knight*'s release, announced that 'former Batman star Adam West' was bidding for a role alongside Christian Bale, as Thomas Wayne. 'The older Batman comes out of the woodwork, when times get really tough', West proposed. 'Maybe a few tips here and there.'[5] Older Batmen keep coming out of the woodwork, adapting and surviving in the strangest forms and the strangest places: in a hand-painted mural on the Berlin wall, in a low-budget fan-film, in a political cartoon. Batman remains anchored by copyright, but at the same time, he has become a cultural virus, a folk icon, a popular fable that exists independently and would no doubt persist independently, if the movie franchise ended and the comic books finally folded.

I have proposed that all Batman texts enter a matrix of cross-platform product, and operate in a dialogue between the other current incarnations, and all previous versions, even if they define themselves against an earlier tradition now judged to be aberrant. They also exist in a network with the future possibilities of the text, as stories, trends and institutional decisions yet to come may rule them out of official continuity, and relegate them from the formal history. But perhaps most important, they enter a dialogue with the reader. It is the reader, finally, who constructs and collages a Batman from all the pieces of the cultural mosaic; the reader who is the ultimate scriptor and author, the editor and compiler of all those different, diverse traces into a single, complex figure. It is the reader's responsibility, I would argue, to retain that complexity, rather than reduce it. Batman is never one thing, and to pretend otherwise is a disservice to the rich, crazy, beautiful life of a cultural icon.

Who is the Batman? You have a sense of him; who he is, what he looks like. Imagine him. Feel free. He's yours. But do him justice.

NOTES

Prologue

1. Eileen R. Meehan, '"Holy commodity fetish, Batman!": The political economy of a commercial intertext', in Roberta E. Pearson and William Uricchio (eds.), *The Many Lives of the Batman: Critical Approaches to a Superhero and His Media* (New York: Routledge, 1991), pp.47–48.
2. Jim Collins, 'Batman: the movie, narrative: the hyperconscious', in Pearson and Uricchio, *Many Lives*, pp.164–5.
3. William Uricchio and Roberta E. Pearson, '"I'm not fooled by that cheap disguise"', in Pearson and Uricchio, *Many Lives*, pp.184–185.

Chapter 1   The Nolan Function: Authorship

1. David A. Gerstner, 'The practices of authorship' in David A. Gerstner and Janet Staiger (eds.), *Authorship and Film* (New York: Routledge, 2003), p.5.
2. John Caughie observes that though Andrew Sarris helped to 'naturalise' the translation in a *Film Culture* article from 1962, he was not the first to use the term '*auteur* theory'. See John Caughie (ed.), *Theories of Authorship* (London: Routledge, 1981), p.62. I use the word 'auteur' without italics throughout this book, because it has been so broadly accepted into English.
3. See Gerstner, 'Authorship'. pp.7–8, and Caughie, *Authorship*, p.61.
4. Robin Wood, 'Shall we gather at the river?; The late films of John Ford', *Film Comment* vol.7, no.3 (Fall 1971), reprinted in Caughie, *Authorship*, p.85.

5. Ibid.
6. Ibid., pp.86–87.
7. Ibid., p.95.
8. Gerstner, *Authorship*, p.5.
9. Jack Boozer, *Authorship in Film Adaptation* (Austin: University of Texas Press, 2008), p.19.
10. See Staiger, op.cit. pp.43–44.
11. See Peter Wollen, *Signs and Meaning in the Cinema* (Bloomington: Indiana University Press, 1972), p.168.
12. Roland Barthes, 'Death of the Author,' from *Image-Music-Text* (originally Paris, 1968) reprinted in Caughie, *Authorship*, p.211.
13. Ibid., p.212.
14. Ibid., p.209.
15. Michel Foucault, 'What is an author?' from *Language, Counter-Memory, Practice* (originally Paris, 1969), reprinted in John Caughie (ed.), *Theories of Authorship* (London: Routledge, 1986), p.285. Note that while Foucault does not subscribe to Barthes' view of (or call for) the author's death, he agrees that the author is a contingent category. See Janet Staiger, 'Authorship approaches' in Gerstner and Staiger (eds.), *Authorship*, p.29.
16. Foucault, 'Author', p.285.
17. Ibid., p.286.
18. Ibid., p.290; See also Gerstner, op.cit. p.14. For an example, see the discussion of Gene Roddenberry and *Star Trek* in John Tulloch and Henry Jenkins, *Science Fiction Audiences* (London: Routledge, 1995), pp.188–91.
19. Boozer, *Authorship*, p.20.
20. Gerstner suggests that Barthes' 'Death of the Author' is 'not so much an end point of a discourse of authorship' as 'a transformative point of departure for theoretical and political intervention.' (*op.cit*, p.12).
21. Barthes, 'Author', p.213.
22. Ibid.
23. Ibid., p.209.
24. Foucault, 'Author', p.286.
25. David A. Gerstner and Janet Staiger. 'Introduction', in Gerstner and Staiger (eds.), *Authorship*, p.xi.
26. Gérard Genette, *Paratexts: Thresholds of Interpretation* (Cambridge: Cambridge University Press, 1997), pp.1–2. Note that while Genette sees the paratext as 'subordinate to "its" text' and 'dedicated to the service of' the text (p.12), Gray argues that 'a film or program is but one part of the text ... it is a larger unit than any film or show that may be part of it'. Jonathan Gray, *Show Sold Separately* (New York: New York University Press, 2010), p.7.
27. Ibid., p.78.
28. http://batmanbegins.warnerbros.com/images/onesheet.jpg (accessed March 2011).

29. See 'The journey begins', documentary feature, *Batman Begins 2-Disc Special Edition* DVD (Christopher Nolan, 2005).

30. Gray provides an excellent, though brief case study of *Batman Begins'* paratexts and their role in rebooting the franchise; see Gray, *Show Sold Separately*, pp.131–135.

31. Anon, *'Batman Begins*: Final production information', Warner Bros. (2005), p.4.

32. In this case, the credits form more of an 'exitway', as title and director's name only appear at the end of the film.

33. Bob Fisher, *'On Film*: Christopher Nolan', Kodak.com, http://motion. kodak.com/US/en/motion/Publications/On_Film_Interviews/ nolan(2).htm (n.d, accessed June 2010).

34. Edward Lawrenson, *'Batman Begins'*, *Sight and Sound* (July 2005).

35. See Lindsay Anderson, *'The Searchers'*, *Sight and Sound* vol.26, no.2 (Autumn 1956), reprinted in Caughie, *Authorship*, p.75.

36. Martyn Palmer, 'Nolan: bringing the Bat back', *The Times* (11 June 2005).

37. Sukhdev Sandhu, 'Dark soul of the night: *Batman Begins'*, *Telegraph* (17 June 2005).

38. Kim Newman, *'Batman Begins'*, *Empire* magazine (June 2005).

39. Todd McCarthy, *'Batman Begins'*, *Variety* (3 June 2005).

40. Christine Geraghty confirms this impression with her observation that reviews of *Atonement* repeated references 'taken from the publicity material promoting the film.' See Geraghty, 'Foregrounding the media: *Atonement* (2007) as an adaptation', *Adaptation* vol.2, no.2 (2009), p.92.

41. Compare to the function that Ang Lee played as director of *Hulk* (2003): M. Keith Booker describes the involvement of this 'esteemed' director, with 'prestigious' literary adaptations and social commentary movies to his name, as part of Marvel's attempt to 'bring superhero films into the realm of truly serious cinema.' See M. Keith Booker, *May Contain Graphic Material: Comic Books, Graphic Novels and Film* (Westport, CT: Praeger Publishers, 2007), p.xxx. Similarly, Linda Hutcheon's *A Theory of Authorship* asserts 'it is evident from both studio press releases and critical response that the director is ultimately held responsible for the overall vision and therefore for the screenplay *as adaptation'*; established directors like Ridley Scott, Federico Fellini and David Lean, Hutcheon suggests, 'make the adaptation very much their own work.' Linda Hutcheon, *A Theory of Adaptation* (London: Routledge, 2006), pp.84–5.

42. These are not the same 19 reviews; both directors are not always mentioned by name in the same piece.

43. Unsurprisingly, in this sample of film reviews for a general readership, the most frequent references are to recent cinema versions of Batman, rather than the early or even the 1980s comic books. Bob Kane is referred to by name four times in this sample.

44. Genette, *Paratexts* pp.5–6.

45. Gray, *Show Sold Separately*, p.23.

46. However, for a proportion of those viewers, the DVD will provide the first encounter with *Batman Begins*. The film's global box-office gross was $372,710,015, while its DVD sales totalled $125,000,000. See http://www.boxofficemojo.com/movies/?id=batmanbegins.htm (accessed March 2011) and http://www.leesmovieinfo.net/Video-Sales.php?type=3 (accessed March 2011).

47. See Dennis O'Neil, *Batman Begins* (London: Titan Books, 2005), front cover and back cover.

48. Ibid. 'Acknowledgements', n.p.

49. As an influential writer, and also editor, of Batman comics, O'Neil's frame of reference is understandable on a personal and professional level.

50. Various, *Batman Begins: The Movie and Other Tales of the Dark Knight* (New York: DC Comics, 2005), n.p.

51. James Mottram, 'Introduction', *Batman Begins: The Screenplay* (London: Faber and Faber 2005), pp.vii–viii.

52. James Mottram, 'Christopher Nolan', *Batman Begins*, p.xix.

53. See 'Genesis of the bat,' documentary feature, *Batman Begins 2-Disc Special Edition* DVD (Christopher Nolan, 2005), 00.00.45–55.

54. I mean 'amateur' in the sense of doing something from love, rather than as a negative value judgement.

55. R. Suarez Glacoman, 'Batman is back', *Amazon.com Customer Reviews: Batman Begins* (5 December 2005), accessed May 2010.

56. Hazen B. Markoe, 'Batman flies high in excellent *Begins*', *Amazon.com* (16 June 2005), accessed May 2010.

57. Jeff Wiley, 'The movie Bat-fans have been waiting for', *Amazon.com* (30 August 2005), accessed May 2010.

58. David Foskin, 'Surprisingly good!', *Amazon.com* (20 November 2005), accessed May 2010.

59. Distant Voyageur, 'Stunning comeback for the caped-crusader', *Amazon.com* (14 October 2005), accessed May 2010.

60. Juha Ylinen, 'The dark revenger's time has come!', *Amazon.com* (15 August 2005), accessed May 2010.

61. L. Clayton Butler Jr, 'They finally got it right!', *Amazon.com* (16 August 2005), accessed May 2010.

62. Michael Acuna, 'Flesh and machinery', *Amazon.com* (17 June 2005), accessed May 2010.

63. BPRK, 'True to its roots', *Amazon.com* (21 August 2005), accessed May 2010.

64. Richard Stoehr, 'The making of a legend – the nature of fear', *Amazon.com*, (30 October 2005), accessed May 2010.

65. Robin Orlowski, 'The bat came back to start cleaning up his town', *Amazon.com* (18 June 2005), accessed May 2010.

66. Wiley, 'Bat-fans.'

67. Orlowski, 'The bat.'
68. See Batman Dark Knight Movie Master Deluxe Action Figure Batman from *Batman Begins* (Crime Scene Evidence), http://www.amazon. com/Batman-Knight-Master-Deluxe-Evidence/dp/B001EY59R0/ ref=sr_1_1?s=toys-and-games&ie=UTF8&qid=1300872522&sr=1-1
69. Glacoman, 'Batman is back!'.
70. Bruce Wayne, 'Not your father's "Batman"', *Amazon.com* (6 September 2005), accessed May 2010.
71. Eddie Lancekick, 'Knight of justice, night of fear, return of the legend!', *Amazon.com* (19 October 2005), accessed May 2010.
72. Robert J. Watkins, 'The dark knight once again!', *Amazon.com* (17 August 2005), accessed May 2010.
73. Neal J. Wertanen, 'Batman has never been so good', *Amazon.com* (3 October 2005), accessed May 2010.
74. Stoehr, 'Legend'.
75. Anon, '*The Prestige*: Final production information', Warner Bros. (2006), p.3.
76. 'Christopher Nolan', *Rotten Tomatoes.com*, http://www.rottentomatoes. com/celebrity/christopher_nolan/.
77. Peter Bradshaw, '*The Prestige*', *Guardian* (10 November 2006).
78. Matt Stevens, '*The Prestige*', *EOnline.com* (19 October 2006).
79. Kenneth Turan, '*The Prestige*', *LA Times* (20 October 2006).
80. Stephanie Zacharek, '*The Prestige*', *Salon.com* (20 October 2006).
81. Dana Stevens, 'Old tricks', Slate.com (20 October 2006).
82. Ben Walters, '*The Prestige*', *Time Out* (8–15 November 2006).
83. 17th October in the United States, and 5th November in the United Kingdom: see http://www.imdb.com/title/tt0482571/releaseinfo.
84. The suggested parallel between film making and magic is picked up in at least two of these reviews.
85. We should note that none of this commentary actually discusses the cultural role of 'Nolan' as a form of classification and a tool of commercial branding; it perpetuates the process that Foucault describes, rather than recognising and analysing it.
86. Similarly, Neil Rae and Jonathan Gray identify a 'distancing from the original medium' of comics in reviews of *X-Men 2*, as many critics sought to show the film 'as capable of standing alone'; *X-Men 2* was to a significant extent reviewed not in relationship to comics or even to superhero films, but within a relocated context of blockbusters, effects-heavy movies and science fiction. Rae and Gray, 'When Gen-X met the X-Men: retextualising comic book film reception", in Jancovich and McAllister, *Film and Comic Books*, pp.113–114.
87. Jonathan Romney, '*The Dark Knight*', *The Independent* (27 July 2008).
88. See Anon, 'The Dark Knight', *Film4.com* (July 2008).
89. See Bill Gibron, '*Dark Knight* is epic entertainment', *Popmatters.com* (18 July 2008).

90. Stephen Hunter, 'This Joker holds all the cards', *The Washington Post* (17 July 2008).
91. See Suhdev Sandhu, *'The Dark Knight'*, *The Telegraph* (25 July 2008).
92. See Mick LaSalle, *'Dark Knight*: Ledger Terrific'', *SFGate.com* (17 July 2008).
93. See for instance Dana Stevens, 'No Joke', Slate.com (17 July 2008).
94. Sonny Bunch, 'Gotham City's War on Terror', *The Washington Times* (18 July 2008).
95. Stevens, 'No Joke'.
96. Anon, *'The Dark Knight*: Final production information', Warner Bros. (2008), pp.1–3.
97. Antony Quinn, *'The Dark Knight'*, *Independent* (25 July 2008).
98. Gibron, *'Dark Knight'*.
99. Romney, *'The Dark Knight'*.
100. Stephanie Zacharek, *'The Dark Knight'*, *Salon.com* (17 July 2008).
101. Peter Bradshaw, *'The Dark Knight'*, *Guardian* (25 July 2008).
102. Quinn, *'The Dark Knight'*.
103. Gibron, *'The Dark Knight'*.
104. Sukhdev Sandhu, *'The Dark Knight'*, *The Telegraph* (25 July 2008).
105. Justin Heath, 'The dark masterpiece surpasses the hype', *Amazon.com Customer Reviews: The Dark Knight* (11 October 2008), accessed May 2010.
106. Woopak, *'The Dark Knight* returns for Gotham City's soul', *Amazon.com* (20 July 2008), accessed May 2010.
107. E. A Solinas, 'Batman has no limits', *Amazon.com* (9 October 2008), accessed May 2010.
108. Thornhillatthemovies, *'The Dark Knight* is going to spoil us', *Amazon.com* (22 July 2008), accessed May 2010.
109. The teaser poster for *The Dark Knight Rises*, first circulated online in July 2011, suggests an interesting further development to Nolan's branding: the image strongly recalls *Inception's* crumbling skyscrapers and silvery blue palette, while also continuing the colour-scheme and 9/11 imagery of *The Dark Knight*. Nolan's oeuvre had gained a new visual and thematic association with steely, cold business architecture and urban environments at risk of collapse: a connotation confirmed by the use of the *Inception* soundtrack on the BBC TV series *The Apprentice* in June–July 2011.
110. 'FAQ', *Batman on Film*, http://www.batman-on-film.com/bof_101.html (accessed March 2011).
111. Will Brooker, *Hunting the Dark Knight Survey*, Q27 (June 2010).
112. Christopher A. Bourassa, aged 37 from Massachusetts, response to *Survey* Q27.
113. Richard Lee Robinson Jr, aged 22 from Troy, Illinois, response to *Survey* Q27.
114. Paul Leslie Kerr, aged 46 from Sydney, Australia, response to *Survey* Q27.

115. Anonymous respondent, aged 26 from Toowoomba, Australia, response to *Survey* Q27.

116. Robert Daniel Anglim II, aged 20 from Eugene, Oregon, response to *Survey* Q27.

117. Will Brooker, *Survey* Q7 and Q11.

118. Occasional mentions of visual style centred around Nolan's use of recurring colour schemes, or the predominance of a single colour in each film. One respondent, for instance, noted that '*Batman Begins* is orange; *The Dark Knight* is blue; *The Prestige* is purple.' Zachary Matheson, age undisclosed from Utah, response to *Survey* Q13.

119. Jonathan Batailles, aged 30 from Chatham, Massachusetts, response to *Survey* Q13.

120. Ryan Wilson, aged 24 from Manchester, UK, response to *Survey* Q13.

121. John Stian Ostrem, aged 30 from Norway, response to *Survey* Q13.

122. Craig Harlow, age undisclosed from Essex, UK, response to *Survey* Q13.

123. Brooker, *Survey* Q16.

124. It has a score of 13 per cent on *Rotten Tomatoes*: see http://www.rottentomatoes.com/m/1077027-batman_and_robin/ (accessed March 2011).

125. 69 per cent and 56 per cent, respectively. Brooker, *Survey* Q16.

126. Note further that only a tiny number – 4 per cent and 2.7 per cent – were influenced by a friend or family member. Compare also to Paul Lazarsfeld's classic 1944 study of media influence, whereby friends, neighbours, teachers and other community leaders shaped opinion in a 'two-step flow'; this group is far more directly influenced by mass media than by personal relationships and recommendations. See Paul F. Lazarsfeld, Bernard Berelson and Hazel Gaudet, *The People's Choice: How the Voter Makes Up His Mind in a Presidential Campaign* (New York: Columbia University Press, 1944).

127. Ben Posnett, aged 20 from Walton-on-Thames, United Kingdom, response to *Survey* Q18.

128. 36 per cent and 37 per cent respectively. Brooker, *Survey* Q16.

129. Javier Moreno, aged 22 from West Covina, California, response to *Survey* Q16.

130. Harlow, *Survey* Q18.

131. See Matt Hills for a similar take on the rebooted *Doctor Who* and the '(de)materialising authorship of showrunner Russell T. Davies', which nevertheless coexists with a 'conventional "author-function"'. Matt Hills, *Triumph of A Time Lord: Regenerating Doctor Who in the Twenty-First Century* (London: I.B.Tauris, 2010), p.48.

132. Batailles, *Survey* Q14.

133. Ostrem, *Survey* Q14.

134. Hugu Seriese, aged 25 from The Hague, Netherlands, response to *Survey* Q14.

135. Jason Spore, aged 29 from Warsaw, Indiana, response to *Survey* Q14.
136. Chris Capel, aged 27 from Oxford, United Kingdom, response to *Survey* Q14.
137. Posnett, *Survey* Q18.
138. This is confirmed by Rae and Gray's study of *X-Men* fans, who approve of comic book films that reinterpret characters and plots if they are fuelled by an admirable 'vision'. 'Effectively ... a comic book film could be in some ways like a new episode or graphic novel of the comic.' Schumacher's 'vision' is criticised as consisting only of 'butt shots and nipple costumes'. See Rae and Gray, 'When Gen-X met the X-Men', pp.93–94.
139. See Umberto Eco, 'The myth of Superman' in *The Role of the Reader* (Bloomington: Indiana University Press, 1979), p.109.
140. Richard Reynolds, *Superheroes: A Modern Mythology* (London: B.T. Batsford Ltd, 1992), pp.47–48.
141. Alan Moore, 'Introduction' to Frank Miller and Lynn Varley, *Batman: The Dark Knight Returns* (London: Titan, 1986), n.p.
142. Joss Whedon, 'Introduction' to Brad Meltzer, Rags Morales and Michael Bair, *Identity Crisis* (New York: DC Comics, 2005), n.p.
143. Bob Schreck, 'Introduction' to Grant Morrison, Frank Quitely and Jamie Grant, *All-Star Superman Volume I* (New York: DC Comics, 2007), n.p.
144. This tradition is confirmed by Nolan himself: 'Indeed, in the comics, one of the things that Paul Levitz at DC Comics first talked about when I first came onboard for *Batman Begins* is that Batman is a character who traditionally is interpreted in very different ways by the different artists and writers who've worked on it over the years. So there's a freedom, and an expectation even, that you will actually put something new into it, that it'll be interpreted in some different way'. See Rebecca Murray, 'Writer/Director Christopher Nolan talks about *The Dark Knight*', About.com, http://movies.about.com/od/thedarkknight/a/darkknight70408.htm (accessed April 2011).
145. See Graham Allen, *Intertextuality* (London: Routledge, 2000), p.14.
146. Gray, *Show Sold Separately*, p.109.
147. The 'Genesis of the bat' DVD documentary makes the parallel explicit by moving from a discussion of Nolan's interpretation to what is essentially a promotion of Frank Miller and Jim Lee's *All Star Batman and Robin the Boy Wonder* comic book series in terms of its 'fresh spin.'

Chapter 2   The Batman Matrix: Adaptation

1. Deborah Cartmell and Imelda Whelehan, 'Adaptations: theories, interpretations and new dilemmas' in Cartmell and Whelehan (eds), *Screen Adaptation: Impure Cinema* (London: Palgrave Macmillan, 2010), p.12.

2. Ibid., pp.20–21.

3. Thomas Leitch, 'Adaptation studies at a crossroads' in *Adaptation* vol.1, no.1 (2008), p.63.

4. Deborah Cartmell and Imelda Whelehan, 'Introduction – literature on screen: a synoptic view' in Cartmell and Whelehan (eds), *The Cambridge Companion to Literature on Screen* (Cambridge: Cambridge University Press, 2007), p.2.

5. Ibid.

6. Leitch, 'Crossroads', p.64.

7. Ibid.

8. Ibid.

9. For recognition of Stam's influence and significance in these debates, see Cartmell and Whelehan, *Screen Adaptation*, p.4, and Christine Geraghty, *Now a Major Motion Picture: Film Adaptations of Literature and Drama* (Plymouth: Rowman and Littlefield, 2008), p.2.

10. Ibid.

11. Robert Stam, 'Introduction: the theory and practice of adaptation' in Robert Stam and Alessandra Raengo, *Literature and Film* (Oxford: Blackwell, 2005), p.3.

12. Ibid., p.4.

13. Ibid., p.14.

14. Ibid., p.46.

15. Ibid., p.8.

16. Ibid., p.27.

17. Ibid., p.46.

18. Genette calls the original source the *hypotext* and the adaptation the *hypertext,* but the terms are not widely used. See Richard Macksey, 'Foreword' to Genette, *Paratexts*, p.xv, and Graham, *Intertextuality*, p.108.

19. See also Stanley Fish's concept of interpretive communities: Stanley Fish, *Is There a Text in this Class?* (Cambridge, MA: Harvard University Press, 1980).

20. Stam, 'Introduction', p.15.

21. Ibid., p.9.

22. Mikhail M. Bakhtin, 'Discourse in the novel' in Michael Holquist (ed.), *The Dialogic Imagination: Four Essays by M.M. Bakhtin* (Austin: University of Texas Press), p.272.

23. Ibid., p.276.

24. Julia Kristeva, 'Word, dialogue and novel' in Toril Moi (ed.), *The Kristeva Reader* (Oxford: Blackwell, 1986), p.37.

25. Luca Somigli, 'The superhero with a thousand faces: visual narratives on film and paper' in Andrew Horton and Stuart T. McDougal (eds), *Play It Again, Sam: Retakes on Remakes* (Berkeley: University of California Press, 1998), pp.284–285.

26. Derek Johnson, 'Will the real Wolverine please stand up? Marvel's mutation from monthlies to movies,' in Ian Gordon, Mark Jancovich and Matthew P. McAllister, *Film and Comic Books* (Mississippi: University

Press of Mississippi, 2007), p.65. Neil Rae and Jonathan Gray, in the same volume, echo and confirm the point.

27. Ibid., p.66.
28. See Gordon, Jancovich and. McAllister, *Film and Comic Books*, p.x.
29. I include *Batman* (1943), *Batman and Robin* (1949), the TV spin-off feature *Batman* of 1966, Burton's *Batman* (1989) and *Batman Returns* (1992), the animated *Batman: Mask of the Phantasm* (1993), Schumacher's *Batman Forever* (1995) and *Batman & Robin* (1997) and Nolan's two films.
30. See Julian Darius, *Batman Begins and the Comics* (Hawaii: Sequart Books, 2005), pp.9–17.
31. Hutcheon, *A Theory*, p.21.
32. Ibid., p.125.
33. Ibid., p.19.
34. Cartmell and Whelehan, *Impure Cinema*, p.6.
35. Ibid., p.7.
36. Dan Georgakas, 'Robin Hood: from Roosevelt to Reagan' in Andrew Horton and Stuart Y. McDougal (eds.), *Play It Again, Sam: Retakes on Remakes* (Berkeley and LA: University of California Press, 1998), p.70. Georgakas further observes that the 1938 version was 'aware of the highly successful Fairbanks 1922 silent *Robin*'.
37. Geraghty, *Major Motion Picture*, p.28.
38. Martin Barker and Roger Sabin, *The Lasting of the Mohicans: History of an American Myth* (Mississippi: University Press of Mississippi, 1995), p.182.
39. Ibid., p.122.
40. Ibid., p.143.
41. Kamilla Elliott, 'Adaptation as compendium: Tim Burton's *Alice in Wonderland*', *Adaptation* vol.3 no.2 (2010), pp.194–5.
42. Hutcheon, *Theory of Adaptation*, p.93.
43. Rebecca Bell-Metereau, 'The three faces of *Lolita*, or how I learned to stop worrying and love the adaptation', in Boozer, *Authorship,* p.204.
44. Cited in R. Barton Palmer, 'From obtrusive narrator to crosscutting: adapting the doubleness of John Fowles's *The French Lieutenant's Woman*', in Boozer, *Authorship,* p.181.
45. Ibid., p.188.
46. Pascal LeFèvre, 'Incompatible visual ontologies? The problematic adaptation of drawn images', in Boozer, *Authorship*, pp.3–4.
47. See Michael Cohen, 'Dick Tracy: in pursuit of a comic book aesthetic', in Gordon, Jancovich and. McAllister, *Film and Comic Books*, p.14.
48. See LeFèvre, 'Ontologies', p.6.
49. And, though it was published five years after the film's release, an academic book: Deborah Cartmell's *Screen Adaptations: Pride and Prejudice: A Close Study of the Relationship Between Text and Film* (London: Methuen, 2010).
50. See Will Brooker, *Batman Unmasked* (London: Continuum, 2000), p.285.

51. Cited in Pearson and Uricchio, 'I'm not fooled,' p.184.

52. See Brooker, *Batman Unmasked*, pp.279–4.

53. Gordon, Jancovich and. McAllister, *Film and Comic Books*, p.ix.

54. Ibid.

55. Ibid., p.viii.

56. Bob Rehak, 'Watchmen: stuck in the uncanny valley', *Graphic Engine*, http://graphic-engine.swarthmore.edu/?p=239 (9 March 2009), accessed March 2011.

57. Andrew Pulver, "He's not a god – he's human", *Guardian* (15 June 2005).

58. Ibid.

59. Quite a change from the fan as 'powerless elite', described by John Tulloch in 1995; see John Tulloch and Henry Jenkins, *Science Fiction Audiences: Watching Doctor Who and Star Trek* (London: Routledge, 2005), p.144. On the other hand, Neil Rae and Jonathan Gray, writing in 2007, continue to characterise comic book fans as an 'intertextually "rich" minority', denied the power to shape a film's reading: see Rae and Gray, 'When Gen-X met the X-Men', p.89. See also Goyer's interview in the published screenplays, where he admits 'we had to appease the comic book fans but also the mainstream audience. And also Warner Bros. It was an interesting balancing act.' James Mottram, 'David S. Goyer', *Batman Begins*, p.xxvii.

60. Anon, '*Batman Begins:* Final production information', p.6.

61. Ibid.

62. Ibid., p.11.

63. Ibid.

64. Ibid., p.13.

65. James Mottram, 'Christopher Nolan', p.xi.

66. According to one interview, Bale's research included gaining the approval of Bob Kane's wife, and drawing on the work of Jeph Loeb and Tim Sale, Frank Miller and artist Alex Ross. See John Hutchins, "Christian Bale", *World of Batman*, http://batman.ugo.com/movies/batman_begins/bale.asp (accessed June 2010).

67. 'The journey begins', 00.01.08.

68. Ibid., 00.02.45.

69. 'Genesis of the bat', 00.00.10.

70. Ibid., 00.01.25.

71. O'Neil and Adams' first Batman story was 'The Secret of the Waiting Graves', which appeared in *Detective Comics* #395 (January 1970).

72. Ibid., 00.02.50.

73. Ibid., 00.03.25.

74. Ibid., 00.04.15.

75. Ibid., 00.07.15.

76. Ibid., 00.07.40.

77. O'Neil worked with several artists on Ra's al Ghul stories between 1971 and 1980, but the 1971 first appearance, drawn by Neal Adams, is singled out in this documentary.

78. With exceptions, such as Mike W. Barr's *In Darkest Knight*, an 'Elseworlds' story from 1994 in which Bruce Wayne gains the cosmic power of Green Lantern.

79. Christine Geraghty observes that the image of the child asking for more, combined with the London setting, are enough to identify an adaptation as *Oliver Twist*; but she qualifies this as a 'starting point'. See Geraghty, *Major Motion Picture*, p.29.

80. Catwoman makes her first appearance during the story, and Joker is first mentioned on the last page.

81. 'The Man Who Falls' in turn summarises various earlier stories, including O'Neil's five-part story 'Shaman', which launched the new *Legends of the Dark Knight* title in 1989 and finds echoes in the film's themes of hallucination and bat-as-totem.

82. Carmine Falcone was created by Miller for *Year One*, but plays a more significant role in *The Long Halloween*; events and dialogue in *The Long Halloween*, in turn, are a more obvious influence on *The Dark Knight* than on *Batman Begins*.

83. The journey begins', 00.03.00.

84. As Dan Georgakas points out, such movies can select elements from a 'vast Robin Hood folklore available to forward the plot'; Georgakas, 'Robin Hood', p.73. Compare also Luca Somigli's comment on the *Superman* movies: 'there is some "source" ... but it stands in a very different relation to the film than, say, E.M. Forster's novel does to Merchant and Ivory's *A Room With a View*.' See Somigli, 'The superhero', p.284.

85. See Julian Darius, *Improving the Foundations* (Illinois: Sequart, 2009), p.6.

86. Ibid.

87. Hutcheon, *A Theory*, p.125.

88. Rae and Gray, 'When Gen-X', p.89.

89. Hutcheon, *A Theory*, p.8.

90. The term 'interpretive community' is usually associated with Stanley Fish: see Fish, *Is There a Text in this Class?* (Cambridge: Harvard University Press, 1980).

91. Darius, *Batman Begins*, p.99.

92. Ibid., p.105.

93. Tim Leighton, aged 30 from Vancouver, BC, response to *Survey* Q22.

94. Andrew Allen, aged 24 from California, response to *Survey* Q22.

95. Robert Daniel Anglim II, aged 20 from Eugene, Oregon, response to *Survey* Q22.

96. Barthes, 'Author', p.213.

97. Lefèvre, 'Ontologies', p.8.

98. Somigli, 'The superhero', p.281.

99. Collins, 'Narrative: the hyperconscious", p.173.

100. Lefèvre, 'Ontologies', p.6.

101. Ibid.

102. Darius, *Batman Begins and the Comics*, p.20.

103. Kerry Gough demonstrates though a case study of *Alien* comic books that 'comics can be faithful to a coherent but complex filmic style'; but the *Batman Begins* adaptation is not such a thoughtful translation. See Kerry Gough, 'Translation creativity and alien econ(c)omics: from Hollywood blockbuster to Dark Horse comic book', in Gordon, Jancovich and. McAllister, *Film and Comic Books*, p.44.

104. Compare with Somigli's 'good example of how the illusion of movement can be created through static images'. 'The superhero', p.281.

105. Collins, 'Narrative: the hyperconscious', p.173.

106. O'Neil, in turn, provides a prose version of the film scene, which was based on his comic book script, which was itself based on Miller's comic book, in his novelisation of *Batman Begins*.

107. Uricchio and Pearson, 'I'm not fooled', p.184.

108. Ibid., p.200.

109. Ibid., p.211.

110. Ibid., p.189.

111. Gough, 'Translation creativity', p.44.

112. Ibid., p.50.

113. Johnson, 'Will the real Wolverine please stand up?', p.85.

114. Ibid., p.80.

115. Ibid., p.81.

116. Ibid.

117. Ibid., p.82.

118. Ibid., p.77.

119. The comic *Arkham City*, launched in May 2011, in turn bridges the video games.

120. See Frank Miller and Jim Lee with Scott Williams, *All Star Batman and Robin the Boy Wonder* (New York: DC Comics, 2008), n.p.

121. See Jeph Loeb and Tim Sale, *Batman: Dark Victory* (London: Titan Books, 2001), pp.242–3.

122. Ibid. p.76.

123. This example is not hypothetical – see Grant Morrison, J.H. Williams III and Tony S. Daniel, *Batman: The Black Glove* (New York: DC Comics, 2008), p.8 – but it neatly echoes Jenette Kahn's example from the late 1980s that 'if Alfred has a broken arm in *Batman*, he's still nursing that broken arm in *Detective.*' See Uricchio and Pearson, "I'm not fooled by that cheap disguise', p.191.

124. See for instance *IGN Comics*, http://uk.comics.ign.com/articles/115/1158120p3.html (accessed April 2011).

125. Uricchio and Pearson, 'I'm not fooled by that cheap disguise,' p.211.

126. *Batman: The Return of Bruce Wayne* part 4 (July 2010) and *Batman and Robin: Batman Vs Robin* part 3 (July 2010), reveal that Wayne Manor is constructed in a stylised 'W', with the adjoining gardens transforming it into a Bat-signal: the Wayne and Bat sigils are therefore depicted as mirrors of each other (though the former is arguably part of the latter).

127. Grant Morrison, David Finch, Batt and Ryan Winn, *Batman: The Return* (New York: DC Comics, 2011), n.p. *Batman and Robin* had already played heavily on the idea through the reintroduction of former Robin Jason Todd as a competitor to the new, Dick Grayson Batman. Todd devotes himself to devising snappy crime-fighting slogans, and is seen reading a book called *Getting the Best Out of Your Brand*. 'That's all Batman is now – a brand, a logo, an idea gone past its sell-by date.'

128. Gray, *Show Sold Separately*, p.210.

129. Italian-American cuisine also fits far more readily within Gotham's culture than does an Asgardian bracelet within a burger chain.

130. 'He introduces himself as *"original* Batman", in *Batman Incorporated* #5 (May 2011).

131. Similarly, cancellations or reboots of existing titles are, as we shall see in later chapters, often motivated within the story universe by a 'Crisis' that kills off swathes of characters, alters others and wipes still others out of recorded history.

132. 1964 saw the introduction of a 'New Look' Batman, distinguished from the old by the yellow oval on his chest; in 2006, Grant Morrison started his run on the monthly comic with a similar statement of intent, rebranding and redesign, titling his first episode 'Building a Better Batmobile'.

133. The appendix to *Batman and Robin Volume 2* shows the extensive design that went into the logo for that title: Rian Hughes supplied Morrison with 'a whole suite of possibilities'. Morrison et al. *Batman and Robin Volume 2* (New York: DC Comics, 2010), p.161.

134. 85 per cent of the total respondents.

135. 60 per cent and 50 per cent respectively.

136. 63 per cent of respondents. Space constraints prohibit me from discussing the ARG in detail. For an extensive study of the contemporary relationship between screen narratives and interactive games, see Elizabeth Evans, *Transmedia Television: Audiences, New Media, and Daily Life* (London: Routledge, 2011).

137. 47 per cent and 57 per cent, respectively.

138. 34 per cent saw it as 'slightly related'.

139. By contrast, the picture book *I Am Batman,* which retells *The Dark Knight* for children, is clearly branded with the ice-blue logo, despite its simplified pictures and text. See Catherine Hapka, Adrian Barrios and Kanila Tripp, *I Am Batman* (London: HarperCollins, 2008).

140. See Henry Jenkins, 'Searching for the origami unicorn: *The Matrix* and transmedia storytelling' in *Convergence Culture* (New York: New York University Press, 2006).

141. The 'Elseworlds' imprint provides another example: though its purpose is tell stories outside normal continuity, it was Mark Waid and Alex Ross' possible-future story *Kingdom Come* (1996) that first introduced the name and costume of Red Robin, now adopted into the monthly comic books.

142. Her role underwent a radical reboot in Autumn 2011: see the Epilogue.

143. See Darius, *Batman Begins*, p.72.

144. See for instance 'The Clown at Midnight' in Morrison et. al., *Batman and Son* (New York: DC Comics 2007), Michael Green, Denys Cowan and John Floyd, *Batman: Lovers and Madmen* (New York: DC Comics, 2008) and Brian Azzarello and Lee Bermejo's *Joker* (New York: DC Comics, 2008).

145. Bruce's first question about the Tumbler in *Batman Begins* is 'Does it come in black?'

Chapter 3   Dark Knight Lockdown:
Realism and Repression

1. Michel Foucault, *The History of Sexuality: Volume 1: An Introduction* (London: Penguin, 1979), p.8.

2. Ibid., p.11.

3. Anon, '*Batman Begins:* Final production information', p.4.

4. Ibid., p.3. Note though that Nolan compares his approach to that of Richard Donner, whose *Superman* (1978) was based in verisimilitude, but was unavoidably about a man who could fly. See Mottram, 'Christopher Nolan', *Batman Begins*, p.xii.

5. James Mottram, 'David S. Goyer', *Batman Begins*, p.xxvi.

6. Wilson Morales, '*Batman Begins*: An interview with director Christopher Nolan', *Blackfilm.com*, http://www.blackfilm.com/20050610/features/chrisnolan.shtml (accessed April 2011).

7. Mottram, *Batman Begins*, p.xxvii.

8. Mottram, 'Christopher Nolan', *Batman Begins*, p.xii.

9. Ibid., p.xviii.

10. Ibid., pp.xiii–xiv.

11. Ibid., p.xii.

12. Peter Travers, '*Batman Forever*', *Rolling Stone* (16 June, 1995).

13. Anon, 'Final production information', p.5.

14. As we saw in Chapter One, this parallel was picked up and developed in the production notes for *The Prestige,* which constructed Nolan's 'journey' in similar terms to Wayne's process of becoming Batman.

15. Mottram, 'Christopher Nolan', *Batman Begins*, p.xvi.
16. See Brooker, *Batman Unmasked,* p.298.
17. Anon, 'Final production information', p.16.
18. Ibid., p.15.
19. Ibid., p.17.
20. Ibid., pp.14–15.
21. Ibid., p.14.
22. Ibid., p.6.
23. Ibid., p.7.
24. Ibid., p.22.
25. Jonathan Gray provides a fascinating parallel in his study of the *Fellowship of the Ring* DVD, which constructs the cast and crew as a 'fellowship', bonded by hard work and dedication, and celebrates director Peter Jackson as a strange combination of Gandalf, Aragorn, Merry and Frodo. See Gray, *Show Sold Separately*, p.93.
26. André Bazin, *What is Cinema vol.2,* trans. Hugh Gray (Berkeley: University of California Press, 1972), p.50.
27. Ibid., p.56. Compare Nolan's encouragement of a 'realistic, naturalistic and low-key style' from his cast.
28. Ibid., p.57.
29. Ibid., p.58.
30. Ibid., p.57.
31. Ibid., p.58.
32. Ibid., p.60.
33. Ibid., p.58.
34. Ibid., pp.57–8.
35. *The Dark Knight*'s IMAX sequences come closest, in Nolan's films, to this aesthetic.
36. See 'The chase", documentary feature, *The Dark Knight Two-Disc Special Edition* DVD (Christopher Nolan, 2008), 00.14.20.
37. Mottram, 'Christopher Nolan', *Batman Begins* pp.xvii–xviii.
38. Anon, 'Final production information', p.24.
39. 'The journey begins', 00.06.30.
40. Anon, 'Final production information' p.21.
41. Ibid., p.26.
42. Ibid.
43. Ibid., p.24.
44. See 'See 'Path to discovery,' documentary feature, *Batman Begins 2-Disc Special Edition* DVD (Christopher Nolan, 2005), 00.05.05.
45. Ibid., 00.11.40.
46. Palmer, 'Nolan: bringing the Bat back'.
47. Ibid.
48. Ibid.
49. Ibid.

50. It was a key reference for 1980s Batman texts such as *The Dark Knight* and Burton's first film, but in 2005, Schumacher and Burton's movies had clearly replaced it as the most obvious points of comparison. Manohla Dargis' reference to *Batman Begins* as 'leagues away from Adam West's cartoony persona' is typical: the two are so distant to hardly be worth comparing. See Manhola Dargis, 'Dark was the young knight battling his inner demons', *The New York Times* (15 June 2005).

51. Anon, 'The Best Batman Yet?' *Empire* (29 July 2004).

52. Anon, *'Batman Begins', Total Film* (16 June 2005).

53. Anon, *'Batman Begins', Film4.com* (June 2005). We could note the association of 'soft-drink peddling' with 'bloated camp', and contrast it to the discourse of lean, stripped down physical fitness that surrounds *Batman Begins*.

54. Kenneth Turan, *'Batman Begins', Los Angeles Times* (14 June 2005).

55. Sandhu, 'Dark soul of the night'.

56. Todd McCarthy, *'Batman Begins', Variety* (3 June 2005).

57. Previews of the 1989 *Batman* also reassured fans of the film's dark, serious tone through masculine, militaristic details such as 'a utility belt, which is a dirty yellow, and the size of a soldier's ammo belt', but these references were more occasional. See Brooker, *Batman Unmasked*, p.286.

58. See Brooker, ibid. p.171.

59. Ibid., pp.281–2.

60. Sandhu, 'Dark soul of the night'. Schumacher's camp interpretation was firmly associated with gay overtones in journalistic discourse of the 1990s: see Brooker, ibid., pp.295–7.

61. See Brooker, ibid., pp.101–70.

62. Fredric Wertham, *Seduction of the Innocent* (London: Museum Press, 1955), p.190. See Brooker, ibid., p.103.

63. George Melly, *Revolt into Style: The Pop Arts In Britain* (Harmondsworth: Penguin, 1970), p.193. See Brooker, ibid., p.162.

64. See Brooker, ibid., pp.166–70.

65. See Gray, *Show Sold Separately*, p.134. My previous chapters confirm Gray's perceptive observations about the reboot process; the way in which production discourses around Nolan foregrounded aspects such as fidelity, realism and Nolan's 'edgy', 'indie' reputation in order to distinguish the new film from the previous franchise.

66. Lawrenson, *'Batman Begins', Sight and Sound*.

67. Alan Sinfield, *Cultural Politics – Queer Reading* (Oxon: Routledge, 2005), p.12.

68. Foucault, *History of Sexuality*, p.43.

69. Sinfield, *Cultural Politics*, p.12.

70. Alan Sinfield, *Faultlines: Cultural Materialism and the Politics of Dissident Reading* (Oxford: Oxford University Press, 1992), p.48.

71. Ibid., p.48.
72. Ibid., p.47.
73. Anon, *Batman Begins:* Comics Vs Movies', http://www.mutantreviewers.com/rbatcvm.html (accessed April 2011).
74. Dargis, 'Dark was the young knight'.
75. Sandhu, 'Dark soul of the night'.
76. Turan, *Batman Begins'*.
77. Anon, *'Batman Begins'*, *Total Film* (16 June 2005).
78. Steve Biodrowski, *'Batman Begins'*, *Cinefantastique* (7 December 2005).
79. Paul Clinton, 'Welcome return for Batman', *CNN.com* (15 June 2005).
80. Felix Vasquez, 'Batman's Report Card', *Cinema Crazed.com* (accessed June 2010).
81. Roger Ebert, *'Batman Begins'*, *Chicago Sun Times* (13 June 2005).
82. Anon, 'The Best Batman Yet?'
83. See Brooker, *Batman Unmasked* pp.275–9, and Pearson and Uricchio, pp.185–6.
84. Raymond Williams, *The Long Revolution* (Harmondsworth: Penguin, 1971), p.66.
85. Ibid., p.67.
86. Ibid., p.69.
87. Ibid.
88. Geoff Klock, *How To Read Superhero Comics and Why* (London: Continuum, 2002); Roz Kaveney, *Superheroes! Capes and Crusaders in Comics and Films* (London: I.B.Tauris, 2008); Richard Reynolds, *Superheroes: A Modern Mythology* (Mississippi: Mississippi University Press, 1994); Will Brooker, 'The best Batman story: *The Dark Knight Returns*' in Alan McKee (ed.), *Beautiful Things in Popular Culture* (London: Blackwell, 2007).
89. There were other Crises before it, and others afterwards, but when I refer to pre- and post-Crisis periods in this book, I mean the *Crisis on Infinite Earths* of 1986.
90. Brooker, 'Hero of the beach: Flex Mentallo at the end of the worlds', add source when published, cited in Klock, *How To Read Superhero Comics and Why*, p.19.
91. See Brooker, *Batman Unmasked*, p.318.
92. Brooker, 'The best Batman story', p.39.
93. Dennis O'Neil, quoted in Sam Hamm, 'Introduction', *Batman: Tales of the Demon* (New York: DC Comics 1991).
94. Ibid.
95. Alan Moore, 'Introduction', Frank Miller, Klaus Janson, Lynn Varley, *Batman: The Dark Knight Returns* (London: Titan Books, 1986).
96. Reynolds, *Superheroes*, p.45.
97. The reference is, of course, to the relationship Ferdinand de Saussure identified between *langue* (language system) and *parole* (specific act of communication); see for instance Allen, *Intertextuality*, p.9.

98. Within the fiction, Batman's identity is equally built around a never-ending cycle of death and rebirth, endings and new beginnings; for example, his original vow to avenge his parents' murder is never resolved, and is acted out symbolically again and again with every crime he tackles.

99. He was born in 1957. Miller's sourcing of the 'never funny', gothic and grim Batman of his childhood to the mid-60s, usually associated with Pop and camp, is itself a puzzle.

100. Frank Miller, 'Introduction', *Batman: Year One* (London: Titan Books, 1988).

101. Hamm, 'Introduction'.

102. Andy Medhurst, 'Batman, deviance and camp' in Pearson and Uricchio, *The Many Lives of the Batman*, pp.161–2.

103. Ibid., p.162.

104. See Brooker, *Batman Unmasked*, pp.300–1.

105. See Brooker, ibid., pp.101–70.

106. Medhurst, 'Batman, deviance and camp', pp.151–2.

107. See Brooker, *Batman Unmasked*, p.166.

108. See Brooker, ibid., p.104.

109. Hamm, 'Introduction'.

110. Medhurst, 'Batman, deviance and camp', p.158.

111. Ibid., p.159.

112. He is featured in a tiny detail of a single frame, in a nostalgic Bob-Kane style portrait alongside pre-Crisis Batman family members such as Batwoman and Ace.

113. See Brooker, *Batman Unmasked*, p.104.

114. Medhurst, 'Batman, deviance and camp', p.152.

115. Raymond Williams, *Marxism and Literature* (Oxford: Oxford University Press, 1977), p.110.

116. Ibid., pp.112–3.

117. Alan Sinfield, *Faultlines*, p.41.

118. Ibid., p.47.

119. Williams, *Marxism and Literature*, p.114.

120. Sinfield, *Faultlines*, p.48.

121. Medhurst, 'Batman, deviance and camp', p.160.

122. Ibid., p.161.

123. Ibid.

124. *The Killing Joke*, too, is not a closed, relentlessly 'dark' text: Brian Bolland's artwork also refers back to and quotes from to pre-Crisis imagery.

125. Klock, *How to Read Superhero Comics and Why*, p.37.

126. Robert Brian Taylor, 'Keeping it real in Gotham' in Dennis O'Neil with Leah Wilson (eds), *Batman Unauthorized: Vigilantes, Jokers and Heroes in Gotham City* (Dallas: BenBella Books, 2008) p.8.

127. Ibid., p.9.
128. Ibid., pp.10–11.
129. Ibid., p.12.
130. Ibid.
131. Ibid., p.14.
132. Williams, *Marxism and Literature*, p.116.
133. Sinfield, *Faultlines*, p.48.

Chapter 4   Carnival on Infinite Earths: Continuity and Crisis

1. Mikhail Bakhtin (trans. Hélène Iswolsky), *Rabelais and His World* (Indiana: Indiana University Press, 1984, p.6.
2. Ibid., p.6.
3. Ibid., p.5.
4. Ibid., p.4.
5. Ibid., pp.5–6.
6. Ibid., p.6.
7. *Batman Incorporated* (2011) shows him solemnly inducting each new member into his global crime-fighting organisation through an identical ritual, a merger of business with religion.
8. Mikhail Bakhtin (trans. Caryl Emerson), *Problems of Dostoevsky's Poetics* (Manchester: Manchester University Press, 1984), p.127.
9. See also Klock, *How to Read Superhero Comics*, p.36.
10. Bakhtin, *Rabelais and His World*, p.8. Roz Kaveney describes him as a 'principle of the universe'. See Roz Kaveney, *Superheroes: Capes and Crusaders in Comics and Films* (London: I.B.Tauris, 2008), p.239.
11. In a further, neat echo of Harleen Quinzel's essential clownishness, the voice actress who helped create the character is named Arleen (Sorkin).
12. See Dick Sprang and Stan Kaye, 'Superman and Batman's greatest foes' (1957), and Sprang and Charles Paris, 'The Joker's utility belt' (1952), reprinted in *The Greatest Joker Stories Ever Told*, (New York: DC Comics, 1988), p.76, p.110.
13. Denny O'Neil and Neal Adams, 'The Joker's five-way revenge', reprinted in *The Greatest Joker Stories Ever Told*, p.175.
14. Bill Finger and Bob Kane, 'Batman vs the Joker', reprinted in *The Greatest Joker Stories Ever Told*, p.20.
15. See for instance Dick Sprang and Charles Paris, 'The Joker's crime costumes' (1951) in which he dresses up as Falstaff, Mr Pickwick, the Connecticut Yankee and Old King Cole to entertain Gotham's citizens. Reprinted in *The Greatest Joker Stories Ever Told*, p.64.
16. The Joker of the 'dark' modern tradition has the same aim, but it is generally only realised on a smaller scale: he becomes king of black

comedy within the already carnivalised confines of a fairground or a madhouse, as in *The Killing Joke*, *Dark Knight Returns* and *Arkham Asylum* respectively.

17. Bakhtin, *Rabelais and His World*, p.11.
18. Bakhtin, Dostoyevsky's Poetics, p.128.
19. Ibid.
20. See Brooker, *Batman Unmasked*, p.243.
21. Bakhtin, *Rabelais and His World*, p.10.
22. Ibid., p.11.
23. Ibid., p.9.
24. Ibid., p.33.
25. Ibid., pp.33–4.
26. Ibid., p.35.
27. Ibid., p.38.
28. Ibid., pp.38–9.
29. Ibid., pp.40–1.
30. Ibid., p.41.
31. Ibid., p.53.
32. Ibid., p.19.
33. Ibid., p.25.
34. Ibid., p.24.
35. Ibid., pp.52–3.
36. Ibid., p.24.
37. Ibid., p.50.
38. Ibid., p.53.
39. Ibid., p.40.
40. Bakhtin, 'Discourse in the novel', p.263.
41. Ibid.
42. Ibid., p.270.
43. Ibid., p.272.
44. Ibid., p.273.
45. Ibid., p.278. See also the *JLA* story 'Tower of Babel', in which Batman's strategies to bring down his own colleagues are used against them, and Ra's al Ghul turns all language to gibberish. Mark Waid et al. *JLA: Tower of Babel* (New York: DC Comics, 2000).
46. Ibid., pp.298–9.
47. Ibid., p.297.
48. Ibid., p.273.
49. Reynolds sees the phrase as encompassing the comic book dynamic between unity and plurality, presumably in an echo of the relationship Eco identified between mythic stability and narrative progression.
50. Bakhtin, 'Discourse in the novel', p.279.
51. Ibid., p.298.
52. Ibid., p.279.

53. Ibid., p.288.

54. Strictly speaking, Owlman's world in *Earth 2* was an antimatter universe, rather than the parallel Earth-3 of pre-Crisis continuity. Earth-3 had appeared briefly in Morrison's *Animal Man* (1988–1990) and made a subsequent cameo in the non-canon, Elseworlds title *Another Nail* (2004).

55. Reynolds, *Superheroes*, p.44. Henry Jenkins uses 'meta-text' in a similar way with regard to *Star Trek*, to describe 'a composite view of many different episodes': see Henry Jenkins, *Textual Poachers* (London: Routledge, 1992), p.101. However, Matt Hills' 'hyperdiegesis' is more similar to canon: see below.

56. See Brooker, *Batman Unmasked*, pp.330–3.

57. Patrick Chappatte, 'Saviour of the economy', *Le Temps* (8 November, 2008).

58. Ben Jennings, 'DIY police', *Guardian* (29 July, 2010).

59. *Dead End* was described as 'for many fans ... the finest cinematic evocation of the character yet.' Anon, *Batman Begins*', *FilmFour.com*, http://www.film4.com/reviews/2005/batman-begins (accessed May 2011).

60. This category, extensive but still narrow and contained in comparison to the sprawling, diverse and contradictory 'myth', corresponds most closely to Matt Hills' 'hyperdiegesis': 'a vast and detailed narrative space, only a fraction of which is ever directly seen or encountered within the text, which nevertheless appears to operate according to principles of internal logic and extension ... this overarching intricacy ... typically displays such a coherence and *continuity* that it can be trusted by the reader' [italics mine]. Hills, *Fan Cultures* (London: Routledge, 2002), p.137.

61. Uricchio and Pearson, 'I'm not fooled', p.192.

62. *Heroes and Villains: Origin Stories: Batman*, http://www.dccomics.com/dcu/heroes_and_villains/?hv=origin_stories/batman&p=1 (accessed June 2011).

63. See *Comic Book Resources*, http://forums.comicbookresources.com/forumdisplay.php?f=5.

64. Eco, 'The myth of Superman', p.116.

65. Ibid., p.114.

66. See Uricchio and Pearson, 'I'm not fooled', p.186.

67. See Brooker, *Batman Unmasked*, p.18.

68. Ibid., p.318.

69. Seth Jones, 'WW Chicago: *Batman: Gotham Knight* world premiere', *Comic Book Resources*, http://www.comicbookresources.com/?page=article&id=17021 (9 June, 2008), accessed May 2011. Neil Gaiman's 'Whatever happened to the Caped Crusader'(2009) makes Batman into a bedtime story, as does the 1996 *Batman Black and White* episode 'Legend'; see Brooker, *Batman Unmasked*, p.330.

70. Gaiman's 'Whatever happened to the Caped Crusader', similarly, has Batman drawn in the style of various artists, his shape changing across subsequent panels.

71. Eco, 'The myth of Superman', p.114.

72. Anon, *'Batman: Year Two'*, *Wikipedia* (http://en.wikipedia.org/wiki/ Batman:_Year_Two#Canonical_status), accessed May 2011.

73. Julian Darius, *Improving the Foundations: Batman Begins from Comic to Screen* (Illinois: Sequart Research and Literacy Foundation, 2009), pp.18–21.

74. Kevin Smith's *Batman: The Widening Gyre* (2010) makes the interesting retroactive addition that Batman suffered a 'bladder spasm' during a climactic moment in Miller's *Year One*: it remains to be seen if this detail will lodge in continuity.

75. Klock, *How To Read Superhero Comics*, pp.30–31.

76. T.S. Eliot, 'Tradition and the individual talent', *Selected Essays* (London: Faber and Faber, 1932), p.15. Quoted in Reynolds, *Superheroes*, p.43.

77. See Brooker, 'Hero of the beach: Flex Mentallo at the end of the worlds', *Journal of Graphic Novels and Comics*, vol. 2, no.1 (June 2011), pp.25–37.

78. 'I hear talk of *alternate universes* where the laws of physics are different and *anything* goes!' muses Bruce: see Grant Morrison, Andy Kubert and Jesse Delperdang, *Batman and Son* (New York: DC Comics, 2007), p.30.

79. Grant Morrison, 'Introduction', *Batman: The Black Casebook* (New York: DC Comics, 2009), n.p.

80. Duncan Falconer, 'A hall of mirrors, II: the Prismatic Age', *Mindless Ones* (August 3, 2008), http://mindlessones.com/2008/08/03/a-hall-of- mirrors-ii-prismatic-age/, accessed May 2011.

81. Recall Sabin and Barker's conclusion (quoted in Chapter Two) that 'our myths have become more and more like a shattered mirror. A million frag- ments of story-glass, each refracting small elements back into our lives.'

82. Marc Singer, *Grant Morrison: Combining the Worlds of Contemporary Comics*, (Mississippi: University Press of Mississippi, 2012), p.283.

83. He includes a visual quotation from the story in *Batman: RIP*, so his claim may be entirely disingenuous.

84. In fact, Morrison adds the tic 'Hh' to Bruce's original, 1939 dialogue: an auteurist motif he introduced during his run on *JLA* to convey Batman's sharp, sceptical intakes of breath.

85. All quotations are from Grant Morrison, Tony S. Daniel et.al. *Batman RIP* (New York: DC Comics, 2010).

86. The Pop references return in *Batman and Son*, as Bruce visits a charity evening decorated with Lichtenstein- and Warhol-style canvases.

87. Grant Morrison, 'The Clown at Midnight', in Morrison, Andy Kubert and Jesse Delperdang, *Batman and Son* (New York: DC Comics, 2007), n.p.

88. Morrison, *Batman RIP*, n.p.

89. This sense of uncertainty is 'queer' in itself in its unsettling of boundaries and refusal of linear narrative trajectory: see Brooker, 'Hero of the beach' for an application of queer theory to Morrison's work.

90. See for instance Uricchio and Pearson, 'I'm not fooled', p.196.

91. Morrison riffs further on this opposition in *Supergods*: 'The pair shared the perfect symmetry of Jesus and the Devil, Holmes and Moriarty, Tom and Jerry'. See Grant Morrison, *Supergods: Our World in the Age of the Superhero* (London: Jonathan Cape, 2011), p.24.

92. She tells Batman, 'I wrote a *thesis* on that man! You will *never never ever* comprehend that artist ... I have a doctorate and I can *kick your ass!*'

93. Particularly playful is the incorporation of Ronnie's black, jet-powered crimefighter from 'The Batman Nobody Knows' as Batwing: see http://www.comicsalliance.com/2011/05/12/batwing-batman-of-africa-exclusive/.

94. Klock, *How To Read Superhero Comics*, p.46.

95. Barthes quotes this line with reference to the dialogic, many-voiced text. See Barthes, *Image-Music-Text* (London: Fontana Press, 1977) p.160; see Allen, *Intertextuality*, p.60.

Chapter 5   The Never-Ending War: Deconstruction and the Dark Knight

1. Christopher Norris notes that Derrida's works 'defy classification according to any of the clear-cut boundaries that define modern academic discourse ... they belong to 'philosophy'... yet Derrida's texts are like nothing else in modern philosophy.' Christopher Norris, *Derrida* (London: Fontana, 1987), p.18.

2. Norris, *Derrida*, p.35.

3. For an introduction to Saussure's theories of linguistics and their relation to structuralism, see for instance John Storey, *Cultural Theory and Popular Culture* (Harlow: Pearson Education, 2006), pp.87–89.

4. Christopher Norris, *Deconstruction: Theory and Practice* (London: Routledge, 1982), p.25.

5. Jacques Derrida, *Writing and Difference* (London: Routledge, 1978), p.25. See also Storey, *Cultural Theory and Popular Culture*, p.98.

6. Norris, *Deconstruction*, p.29.

7. Mottram, 'Introduction', pp.vii–ix.

8. See Brooker, *Batman Unmasked*, pp.285–6.

9. Ibid., p.299.

10. Darius, *Batman Begins and the Comics*, p.149.

11. See also Bakhtin, *Problems of Dostoevsky's Politics* (Manchester: Manchester University Press, 1984), p.202. Just as *'e pluribus unum'* is a motto on

the Seal of the United States (not the 'the U.S. Constitutional motto' as Reynolds has it: *Superheroes* p.45), so *'cui bono'* is the motto of Owlman's alternate-universe Crime Syndicate of America.

12. Norris, *Deconstruction*, p.31.
13. Jacques Derrida, *Positions* (London: The Athlone Press, 1972), p.41.
14. Norris, *Deconstruction*, p.48: Norris notes that Derrida selects texts precisely for their 'rigour and tenacity'.
15. Such as 'hymen' as a term that both connects and divides, and 'supplement' as both an addition and replacement; see for instance Simon Morgan Wortham, *The Derrida Dictionary* (London: Continuum, 2010), p.44, p.203.
16. Norris, *Deconstruction*, p.49.
17. Ibid., p.51.
18. Grant Morrison et al. *Final Crisis* (New York: DC Comics, 2009).
19. Bob Kane et al. 'The case of the chemical syndicate', *The Batman Archives Volume 1* (New York: DC Comics, 1990), p.8.
20. Bakhtin notes that the Socratic dialogue 'grows out of a folk-carnivalistic base and is thoroughly saturated with a carnival sense of the world'; see *Dostoyevsky's Poetics*, p.109.
21. More commonly known as 'Thoth'.
22. Jacques Derrida, *Dissemination* (London: The Athlone Press, 1981), p.75.
23. Ibid., p.102.
24. Ibid.
25. Norris, *Derrida*, p.31.
26. Ibid.
27. Derrida, *Dissemination*, p.85.
28. Ibid., p.103.
29. Norris, *Derrida*, p.34.
30. Derrida, *Dissemination*, pp.74–5.
31. Ibid., p.148.
32. Ibid., p.149.
33. Norris, *Derrida*, p.35.
34. Derrida, *Dissemination*, pp.71–2.
35. Ibid., p.97.
36. Ibid.
37. Poison is 'not the only other thing *pharmakon* means', ibid. p.98.
38. Ibid.
39. Ibid., p.99.
40. See Norris, *Derrida*, p.43.
41. See Derrida, *Dissemination*, pp.130–2.
42. Ibid., p.133.
43. Cf. Batman, 'This isn't a mudhole. It's an operating table' (*The Dark Knight Returns*) and 'This isn't a restaurant. It's an arsenal.' (Mark Waid and Ariel Olivetti, *The Kingdom* #2, New York: DC Comics, 1999).

44. This relationship is neatly captured in the sequel to the *Arkham Asylum* video game, *Arkham City* (2011).
45. Derrida, *Dissemination*, p.142.
46. See Uricchio and Pearson, 'I'm not fooled,'p.198. Morrison describes Joker as 'some unhallowed marriage of showbiz, drag culture and the art of the mortician.' *Supergods*, p.24.
47. The Alternate Reality Game encouraged players – most of whom were young men – to send in photographs of themselves wearing Joker make-up, in a subversive carnivalisation of teenage male masculinity. The Jokerised posters of Barack Obama, which according to their original creator had no racist or even political intention, could also be seen as an extension of this carnival impulse, a playful decrowning of the chief. See Daniel Nasaw, 'US student comes forward as creator of Obama-Joker image', *Guardian* (18 August 2009), http://www.guardian.co.uk/world/2009/aug/18/obama-joker-image-creator (accessed June 2011).
48. Derrida, *Dissemination*, p.143.
49. Ibid., p.144.
50. Ibid., p.143.
51. Ibid.
52. Ibid., p.152.
53. Ibid., p.150.
54. Ibid., p.152.
55. Ibid., p.93.
56. *Batman RIP* stages a literal rebirth, as Batman breaks out of a shallow grave.
57. Nick Mamatas argues that 'Batman is nothing in particular and thus nothing at all ...'. Nick Mamatas, 'Holy signifier, Batman', in O'Neil, *Batman Unauthorised*: p.51.
58. See for instance the flashbacks in Loeb and Sale's *Dark Victory*.
59. 'Batman versus the Joker', in *The Greatest Joker Stories Ever Told*, p.18.
60. Loeb and Sale, *The Long Halloween*, p.87.
61. James Robinson, Don Kramer, Leonard Kirk, *Batman: Face the Face* (New York: DC Comics, 2006), p.55.
62. Azzarello et al. *Joker*, n.p.
63. Justine Toh, 'The tools and toys of (the) war (on terror): consumer desire, military fetish, and regime change in *Batman Begins*', in Jeff Birkenstein, Anna Froula and Karen Randell (eds.), *Reframing 9/11: Film, Popular Culture and the 'War on Terror'* (London: Continuum, 2010).
64. Derrida, *Dissemination*, p.93.
65. Ibid.
66. Ibid., p.120.
67. Benjamin Kerstein, 'Batman's war on terror', *AzureOnline* (Autumn 2008), http://www.azure.org.il/article.php?id=477, accessed May 2011.

68. Cosmo Landesman, '*The Dark Knight*', *Sunday Times* (27 July 2008).
69. Carrie Rickey, 'Brooding, brilliant *Dark Knight*', *Philadelphia Inquirer* (16 July 2008).
70. John Ip, '*The Dark Knight*'s War On Terrorism', *Ohio State Journal of Criminal Law* (April 2010), p.5.
71. Ibid., p.6.
72. Ibid., p.7.
73. Ibid., p.10.
74. Spencer Ackerman, 'Batman's *Dark Knight* Reflects Cheney Policy: Joker's Senseless, Endless Violence Echoes Al Qaeda', *The Washington Independent* (21 July 2008).
75. Matthew Yglesias, '*Dark Knight* Politics', *The Atlantic* (24 July 2008).
76. Ackerman, 'Batman's *Dark Knight*', ibid.
77. Yglesias, '*Dark Knight* politics', ibid.
78. Andrew Klavan, 'What Bush and Batman have in common', *Wall St Journal* (25 July 2008).
79. Transcribed in 'The new Batman and the war on terror,' *JeremySarber. com*, http://jeremysarber.com/2008/08/04/the-new-batman-and-the-war-on-terror/, accessed May 2011.
80. Steve Schneider, 'Cape, cowl and camelot: Batman and the audacity of hope', *Orlando Weekly* (25 July 2008).
81. Steve Biodrowski , 'Sense of wonder: Dark Knight's politics of noir", *Cinefantastique* (21 September 2008).
82. Ibid.
83. Ip, '*The Dark Knight*'s War on Terrorism', p.9.
84. Ibid.
85. Lucius and Wayne also enjoy linguistic games when Wayne smiles at the use of 'sonar, just like a [bat]' and Lucius interrupts, 'like a submarine, Mr Wayne. Like a submarine.'
86. Morrison's *Batman and Robin* #13 (August 2010) makes this point intertextually, with Robin declaring to Joker 'you say you're a force of chaos and you don't *plan* anything, it just *happens*. But I've read your files and *everything's* a plan. ... I don't think you know what chaos *is*.'
87. Another pop cultural quotation, this time from Eminem, who dressed as a Burt Ward-style Robin in the video for 'Without Me'.
88. Giovanna Borradori, *Philosophy in a Time of Terror: Dialogues with Jurgen Habermas and Jacques Derrida* (London: University of Chicago Press, 2003) p.106. See also Toh, 'The tools and toys', p.131.
89. Borradori, *Philosophy in a Time of Terror.* p.94 . See also Martin McQuillan, *Deconstruction after 9/11* (London: Routledge, 2009), pp.10–11.
90. Ibid., p.95.
91. Ibid., p.99.
92. Ibid., p.124.

93. Ibid., p.107.
94. Ibid., p.105.
95. Ibid., p.151.
96. Sinfield, *Faultines*, p.45. See also Alex Evans, 'Superman *is* the fault-line: Fissures in the monomythic man of steel' in Birkenstein, Froula and Randell, *Reframing 9/11*, p.124.
97. Ibid., p.48. For further examples and examinations of other 9/11 'faul-tine' narratives, see Birkenstein, Froula and Rondell, *Reframing 9/11*. Stephen Prince, *Firestorm: American Film in the Age of Terrorism* (New York: Columbia, 2009), Marc diPaolo, *War, Politics and Superheroes: Ethics and Propaganda in Comics and Film* (North Carolina: McFarland, 2011).
98. Sinfield, *Faultlines*. p.46.
99. 'Really my co-writers David Goyer and my brother, Jonah, and myself, try and be pretty rigidly not aware and not conscious of real world parallels in things we're doing,' Nolan claimed in one interview. Anon, *'The Dark Knight* – Christian Bale and Christopher Nolan interview', *IndieLondon* (n.d.), http://www.indielondon.co.uk/Film-Review/the-dark-knight-christian-bale-and-christopher-nolan-interview, accessed June 2011.
100. 'This heavy-handed, wearisome 9/11 connection is the artistic equiva-lent of a fake tan: it provides the film with instant, spray-on serious-ness.' See Landesman, *'The Dark Knight'*.
101. And, to an extent, in *Batman Begins*, as Toh demonstrates.

EPILOGUE

1. Brian Truitt, 'DC Comics unleashes a new universe of comics titles,' *USA Today* (31 May 2011), http://www.usatoday.com/life/comics/2011–05-31-dc-comics-reinvents_n.htm, accessed June 2011.
2. Alan Moore, Curt Swan and George Perez, *Superman: Whatever Happened to the Man of Tomorrow* (New York: DC Comics, 1997).
3. Jason Cowley, 'Joker David Cameron is having a laugh', *The Mirror* (11 April 2010); Alison Maloney, 'Jedward meet the dynamic duo', *The Sun* (15 March 2010); Chris Irvine, 'Eddie Murphy "to play Riddler in Batman sequel"', *Daily Telegraph* (18 December 2008); Anon, 'Batman to take on Al Qaeda', *Daily Mail* (16 February 2008).
4. Jody Thompson, 'Batman star Val Kilmer more of a Fatman as he poses at film festival', *The Mirror* (17 March 2010).
5. Alison Maloney, 'West wants to be Batdad', *The Sun* (27 June 2008).

SELECT BIBLIOGRAPHY

Allen, Graham, *Intertextuality* (London: Routledge, 2000).

Bakhtin, Mikhail M., 'Discourse in the novel' in Michael Holquist (ed.), *The Dialogic Imagination: Four Essays by M.M. Bakhtin* (Austin: University of Texas Press).

—— (trans. Hélène Iswolsky), *Rabelais and His World* (Indiana: Indiana University Press, 1984).

—— (trans. Caryl Emerson), *Problems of Dostoevsky's Poetics* (Manchester: Manchester University Press, 1984).

Barker, Martin and Sabin, Roger, *The Lasting of the Mohicans: History of an American Myth* (Mississippi: University Press of Mississippi, 1995).

Bazin, André, *What is Cinema vol.2*, trans. Hugh Gray (Berkeley: University of California Press, 1972).

Birkenstein, Jeff, Froula, Anna and Randell, Karen (eds), *Reframing 9/11: Film, Popular Culture and the 'War on Terror'* (London: Continuum, 2010).

Booker, Keith M., *May Contain Graphic Material: Comic Books, Graphic Novels and Film* (Westport, CT: Praeger Publishers, 2007).

Boozer, Jack, *Authorship in Film Adaptation* (Austin: University of Texas Press, 2008).

Borradori, Giovanna, *Philosophy in a Time of Terror: Dialogues with Jurgen Habermas and Jacques Derrida* (London: University of Chicago Press, 2003).

Brooker, Will, *Batman Unmasked* (London: Continuum, 2000).

—— 'The best Batman story: *The Dark Knight Returns*' in Alan McKee (ed.), *Beautiful Things in Popular Culture* (London: Blackwell, 2007).

—— 'Hero of the beach: Flex Mentallo at the end of the worlds', *Journal of Graphic Novels and Comics* vol.2 no.1 (June 2011).

Cartmell, Deborah and Whelehan, Imelda (eds), *Screen Adaptation: Impure Cinema* (London: Palgrave Macmillan, 2010).

—— and —— (eds), *The Cambridge Companion to Literature on Screen* (Cambridge: Cambridge University Press, 2007).

Caughie, John (ed.), *Theories of Authorship* (London: Routledge, 1981).

Darius, Julian, *Batman Begins and the Comics* (Hawaii: Sequart Books, 2005).

—— *Improving the Foundations* (Illinois: Sequart, 2009).

Derrida, Jacques, *Writing and Difference* (London: Routledge, 1978).

—— *Positions* (London: The Athlone Press, 1972).

—— *Dissemination* (London: The Athlone Press, 1981).

Ebert, Roger, *The Dark Knight, Chicago Sun-Times* (16 July 2006).

Fish, Stanley, *Is There a Text in This Class?* (Cambridge, MA: Harvard University Press, 1980).

Foucault, Michel, *The History of Sexuality: Volume 1: An Introduction* (London: Penguin, 1979).

Genette, Gérard, *Paratexts: Thresholds of Interpretation* (Cambridge: Cambridge University Press, 1997).

Geraghty, Christine, *Now a Major Motion Picture: Film Adaptations of Literature and Drama* (Plymouth: Rowman and Littlefield, 2008).

Gerstner, David A. and Staiger, Janet (eds), *Authorship and Film* (New York: Routledge, 2003).

Gordon, Ian, Jancovich, Mark and McAllister, Matthew P., *Film and Comic Books* (Mississippi: University Press of Mississippi, 2007).

Gray, Jonathan, *Show Sold Separately* (New York: New York University Press, 2010).

Hills, Matt, *Triumph of a Time Lord: Regenerating Doctor Who in the Twenty-First Century* (London: I.B.Tauris, 2010).

Horton, Andrew and McDougal, Stuart T. (eds), *Play it Again, Sam: Retakes on Remakes* (Berkeley: University of California Press, 1998), pp.284–5.

Hutcheon, Linda, *A Theory of Adaptation* (London: Routledge, 2006), pp.84–5.

Jenkins, Henry, *Convergence Culture* (New York: New York University Press, 2006.

Kaveney, Roz, *Superheroes! Capes and Crusaders in Comics and Films* (London: I.B.Tauris, 2008).

Klock, Geoff, *How to Read Superhero Comics and Why* (London: Continuum, 2002).

Kristeva, Julia, 'Word, dialogue and novel' in Toril Moi (ed.), *The Kristeva Reader* (Oxford: Blackwell, 1986).

Morrison, Grant, *Supergods: Our World in the Age of the Superhero* (London: Jonathan Cape, 2011).

Norris, Christopher, *Derrida* (London: Fontana, 1987).

—— *Deconstruction: Theory and Practice* (London: Routledge, 1982).

O'Neil, Dennis with Wilson, Leah (eds), *Batman Unauthorized: Vigilantes, Jokers and Heroes in Gotham City* (Dallas: BenBella Books, 2008).

Pearson, Roberta E. and Uricchio, William (eds), *The Many Lives of the Batman: Critical Approaches to A Superhero and His Media* (New York: Routledge, 1991).

Reynolds, Richard, *Superheroes: A Modern Mythology* (London: B.T. Batsford Ltd, 1992).

Sinfield, Alan, *Cultural Politics – Queer Reading* (Oxon: Routledge, 2005).

—— *Faultlines: Cultural Materialism and the Politics of Dissident Reading* (Oxford: Oxford University Press, 1992).

Singer, Marc, *Grant Morrison: Combining the Worlds of Contemporary Comics*, (Mississippi: University Press of Mississippi, 2012).

Stam, Robert and Raengo, Alessandra, *Literature and Film* (Oxford: Blackwell, 2005).

Tulloch, John and Jenkins, Henry, *Science Fiction Audiences* (London: Routledge, 1995).

Wertham, Fredric, *Seduction of the Innocent* (London: Museum Press, 1955).

Wollen, Peter, *Signs and Meaning in the Cinema* (Bloomington: Indiana University Press, 1972).

INDEX